HEALTH and HEALING

HEALTH and HEALING

Studies in New Testament Principles and Practice

JOHN WILKINSON
B.D., M.D., F.R.C.P.

The Handsel Press

1980

Published by
The Handsel Press Ltd.
33 Montgomery Street, Edinburgh

ISBN 0 905312 08 2

Printed in Great Britain by
R. & R. Clark Ltd., Edinburgh

CONTENTS

TO JEAN

PREFACE

Health and Healing have been topics of personal and abiding interest to all men and women over the years, and they have inspired the writing of many books and articles. There are few books, however, which have considered these subjects systematically in a Biblical context and in a comprehensive way. This is the purpose of the present volume and may be allowed to provide its justification.

The reader of this book will soon become aware that the terms health and healing are used within its pages in a comprehensive sense and are not confined to only one aspect of man's being, although it may on occasions be difficult to rid the words entirely of the restriction to purely physical health and healing which is common in popular usage. The reason for using the term healing in this comprehensive way may be stated simply as the need for an all-embracing term which includes all three forms of restoration to normality which we find in the New Testament, namely, physical healing, the casting out of demons and the raising of the dead. The English language has no one word which covers all these three activities, and the term healing appeared to be the nearest approximation to the word which was required. Furthermore, there is no single term in English which describes the restoration to wholeness or well-being in every sphere of man's being whether it be body, mind, spirit or community. Healing and health appeared to be the closest to what was required in this sense also, for they had not been given the specialised theological meaning that a word like salvation had acquired in modern usage.

If we are accused of extending the meaning of the words health and healing beyond what is permissible, we can only plead in defence the following three facts. First, that in the New Testament the verb sōzō, save, is used for the healing of man's whole being, body, soul and spirit, and we need a translation-equivalent for it when it is used in this comprehensive way. Second, the semantic tendency in modern usage is to extend the meaning of health and healing to include the whole man as we can see from the definition of health prepared by the World Health Organisation which is discussed on page five. Finally, there is the plain fact that the Biblical concept of health and healing is much more comprehensive than the modern concept, and we do not have an English term which embraces this wider concept. The alternative to using the terms in this more comprehensive way is to allow them to become emptied of their meaning until they become synonymous with quackery and charlatanism, a process which has already occurred according to some modern authors.[1] However, they are words of noble ancestry in our linguistic heritage and should not be allowed to be diluted of their meaning in this way.

1. See, e.g., E. J. Cassels, *The Healer's Art* (Penguin Books, Harmondsworth, 1978), p. 14.

If the book is felt to lack unity, this can be explained by its origin. It is basically a collection of articles which have been published in various journals over a number of years. These articles have been revised, and in some cases reorganised and expanded, and several new studies have been added to the original ones in order to produce a more adequate coverage of the subject of health and healing in the New Testament. The articles which still retain much of their original form were published in the following journals:

The Scottish Journal of Theology

    1. 'Healing in the Epistle of James', vol. 24, pp. 326-345 (August 1971).
        This appears as chapter twelve of the present book.
    2. 'The Mission Charge to the Twelve and Modern Medical Missions'.
        vol. 28, pp. 313-328 (August 1975).
        This forms part of chapter thirteen.

The Expository Times

    'The Case of the Epileptic Boy', vol. 79, pp. 39–42 (November 1967).
        This is included as chapter seven.

The Evangelical Quarterly

    'The Case of the Bent Woman in Luke 13.10-17', vol. 49, pp. 195-205
        (October-December 1977).
        This forms chapter eight.

We have tried to reduce notes to a minimum, and have used them in most cases simply to provide source references. A few common forms of abbreviation have been used and a list of these is included.

Scripture quotations are usually given in the words of the Revised Standard Version of the Bible, but on occasions other translations have been preferred, and where this occurs it is indicated in the text.

Edinburgh   JOHN WILKINSON
November, 1979

LIST OF ABBREVIATIONS

Arndt and Gingrich — *A Greek-English Lexicon of the New Testament and Other Early Christian Literature*, edited by W. F. Arndt and F. W. Gingrich (Cambridge University Press, 1957).

AV — The Authorised Version of the Bible of 1611.

Barclay — *The New Testament. A New Translation* by William Barclay (Collins, London, 1968).

BDB — *A Hebrew and English Lexicon of the Old Testament* by F. Brown, S. R. Driver and C. A. Briggs (Oxford University Press, 1907).

ET — English Translation.

Knox — *The Holy Bible. A Translation from the Latin Vulgate* by R. A. Knox (Burns and Oates, London, 1955).

LXX — The Septuagint or the Greek Version of the Hebrew Old Testament.

NEB — *The New English Bible* (Oxford and Cambridge University Presses, 1970).

Phillips — *The New Testament in Modern English* by J. B. Phillips (Geoffrey Bles, London, 1960).

RSV — The Revised American Standard Version of the Bible (Nelson, London, 1952).

RV — The Revised Version of the Bible of 1885.

RVm — Reading from the margin of the Revised Version.

TEV — Today's English Version, or *The Good News Bible* (Collins, London, 1976).

Vulgate — The Latin Version of the Bible (*editio vulgata*) prepared by Jerome.

Part One

THE BIBLICAL UNDERSTANDING OF HEALTH

HEALTH *is such a perennial source of interest and concern to man in the modern world that it comes as a great surprise to find that the Bible appears to say little about it. This lack of interest, however, is more apparent than real for in the widest sense of man's wholeness, health is the main topic of the Bible. What modern man confines to the body, the Bible extends to the whole of man's being and relationships. It is only when man's being is whole and his relationships right that he can be truly described as healthy. The basic relationship of all is man's relationship to God and when this is disturbed all human relationships are disturbed whether they are of man to himself, to his fellows, or to his environment.*

Our concern in this book is principally with the concept of health and the practice of healing in the New Testament, but we cannot understand the New Testament unless we read it in the light of the Old. If the Old Testament is the lexicon whence the New derives many of its words and their meanings, the New Testament is the encyclopaedia of the Old in which these words are given fuller significance in concepts which, though already present in the Old Testament, are nevertheless only fully expressed and illustrated in the New, and supremely in the person, teaching and work of Jesus Christ. To quote Augustine's famous aphorism, The New Testament is latent in the Old, and the Old Testament is patent in the New.[1] *In the Old Testament is set out that perfect pattern and high quality of life which is health, and which was God's intention that man should enjoy. It was man's failure to attain that pattern and quality of life which made the New Testament necessary. This means that in general the Old Testament has more to say about health than about healing, and the New Testament says more about healing than about health. The New Testament presupposes the Old Testament concept of health and so any study of the New Testament understanding of health must begin with that of the Old Testament.*

REFERENCES

1. Augustine, *Quaestiones in Exodum*, 73.

Chapter One

THE CONCEPT OF HEALTH IN THE OLD TESTAMENT

The concordance to any English version of the Old Testament will readily reveal how rarely the word *health* occurs in its pages. The 'AV uses the word fifteen times in its translation of the Old Testament, whilst the RSV uses it only six times. Even those modern versions which do not stand in the tradition of English Bible translation which goes back to William Tyndale do not use the word any more often. James Moffatt in the revised edition (1935) of his translation used the word health on only twelve occasions.

The occurrence of a word so infrequently in a volume which runs to well over a thousand pages of double columns of print would normally suggest that such a book had little to say on the subject and could safely be ignored in any serious study of it. This conclusion would, however, only be valid if we were to insist on the Old Testament speaking our modern language, using our modern concepts, and presenting its teaching in a modern systematic way. It is obviously unreasonable to expect it to do any of these things. It is an ancient book which must be interpreted on its own terms and not ignored because its relevance is not immediately appreciated by the modern mind. The most striking feature of the Old Testament is that it presents its teaching not by definition and argument, but by illustration and example. It lays before its readers not a definition of health systematically expounded, but a picture of the characteristics of healthy people illustrated by their life, their character and their actions.

The modern reader of the Old Testament who is interested in the subject of health will also be surprised at the virtual absence of the word *body* from its pages. It is rare enough in the English versions where it is used to translate a number of words of very different meanings. In the Hebrew text there are names for about eighty parts of the body, but no word for the body as we think of it today. The word which comes nearest to meaning the physical body in Hebrew is the word *g viyyāh* which occurs thirteen times in the Hebrew Bible. On eight occasions it refers to a dead body, on three to a being seen in a vision or dream, and only on two occasions to living bodies as the potential subjects of starvation (Genesis 47.18) or of slavery (Nehemiah 9.37). It is the only Hebrew anthropological term which does not have any psychical meaning but only a purely physical one.[1] The rarity of its usage is therefore very significant, for it means that Hebrew does not feel the need of a word for the body regarded as a purely physical object. However, the Old Testament does have a word for the material of which the body is made. This is the word *bāsār* which is the visible

part of the physical substance which makes up the body. It is this word which
the RSV sometimes translates as body, but as Wolff points out,[2] it means not so
much the body, as man in his bodily aspect. It is not used for the body as a
separate physical entity although since there is no word for this, the word *bāsār*
is used in this sense on the rare occasions when such a word is required as, for
example, in Leviticus 13 *passim*, Numbers 8.7; 1 Kings 21.27; Job 4.15 and
Proverbs 4.22. The significance of the virtual absence of the word body from
the pages of the Old Testament is that health is not presented there in primarily
physical terms. This is in contrast to the modern popular concept of health
which is mainly physical in character.

Old Testament thought is usually regarded as predominantly synthetic in
nature and always concerned with different aspects of the whole rather than
dividing it up into distinct parts.[3] Its concept of man recognises no distinctions
in his being, but only aspects of man regarded as a whole. Nevertheless, for
purposes of analysis and understanding it is convenient to use terms and distinctions which in other contexts would denote parts rather than aspects of a whole.
This must be borne in mind as we now proceed to attempt to separate the
various strands which together compose the Old Testament concept of health.

The concept of health which we find in the Old Testament may be summarised in four propositions:

1. Health is basically a state of wholeness and fulfilment of man's being
   considered as an undivided entity.
2. Health on its ethical side consists of complete obedience to God's law.
3. Health on its spiritual side consists of righteousness which is basically a
   right relationship of man to God.
4. Health on its physical side is manifested by strength and long life.

*1. Health is basically a state of wholeness and fulfilment of man's being
considered as an undivided entity*

For the Old Testament writers the basic characteristic of man is life. At its
lowest level this is physical and biological existence, and it is with an account
of how this began that the Old Testament opens. However, the Old Testament
writers are not very interested in the purely biological level of life. They take
it for granted rather than describe or investigate it. They refer to different
physical organs of the body, but are not interested in their anatomical structure
or physiological function so much as in the moral and spiritual significance
which has been given to them. For them life consists not of physical anatomy or
physiological function, but of moral activity and spiritual achievement. Its
important dimension is its quality rather than its quantity, although it is
accepted that its quantity may reflect its quality. The Hebrew word which
expresses the fullness and well-being of life, and which therefore comes nearest
to expressing the Old Testament concept of health is the word *shalōm*. This
word occurs about two hundred and fifty times in the Hebrew Bible, and most
frequently in the Psalms (twenty-seven times), and in the prophetical books of
Isaiah (twenty-seven times) and Jeremiah (thirty-one times). In the English
versions it is commonly translated as 'peace', but its essential meaning is not of
peace understood simply as the absence of war, for this is its meaning in only

thirty-eight of the occurrences of the word in the Old Testament. Briggs gives
its meaning as 'completeness, soundness, welfare, peace'.[4] Burton in the lexico-
graphical appendix to his commentary on the Epistle to the Galatians says that
shalōm 'has as its fundamental idea "soundness", "prosperity", "well-being"
and acquires the sense of harmony between persons or nations, freedom from
strife and war, only as a secondary meaning and apparently because such freedom
from strife is conceived of as a necessary condition of well-being'.[5] Von Rad
gives its root meaning as 'well-being' with a strong emphasis on the material
side, and quotes the following references in support of this latter point: Judges
19.20; 1 Samuel 16.5; 2 Samuel 18.28 and Ezra 5.7.[6] There is therefore general
agreement that the root meaning of *shalōm* is that of wholeness, completeness
and well-being, and that it may denote the occurrence of these characteristics
in every sphere of life whether physical, mental and spiritual, or individual,
social and national. In most cases in which the word is used, *shalōm* means an
active dynamic condition or relationship of wholeness and fulfilment. It is true
that in the poetical books we read of the *shalōm* of the wicked in such verses as
Job 15.21; 21.9 and Psalm 73.3, but this is usually in the sense of their material
prosperity. The general view is that there is no true *shalōm* for the wicked
(Isaiah 48.22; 57.21 and 59.8). One of the covenant names of God which Gideon
used when he built his altar to the Lord at Ophrah was *Yahweh-shalōm*, the Lord
is *shalōm* (Judges 6.24). He it is who offers his people a covenant of *shalōm*, that
is, a covenant which will secure *shalōm* for them (Numbers 25.12; Isaiah 54.10;
Jeremiah 32.40; Ezekiel 34.25; 37.26, and Malachi 2.5). True *shalōm* comes from
God, for man finds his true wholeness and complete fulfilment only in God. In
God alone can he know that wholeness in all his being and of all his relationships which is what the Old Testament means by health. If this presentation of
the Old Testament concept of *shalōm* is correct, then it explains why it is so
difficult to translate this word into the terms which we use to express our
modern ideas of health, for the concept of *shalōm* is much more comprehensive
than our modern popular idea of health, and is not related primarily to the state
of the body.

2. *Health on its ethical side consists of complete obedience to God's law*

The World Health Organisation defined health as 'a state of complete
physical, mental and social well-being and not merely the absence of disease or
infirmity'.[7] According to this definition health has a positive and a negative
aspect. Health is the absence of disease or illness: this is its negative aspect. Far
more significantly, however, health is the presence of well-being in all the
departments of human life, and this is its positive aspect. This two-fold definition is true to the Old Testament understanding of health although this may
not have been evident to the framers of the definition drawn, as they were,
from all the nations of the world.

In the Old Testament these two aspects of health are both related to obedience to God's word and law. Obedience to God's law means freedom from
disease, whilst disobedience means liability to disease. This is set out explicitly
in such passages as Exodus 15.26; 23.20-26; Leviticus 26.14-16, 23-26; Deuteronomy 7.12-15; 28.27-29, 58-62, and Proverbs 3.7-8. In these passages God tells

his people Israel that if they will listen to his voice, do what is right in his eyes and obey his law then he will not bring disease of any kind upon them and will take away sickness from their midst. Conversely, if they disobey his law he will bring upon them and on their descendants 'extraordinary afflictions, afflictions severe and lasting, and sicknesses grievous and lasting' (Deuteronomy 28.59 RSV). What is explicitly stated in these passages about the relationship of obedience and disease is also implied in many other situations described in the Old Testament. In the nature of the case, the commoner situation described is that in which disobedience produces disease. We find examples of this kind of situation in the experience of the children of Israel during their desert wanderings. The outbreak of a severe and fatal plague (*negeph*) followed the rebellion of Korah and the sympathy the people showed to the rebels (Numbers 16.41-50). Poisonous snakes afflicted the people when they spoke against God and against Moses (Numbers 21.4-9). A fatal plague followed the defection of the people from God to the worship of the Baal of Peor (Numbers 25.1-9). We see the connection between obedience and sickness illustrated too in the case of individuals. Miriam spoke against Moses and was smitten with an unclean skin disease (Numbers 12.1-15). Gehazi became the victim of a similar disease because of his greed and deceit (2 Kings 5.26-27), and Jehoram king of Judah was stricken with a fatal intestinal disease because of his unfaithfulness to God (2 Chronicles 21.11-19). Disobedience results in disease, but health is the product of obedience.

Health is more than the absence of disease, and so obedience produces a positive state and condition of well-being, blessing and the consciousness of belonging to God. This is explicitly taught in such verses as Exodus 19.5; Deuteronomy 11.27; I Samuel 12.14; Psalm 119.165; Jeremiah 7.23; 42.6, and Zechariah 6.15. As with the negative aspect, the positive aspect of health is implicit in almost all the teaching of the Old Testament. Obedience of God's law results in the blessing of God on human life which is the basis of that human well-being which is health. 'The blessing is the power by which life is maintained and augmented. The result of the blessing is the condition defined by the word *shalōm*.'[8]

3. Health on its spiritual side consists of righteousness which is basically a right relationship of man to God

Righteousness is the regular translation-equivalent of the Hebrew word *tsedeq* and its feminine form *tsᵉdāqāh* in the Old Testament. Both words come from the root *ts-d-q* which is usually regarded as expressing the meaning of straightness. The words therefore mean straightness or conformity to a norm, and so they basically describe a relationship. To be righteous in the Old Testament view is to conform to a norm, to be in a right relationship. In the case of man this norm is the character of God, and this relationship is to God and his will. The righteous man fulfils all the demands which are laid upon him by the relationship in which he stands to God. In the case of the righteousness of God, the norm is his own nature and character and this is expressed in his faithful fulfilment of the terms of the covenant he has made with man.

Righteousness is fundamental to the Old Testament concept of health. A right relationship to God produces *shalōm* (Isaiah 32.17). Righteousness and *shalōm* flourish together (Psalm 72.7; 85.10; Isaiah 48.18, and Malachi 2.6). The pursuit of righteousness is the pursuit of life (Proverbs 11.4, 19, 28, 30). Righteousness is illustrated in the life of Enoch (Genesis 5.22), Noah (Genesis 6.9), and Joseph (Genesis 39.2, 21, 23), but supremely in the life of Abraham. In Abraham are linked together faith, obedience and righteousness (Genesis 12.4; 15.6; 17.23; 18.19; 22.16-18), and he was the supreme example of health in the Old Testament understanding of that word. At the end he was to go to his fathers in *shalōm* (Genesis 15.15).

4. *Health on its physical side is manifested by strength and long life*

In Psalm 29.11 strength is equated with *shalōm*, and in several places is regarded as the gift of God (Psalm 28.7-9; 68.35; 138.3; Isaiah 40.29-31; 41.10; Zechariah 10.6). It is clear, however, that when the Old Testament speaks of strength it does not mean simply physical strength, but the strength of man throughout his whole being which of course includes the strength of his body. When Karl Barth came to define health he did so in terms of strength. For him health was 'the strength to be as man'.[9] It is evident that strength in this sense is more than purely physical energy and power. The opposite of strength is weakness and this is the term by which sickness and disease are denoted in the Hebrew Bible. Although sickness is weakness and health is strength, neither is confined to the purely physical aspect of man. They may be most obvious to others by their physical manifestations, but they affect all parts of man's being. When we say that health is strength in the Old Testament sense we mean that it is experienced and manifested as power and energy in all parts of man's being and life.

The other main expression of health on its physical side is length of life. This was promised to Abraham along with *shalōm* (Genesis 15.15), and in due course we are told that he 'died in a good old age, an old man and full of years' (Genesis 25.8). It is also promised to all those who obey God's law (Deuteronomy 6.2; 30.20; 32.46-47; 1 Kings 3.14; Psalm 34.12-14; 91.16; Proverbs 3.1-2; 9.10-11; 10.27).

Although it is possible to distinguish these four aspects of health in the thought of the Old Testament and useful to do so for the purpose of systematic exposition, they are but separate aspects of a single whole. Health characterises the whole of man in much the same way as Reformed theology regards holiness not as one attribute of God among others, but as the absolute perfection of his being which is expressed in his attributes. Indeed, we may summarise the Old Testament concept of health as consisting of wholeness and holiness. The etymological and semantic connection between these two words which exists in English and the Teutonic languages does not hold for the Hebrew language. Nevertheless there is a real connection in thought between the two concepts in the Old Testament. Health is the wholeness of man's being and personality, and the holiness of his character and actions expressed in righteousness and obedience to God's law. Man's wholeness derives from God's wholeness, and man's

8   BIBLICAL UNDERSTANDING OF HEALTH

holiness reflects the holiness of God. The supreme call of the Old Testament is expressed in the oft-repeated demand by God of his people:

'Be holy, because I, the Lord your God, am holy' (Leviticus 19.2 TEV).

Wholeness and holiness are terms of relationship, and the relationship they express in this context is the relationship of man to God. Both words imply a standard, and that standard is the wholeness and perfection of the character of God. This same idea of relationship belongs to the other words which express the different aspects of health such as obedience, righteousness, strength and length of life. As Robinson points out, the question of the relation of the whole man to God is the basic interest of the Old Testament.[10] The Hebrew mind was not interested in the body for its own sake or in the constitution of man. It would find modern psychology and modern physiology equally irrelevant. The important question was man's relationship to God. It was this question with which the historians, poets and prophets of the Old Testament were concerned. It was this question which determined their view of man's health. For them, health consisted in the wholeness of being and the holiness of character which found their origin in man's relationship to God and reached their fullest and finest flowering as that relationship developed and deepened. This relationship, and therefore the health which springs from it, was not static but dynamic as men walked with God and shared his nature in their being and expressed his character in their actions.

REFERENCES

1. W. D. Stacey, *The Pauline View of Man* (Macmillan, London, 1956), p. 94.
2. H. W. Wolff, *Anthropology of the Old Testament* (SCM Press, London, 1974), p. 28.
3. A. R. Johnson, *The Vitality of the Individual in the Thought of Ancient Israel* (University of Wales Press, Cardiff, 1949), p. 7.
4. BDB, p. 1022, s.v. *shalōm*.
5. E. de W. Burton, *International Critical Commentary on the Epistle to the Galatians* (T. & T. Clark, Edinburgh, 1921), p. 425.
6. G. von Rad in *Theological Dictionary of the New Testament*, ed. G. Kittel (Eerdmans, Grand Rapids, 1964), vol. 2, p. 402, s.v. *eirēnē*.
7. World Health Organisation, *Basic Documents* (WHO, Geneva, 1948), p. 1.
8. Edmond Jacob, *Theology of the Old Testament* (Hodder & Stoughton, London, 1958), p. 179.
9. K. Barth, *Church Dogmatics* (T. & T. Clark, Edinburgh, 1961), ET by H. A. Kennedy, vol. III, 4, p. 357.
10. J. A. T. Robinson, *The Body: A Study in Pauline Theology* (SCM Press, London, 1952), pp. 15-16.

Chapter Two

THE WORDS FOR HEALTH IN THE NEW TESTAMENT

Once it is realised that the New Testament understanding of health is a much more comprehensive one than that which is current in modern popular thought, it will occasion no surprise that the terms which are used to denote the whole or a part of this understanding in the New Testament are relatively numerous. The absence of the usual Classical Greek word for health (*hugieia*) from the pages of the New Testament is reflected in the rare use of the word in the English versions. A survey of the occurrence of the word health and its synonyms in the three major English versions will provide a convenient starting-point for our consideration of the words which are used to denote health in the New Testament.

Reference	Greek	AV	RSV	NEB
Matthew 15.28	*iaomai*	made whole	healed	restored to *health*
Luke 7.10	*hugiainō*	whole	well	in good *health*
John 7.23	*hugiēs*	made whole	made well	giving *health*
Acts 3.16	*holoklēria*	perfect soundness	perfect *health*	completely well
Acts 27.34	*sōtēria*	*health*	strength	life
1 Peter 2.2	*sōtēria*	—	salvation	soul's *health*
3 John 2	*hugiainō*	be in *health*	be in *health*	enjoy good *health*

The table illustrates the many-sided nature of the New Testament understanding of health, for only in the case of 3 John 2 do all the versions agree to use the same word. The synonyms used in the different translations show how similar it is to the Old Testament concept. Health is thought of in terms of wholeness, well-being, soundness, life, strength and salvation. All these are facets of the New Testament understanding of health and express ideas which have already been found in the Old Testament. The comprehensive nature of the idea of health is also seen in the words which are used to express it in the New Testament, and we now proceed to examine these in more detail.

The first word we must consider is the word *hugiēs* which means having the quality of soundness, and represents a group of words of which the adjective and the verb occur in the New Testament. The noun *hugieia* is the classical Greek word for health, but it had become the name of the Greek goddess of health, the daughter of Aesculapius, and this pagan association may explain its absence from the pages of the New Testament. The verb is used mainly in the

Pastoral Epistles in a metaphorical sense for the soundness or wholesomeness of teaching, but it does occur in its literal sense three times in Luke's gospel where it is used, for instance, by Jesus to describe those who are whole and do not need a physician (Luke 5.31). It is, however, the adjective *hugiēs* which is the most commonly used of this group in its literal sense especially in the fourth gospel. In most cases the emphasis is on the physical aspect of soundness as when we are told that the withered hand of the man in the synagogue was restored *hugiēs* or sound like the other one (Matthew 12.13; Mark 3.5 and Luke 6.10) or when the impotent man's limbs were made sound enough for him to take up and carry his mattress (John 5.9). On ten occasions, words of this group are used by the LXX to translate the Hebrew word *shalōm* in the Old Testament. In most of these cases the word occurs in an enquiry about a person's general welfare, e.g. Genesis 29.6; 37.14; 43.27 and 2 Samuel 20.9. The emphasis is not so much on the physical well-being as on the general state of the person about whom the enquiry was made. The significant point is that both *shalōm* and *hugiēs* coincide in expressing the idea of the soundness or wholeness of man's being which is of the essence of health.

The second word is the word *eirēnē* which is used to describe a state of peace or rest as opposed to a state of war or disturbance. It is the commonest word used in the LXX to translate the word *shalōm*, and this usage is probably the origin of the common Vulgate translation of *shalōm* by *pax*, which explains the preference of the English versions for the translation of the word *shalōm* by peace. Because of its association with *shalōm* as its equivalent in Biblical Greek, the word *eirēnē* in the New Testament has a much fuller and more positive content than simply the absence of war which is its primary meaning in Classical Greek. The Biblical concept of peace is primarily one of wholeness, and in the New Testament usage of *eirēnē* this meaning is applied to man's relationships, especially his relationship to God, e.g. in Romans 5.1; Ephesians 2.14-18 and Colossians 1.20, and to his relationship with his fellows, e.g. in Mark 9.50; Romans 12.18 and 2 Corinthians 13.11. On the basis of this wholeness which characterises a man's relationship to God and his fellowmen, and which results from faith in the atoning work of his Son Jesus Christ, there arises what appears to be a distinctively Christian meaning of *eirēnē* as peace or serenity of mind referred to in John 14.27; 16.33; Romans 8.6 and Philippians 4.7.[1] This inner tranquillity and the harmonious relationship between God and man, and man and man from which it springs are the essential meaning of *eirēnē* in the New Testament and are a vital element in any understanding of the concept of health in the New Testament.

The third word which expresses the New Testament concept of health is *zōē*, life. There are three words for life in Greek but *bios* and *psuchē* generally refer to our common human life lived under the conditions of time and sense. This kind of life is taken for granted in the New Testament which is interested in life in its highest and fullest sense, and for this it uses the word *zōē*. Indeed, it may be truly said that the principal theme of the New Testament is the meaning and content of the word *zōē*. John and Paul are the New Testament writers who have most to say about it. It was what Jesus came to bring as the gift of God to men (John 3.16; 10.10). It was the reason why John wrote his gospel

(John 20.31). For him life consists of knowledge of the Father through the Son and this implies a conscious relationship of man with God (John 17.3). For Paul the basis of true life is righteousness which is a right relationship with God (Romans 1.17; Galatians 3.11), which is the gift of God through his Son (Romans 6.23), and by which we have peace with God (Romans 5.1) and new life in Christ (2 Corinthians 5.17). To make it quite clear what kind of life is in view, both John and Paul speak not simply of life, but of *zōē aiōnios* or eternal life. This is life, not with the quantity of time of which the Old Testament spoke, but with the quality of eternity unlimited by time. It begins now in time but does not belong to time, for it continues into eternity when time is no more. It is a concept of life which is not primarily temporal but eternal, and not primarily physical but spiritual. It is the life of God himself which men share through faith in his Son Jesus Christ. The New Testament concept of health expresses the quality and character of this eternal life, for health is the fullness and completeness of life.

We come now to the fourth word which expresses another facet of the New Testament idea of health. It is *teleios* which describes that which is mature, a word which is usually translated as *perfect* in the English versions, and which means that which is perfect and complete having attained the end for which it was created. As with the adjective *aiōnios*, we have in *teleios* the two aspects of the future and the present. When we think of the *telos* as the end of the process with the stage of complete perfection and maturity finally achieved, then *teleios* refers to the future. But we are to be *teleios* in the present. This means that we are to be mature, perfect, complete and whole here and now. There is no suggestion in the New Testament that maturity is progressive and reached by a process. It is rather a wholeness which is at once given to us now and also promised to us at the end, so that we are to be now and shall be hereafter *teleios* in the same manner in which God is (Matthew 5.48).

The final word we shall discuss and which expresses the concept of health in the New Testament is *sōtēria*. The adjective *sōs* from which it is derived means safe and sound, and so the noun *sōtēria* is the condition of being safe and sound. In the papyri which came from the rubbish heaps of Hellenistic Egypt at the end of last century the commonest meaning of *sōtēria* is health or well-being, and this would be the commonest meaning of the word in the Hellenistic world in which the New Testament was written. However, the word had been used by the translators of the Old Testament into Greek in the third century B.C. to denote God's deliverance of the Israelites at the Red Sea (Exodus 14.13), and at other times in their national history (Judges 15.18 and 1 Samuel 11.13), as well as his deliverance of the individual believer who trusted in God to deliver him from his enemies (Psalm 18.46; 38.22; 51.14 and 88.1). Consequently it came to have a rich religious content and application, and to mean the act of deliverance by which the condition of being safe and sound was attained. In the New Testament it is this meaning of deliverance to a safe and sound condition which prevails. In the gospels the noun *sōtēria* occurs only five times, four times in Luke (1.69, 71, 77 and 19.9) and once in John 4.22, and in each case it is used in the Old Testament sense of deliverance. The verb *sōzō* on the other hand includes both healing and salvation in the gospels. When we come to the epistles, however, we find that Paul deliberately limits the application of both the noun and the verb to man's relationship to God as the main area where *sōtēria* is required and it was this usage which came to predominate in theological writing. However, this is not to say that the body and health are excluded from Paul's thought about salvation, for he clearly looks forward to the redemption of the body as part of the salvation and renewal of the whole man as we see from Romans 8.23. Salvation in the New Testament sense is total and includes the whole man producing in him that condition of safety and soundness which forms part of the New Testament concept of health.

The five words which we have now briefly discussed all express some aspect of the New Testament understanding of health. It is significant that all of them except *zōē* had already been used by the Greek translators of the Old Testament to translate the Hebrew word *shalōm*. They had each brought their own contribution to the understanding of that comprehensive word, and in turn they had absorbed some of the other facets of its meaning, and these passed over into the New Testament to enrich and express its concept of what belonged to the true health and well-being of man.

REFERENCE

1. C. L. Mitton, *Interpreter's Dictionary of the Bible* (Abingdon Press, Nashville, 1962), vol. 3, p. 706, art. 'Peace in the New Testament'.

Chapter Three

THE DEFINITION OF HEALTH IN
THE NEW TESTAMENT

The Bible is a plain book so far as 'those things necessary to be known, believed and observed for salvation' are concerned, as the Westminster Confession reminds us.[1] It is not, however, a book which provides neat definitions of the ideas and matters with which it deals. If it were, theology would be a less demanding study, and Church history a path less strewn with heresy and schism. Nevertheless it is possible to derive some definitions from it for our own guidance and this we shall now attempt to do in the matter of the New Testament understanding of health. The predominant interest of the New Testament is, of course, in healing and it assumes and accepts the concept of health already set forth in the Old Testament. If there is any difference, it does not lie in the substance of the concept, but in the place where the emphasis is laid and in the fuller light shed by the New Testament revelation.

Several definitions relating to health are to be found in the pages of the New Testament, but all are partial and even fragmentary, and all overlap since the words they each use can often only be fully understood in the light of those used in the other definitions. In other words, the understanding of health in the New Testament is as many-sided as it is in the Old Testament. This is because any adequate definition of man's health and wholeness can only be in terms of the life and perfection of God who created him for fellowship with himself, and whose will it is that man should share and enjoy the same life and perfection as his own.

1. *Health as life*

The first definition we consider is that of health as life. In the tenth chapter of John's gospel Jesus is speaking about sheep and shepherds in what is the nearest approach to a parable which the fourth gospel affords. In verse ten he contrasts the motive of the sheep stealer with the purpose of himself as the good shepherd, and he states his own purpose in the following words:

'I came that they might have life, and have it abundantly' (RSV).

This statement by Jesus of the purpose for which he came has frequently been taken as a definition of health. Health is regarded as the abundance of life of which he speaks. The word he uses for life is *zōē*, the meaning of which we have already considered. It emphasises the quality of life as opposed to *bios* which emphasises the quantity or duration of life. It was not only life which Jesus came to bring, but life with a special quality, and even a special quantity of that quality for the adjective *perissos* which the RSV translates as 'abundantly' means 'more than a sufficient quantity'. The NEB translates this phrase as 'life in all its fullness'. The life which Jesus has in mind is eternal life, which is life with no horizon and of which time is not a measure. It is life with the quality of eternity where God himself dwells. It is the life of God himself.

Nothing could be healthier than the life of God in man producing in him that wholeness, soundness and righteousness which constitute true health and holiness. The relationship of God's life to man's life is a vital and basic element in the New Testament concept of health. The life of man apart from God is mere existence and duration. Health forms no necessary part of it, and men may therefore lack health all the days of their life. But where the life of man is infused with the life of God and lived in a close and constant relationship with him, there is life which is health indeed. Here life means health, and health is life itself.

2. *Health as blessedness*

In the Sermon on the Mount we have a second definition of health. In its opening verses Jesus gives an analysis of what he regards as perfect spiritual well-being. These verses have been known as the beatitudes ever since the time of Ambrose of Milan who gave them this name in his commentary on Luke's gospel. In the fuller version given in Matthew 5.3-12 it is commonly accepted that there are eight beatitudes and that these set out eight different elements of excellence which may be combined in one individual.

The common Classical Greek word for the blessedness or highest well-being of man was *eudaimonia* which literally means to have a good *daimōn*, but Jesus did not use this word nor is it used in the New Testament, probably because of its obvious pagan background. The term which Jesus used was *makarios* which Aristotle ranked lower than *eudaimōn*[2] but which in the New Testament was filled with a new content and given a new dignity when Jesus used it of the truly blessed man and Paul used it of God himself (1 Timothy 1.11 and 6.15).

If it is true that here in the beatitudes we have a definition of health in terms of blessedness, then the qualities of the healthy man are very different from what we might expect. The beatitudes represent a complete reversal of our earthly values and standards, and today the blessed man whom they portray would be regarded as down-trodden, persecuted, under-privileged and even psychologically abnormal. The meaning of the beatitudes is that blessedness and health come from within and not from without. The important thing in blessedness is not the human environment, but the human heart and that not in its physical sense but in the sense of the seat of the whole of man's life, physical, intellectual and spiritual. The only mention of the environment in the beatitudes is in terms of persecution and slander which are at once the product and occasion of blessedness.

When we speak of health as life, and of health as blessedness we are really saying the same thing, for the blessedness of the beatitudes is but another expression for eternal life. Both blessedness and eternal life belong to God, and through Jesus Christ his Son they are offered to men that they might share in the blessedness and life of God which is his purpose for man whom he has created.

3. *Health as holiness*

The nearest approach to a definition of health in the New Testament epistles is in the prayer with which Paul closes his first letter to the Thessalonian Church. The NEB version of 1 Thessalonians 5.23 reads as follows:

'May God himself, the God of peace, make you holy in every part, and keep you sound in spirit, soul, and body, without fault when our Lord Jesus Christ comes.'

The title 'the God of Peace' is a characteristic one in Paul's letters by which he reminds his readers of the author and giver of peace. It contains more than an echo of the *shalōm* of the Old Testament.

This is the only verse in the New Testament where the three terms for body, soul and spirit are brought together, but as Wheeler Robinson comments, 'This is not a systematic dissection of the distinct elements of personality'.[3] Paul is emphasising the total nature of the preservation which he requests from God for his readers, and his use of the three terms simply underlines the all-inclusiveness of his conception of the whole man.

The most significant aspect of this verse is the association of four qualities or attributes which by implication are to be found in God, and which through Jesus Christ can also be found in man. These are peace, holiness, soundness and blamelessness. They are to be found in every part of man, in his body, his soul and his spirit. This is true wholeness and real health, and of its comprehensive nature there can be no doubt.

4. *Health as maturity*

The word which more than any other summarises Paul's view of health in his epistles is the word *teleiōsis* or maturity. The noun itself does not appear in his writings, but he uses the adjective *teleios* and less often the verb *teleioō* to describe the state of maturity and perfection which should be the aim of the Christian believer. It is Paul's desire that his preaching of the gospel might produce men who are *teleios* or mature in Christ Jesus (Colossians 1.28, cp. 4.12). In Ephesians 4.13 he tells his readers that the aim of office-bearers in the Church should be to produce mature men. The phrase he uses is a very significant one. He speaks of *anēr teleios* which means a man of adult maturity and complete development. The standard by which this maturity is to be measured is the fullness of Christ. Paul does not regard himself as having reached this standard of maturity but in Philippians 3.12 states that this is what he is aiming at. It is clear from the previous verse that this state will only be fully attained after the resurrection of the dead. Even so, a relative *teleiōsis* is possible in this present life as we see from verse fifteen where the adjective *teleios* describes a maturity which is related to the stage which Paul and the Christians of the Church at Philippi have reached in their Christian experience.

An indication of how this maturity might be sought and attained is provided by Paul in Romans 12.1-2. At this point in the epistle he passes from the doctrinal part to the practical part of his letter. In the first eleven chapters he has set forth the mercies of God bestowed on both Jew and Gentile by their redemption in Christ, and now on the basis of this demonstration he appeals to the Roman Christians to dedicate themselves to God. He exhorts them to present their bodies as a sacrifice to God as the logical response in worship to what God has done for them. He describes this sacrifice as living, holy and acceptable to God, a description which must also apply to the state of the body to be offered in sacrificial worship. He then speaks of the mind or *nous* by which he means their moral consciousness, whose content and activity have been governed by the fashions of the present world (*aiōn*) which are opposed to the things of God and result only in disobedience to his will. Paul entreats his readers to be radically transformed by the renewal of their minds by the Holy Spirit so that they are governed, not by the changing fashions of the world, but by the will of God which they will now be able to discern and obey. It is in these terms involving both the body and the mind that Paul exhorts the Roman Christians to respond to the mercies of God and so to press on to attain the maturity of the whole man as measured by the standard of the fullness of Christ. A maturity which implies not only full growth and perfect development but also the wholeness, health and well-being of what is mature.

The New Testament presupposes the Old Testament concept of health and accepts its expression in terms of wholeness, obedience, righteousness and life. However, the content of these terms was transformed by the fuller revelation given in Jesus Christ. Each of them was personified and filled out for us by him. It was he who provided in his person a new standard of wholeness, obedience, righteousness and life. It was he who showed in his death how these might be achieved, and in his resurrection demonstrated the source of the power by which they might be attained. In particular he changed the concept of life. In Old Testament terms this had meant life measured by the quantity of time and the quality of this world, but Jesus came to bring eternal life, life measured by the quality of eternity where quantity and duration have no relevance.

REFERENCES

1. Chapter I, section vii.
2. Aristotle, *Nicomachean Ethics*, I. 10, 14 and 16.
3. H. W. Robinson, *The Christian Doctrine of Man* (T. & T. Clark, Edinburgh, 1911), p. 108.

Part Two

HEALING IN THE GOSPELS

THE STUDIES which form the second part of this volume are concerned with healing in the four gospels. In the first part of the book we have been considering concepts and principles. In the gospels we have these concepts and principles expressed in practice, as we have described for us the healing activity of Jesus.

In his book on The Mission and Expansion of Christianity, Harnack declared that 'Jesus appeared among his people as a physician'. He quoted the saying of Jesus that those who are well have no need of a physician, but those who are sick, recorded in Mark 2.17 and Luke 5.31, to support his statement, and went on to say that 'the first three gospels depict him as the physician of soul and body'.[1] Whilst this is true, it is of interest to note that Jesus is never called a physician (iatros) in the New Testament, although the verb iaomai from which the Greek word for physician is derived is frequently used of his healing activity.

The first author to call Jesus a physician was Ignatius of Antioch (A.D. 35-107) who wrote a letter to the Church at Ephesus before his martyrdom in which he said that there was only one physician, namely Jesus Christ our Lord (Ignatius to the Ephesians 7.2). It must be noted, however, that the reference here is metaphorical, for those who were to be cured (therapeuō) were afflicted with heresy and not with disease of the body or the mind. Clement of Alexandria (A.D. 150-215) in the first book of his Paedagogus has several references to Jesus as the physician who heals suffering, and here the reference is to the healing of the body and the soul (Book I, 1.1; 2.6; 6.36; 12.100, and 8.64). Clement calls him 'the all-sufficient (panakēs) physician of humanity' (2.6). There are other occasional references to Jesus as a physician in early Christian literature, but it was Origen (A.D. 185-254) who more frequently and fully than anyone else spoke of Jesus as the physician, and in his work Contra Celsum called him 'the good physician' (Book II, para. 67, end). In his enthusiasm, Origen went so far as to say that Jesus was called a physician in the Holy Scriptures,[2] which as we have already seen is not strictly correct. Finally, Eusebius of Caesarea (A.D. 260-340) spoke of Jesus as 'the great physician' in his panegyric addressed to Paulinus, the bishop of Tyre.[3] These two names of Jesus as 'the good physician' and 'the great physician' are names which have persisted to this day.

Although Jesus may not have been given the name of physician in the New Testament, there is no doubt that he is described as carrying out the work of a physician and healing men and women of disease. It is to a consideration of the description of this work in the four gospels that we now turn.

REFERENCES

1. A. Harnack, *The Mission and Expansion of Christianity in the First Three Centuries* (Williams and Norgate, London, 1908) ET by J. Moffat, vol. 1, p. 101.
2. Origen, *Homily on Leviticus*, 8, 1.
3. Eusebius, *Ecclesiastical History*, x, 4, 11.

Chapter Four

THE RECORDS OF HEALING

I. THE SPACE DEVOTED TO HEALING

A convenient measure of the space which the gospels devote to the description of the healing activity of Jesus is the number of verses in which it is described. By its very nature this cannot be an exact measure, for the verses vary in length, but it is sufficiently approximate for our purpose at present.

If we take the text of the gospels in the AV and count first the total number of verses in each, and then the total number of verses devoted to healing, we obtain the following results.

Gospel	Matthew	Mark	Luke	John
Total verses	1068	678	1149	879
Verses on healing	99	139	134	112
Percentage	9%	20%	12%	13%

This comparison is however a very crude one and takes no account of the nature of the contents of the four gospels. An obvious and relevant division of the contents is into narrative and discourse, the relative proportions of which differ between the gospels as the following table shows.

	Matthew	Mark	Luke	John
Narrative:				
Total verses	267	339	339	312
Percentage	25%	50%	34%	36%
Discourse:				
Total verses	801	339'	810	567
Percentage	75%	50%	66%	64%

The descriptions of the healing miracles belong to the narrative portion of the gospel record, and we shall obtain a truer picture of the amount of space given by each gospel to healing if we now compare the amount of the narrative which the accounts of the healing activity of Jesus take up in each one. When we make this comparison we obtain the results set out in this table.

	Matthew	Mark	Luke	John
Total narrative	267	339	339	312
Healing narrative	99	139	134	112
Percentage	40%	40%	35%	33%

These statistics are by no means exact and can only be rough indicators of significance, but they are of great interest in showing how relatively constant is the amount of narrative space in each gospel which is devoted to healing. Also, they reveal that all four of the evangelists regard the healing activity of Jesus as an important part of his ministry and give it a significant amount of space in their narrative.

II. THE NARRATIVES OF HEALING

The narratives of healing in the gospels can be divided into two main categories. There are those which describe the healing of an individual sick person, or more rarely of two or more sick people, in a variable amount of detail, and there are those which refer usually only briefly to the healing by Jesus of a group of people suffering from sickness or demon possession.

THE ACCOUNTS OF THE HEALING OF INDIVIDUALS

The accounts of the healing of sick or possessed individuals in which some clinical detail of the disease and its healing is given may be further classified into three distinct groups according to the nature of the healing. These groups include examples of physical healing, the exorcism of demons, and the raising of the dead. These groups may be classified as follows in accordance with their occurrence in the four gospels.

	Matthew	Mark	Luke	John
1. *Accounts of physical healing*				
A. In one gospel only.				
1. The two blind men	9.27-31			
2. The deaf mute		7.31-37		
3. The blind man of Bethsaida		8.22-26		
4. The woman with a spirit of infirmity			13.11-17	
5. The man with dropsy			14.1-6	
6. The ten leprosy patients			17.11-19	
7. The ear of Malchus			22.50-51	
8. The nobleman's son				4.46-54
9. The impotent man				5.1-16
10. The man born blind				9.1-41
B. In two gospels only.				
11. The centurion's servant	8.5-13		7.1-10	
C. In three gospels (In the order of Mark).				
12. Peter's mother-in-law	8.14-15	1.30-31	4.38-39	

13. The man full of leprosy	8.1-4	1.40-45	5.12-15
14. The paralytic	9.1-8	2.1-12	5.18-26
15. The man with the withered hand	12.10-13	3.1-6	6.6-11
16. The woman with the flow of blood	9.20-22	5.25-34	8.43-48
17. Blind Bartimaeus	20.29-34	10.46-52	18.35-43

2. *Accounts of the exorcism of demons*

   A. In one gospel only.

1. The dumb demoniac	9.32-34		

   B. In two gospels only.

2. The blind and dumb demoniac	12.22-24		11.14-16
3. The synagogue demoniac		1.21-28	4.31-37
4. The Syrophoenician girl	15.22-28	7.24-30	

   C. In three gospels.

5. The Gadarene demoniac	8.28-34	5.1-20	8.26-39
6. The epileptic boy	17.14-21	9.14-29	9.37-43

3. *Accounts of the raising of the dead*

   A. In one gospel only.

1. The widow's son at Nain			7.11-18	
2. Lazarus				11.1-46

   B. In three gospels.

3. Jairus' daughter	9.18-19, 23-26	5.22-24, 35-43	8.41-42, 49-56

According to this list there are twenty-six accounts of the healing of individuals in the four gospels. If we count the number recorded in each gospel and add them together we obtain a total of forty-eight accounts, but a careful reading of the gospels will reveal that there are four duplicate accounts and nine triplicate accounts of the same incidents and this can be seen from the list above. When we subtract these from the total of forty-eight we arrive at the figure of twenty-six. There is doubt about only two of the triplicate accounts. The first is the case of the Gadarene demoniac, and the second is the healing of Bartimaeus. In both cases it is reasonable to suppose that two men were healed as Matthew records, but Mark and Luke concentrated on one of them because they had more details about him or knew him personally so that in the case of the blind man Mark could even name him as Bartimaeus. There are differences between the accounts of two of the duplicate accounts which should be noted, but they are not significant enough to require a conclusion that they refer to different incidents. In one case Matthew speaks of a blind and dumb demoniac (12.22), whilst Luke speaks only of a demon that was dumb (11.14). In the other case Matthew speaks of a centurion approaching Jesus personally (8.5) where Luke says that he sent Jewish elders to Jesus (7.3). No fewer than nine of the other accounts of healing have been regarded by various authors as doublets or duplicate accounts, and it is true that some accounts do show points of resemblance to others which are not usually regarded as their duplicates. However, we remain unconvinced of the probability of these other suggested identifications. There are similarities of language in the descriptions which is understandable when it is realised that the accounts come from a common linguistic tradition and milieu, but it seems incredible that a withered hand could be confused with the swollen ankles of dropsy as Beare suggests,[1] or that Mark should record the healing of the same man on two occasions, first as a deaf mute (7.31-37) and then as a blind man (8.22-26) as Bultmann suggests.[2] We are, of course, assuming that these accounts of healing by Jesus are historical and that the incidents are not invented.

THE REFERENCES TO THE HEALING OF GROUPS

In addition to the twenty-six accounts of the healing of individuals which occur in the gospels, there are twelve other references to occasions when Jesus healed sick people. In these we are given few details and simply told that he healed an unspecified number of sick people in a group.

	Matthew	Mark	Luke
A. References in one gospel only.			
1. In an unnamed city			5.15
2. In the Temple	21.14		
B. In two gospels only.			
3. On a tour in Galilee	9.35	(6.6)	
4. In answer to John the Baptist	11.1-6		7.18-23[*]
5. At Gennesaret	14.35-36	6.54-56	
6. In the hills	15.30-31	7.31-37	
7. In Judaea	19.2	(10.1)	
C. In three gospels.			
8. At Capernaum	8.16-17[*]	1.32-34[*]	4.40-41[*]
9. On another tour in Galilee	4.23-25[*]	1.39[*]	(4.44)
10. By the seaside	12.15-16	3.10-12[*]	6.17-19[*]
11. At Nazareth	13.58	6.5	(4.24)
12. After the return of the Twelve	14.14	(6.34)	9.11

Some of the above references mention both physical healing and exorcism as occurring in the same collective incident, and these are indicated by an asterisk. Where there is no asterisk the reference is to physical healing alone. In some of the parallel references any mention of healing may be omitted although we are told in the other accounts of the same incident that healing did occur. These references which speak only of preaching or teaching are those included within brackets in the above list. It is noteworthy that Matthew never omits a reference to healing in all the eleven incidents which he records, whilst Mark omits such a reference on three occasions and Luke on two. On the other hand Matthew omits a reference to exorcism on two occasions where it is said to have occurred in the parallel account in Luke.

Amongst the references to occasions on which Jesus healed groups or crowds of sick people there is no mention of any incident in which he raised the dead. In his answer to John the Baptist, Jesus mentioned the fact that the dead were raised up by him as an indication that he was indeed the Messiah, the one who was to come (*ho erchomenos*, Matthew 11.3-5 and Luke 7.20-22), but we are not told that he raised the dead on that occasion. This may mean that cases in which Jesus raised the dead were always reported in full since they were so important. If this is so then it means that Jesus raised only three people from the dead during his ministry on earth, and the reference to raising the dead in his answer to the Baptist was to the raising of the widow's son from the dead at Nain, an incident which immediately precedes the Baptist's question in Luke (see 7.11-17). However, this may not be so and Jesus may have raised others from the dead of whom we are not told. Certainly it is very probable that he healed more people than we are told about in the gospels. John tells us in the conclusion of his gospel that Jesus did many other things including many other *sēmeia* or signs, which is the word by which he refers to miracles, over and above the number of those he had recorded in order that men might believe that Jesus was the Christ, the Son of God (John 20.30 and 21.25).

We have therefore in all some thirty-eight accounts of healing by Jesus recorded in the gospels. Twenty-six of these are concerned with individual sick persons of whom some details are usually provided, and twelve with the healing of groups of sick people of whom no individual detail is recorded. These accounts form the basis of our study of the healing practice of Jesus in the gospels.

III. THE DISEASES HEALED

IN THE HEALING OF INDIVIDUALS

Now that we have identified the twenty-six accounts of the healing of individuals by Jesus in which details are given of the sick and their sickness, it is possible to classify them according to the nature of the disease from which they suffered. In most cases the diagnosis cannot be any more than a general or symptomatic one, but in a few cases sufficient significant details have been recorded which allow a more specific diagnosis to be made. In the following classification of the diseases healed by Jesus the references given are those of the verses which contain the relevant information about the diagnosis.

1. *Physical disease*

    A. Acute disease.
        1. Fever: The nobleman's son (John 4.52).
            Peter's mother-in-law (Matthew 8.14; Mark 1.30; Luke 4.38).
        2. Acute anterior poliomyelitis:
            The centurion's servant (Matthew 8.6; Luke 7.2).
        3. Incised wound: Malchus' ear (Luke 22.50).
        4. Unknown fatal diseases:
            Widow's son at Nain (Luke 7.12).
            Jairus' daughter (Matthew 9.18; Mark 5.23; Luke 8.42).
            Lazarus (John 11.3 and 13).
    B. Chronic disease.
        1. Nervous disease:
            a. Paraplegia or paralysis of the lower limbs:
                The paralytic (Matthew 9.2; Mark 2.3; Luke 5.18).
                The impotent man (John 5.5-7).
            b. Paralysis of the hand:
                The man with the withered hand (Matthew 12.10; Mark
                    3.1; Luke 6.6).
            c. Blindness:
                The two blind men (Matthew 9.27).
                The blind man of Bethsaida (Mark 8.22).
                The man born blind (John 9.1).
                Blind Bartimaeus (Matthew 20.30; Mark 10.46; Luke 18.35).
            d. Deafness and defective speech:
                The deaf mute (Mark 7.32).
        2. Rheumatic disease of the spine (spondylitis ankylopoietica):
            The woman with a spirit of infirmity (Luke 13.11).[3]
        3. Chronic heart failure:
            The man with dropsy (Luke 14.2).
        4. Gynaecological disease: Fibroid tumours of the uterus.
            The woman with the flow of blood (Matthew 9.20; Mark
              5.25; Luke 8.43).
        5. Skin disease:
            The ten leprosy patients (Luke 17.12).
            The man full of leprosy (Matthew 8.2; Mark 1.40; Luke 5.12).

A close examination of the references in these cases will reveal how often it is Luke who records the significant detail. It is he who tells us that Peter's mother-in-law had a *high* fever (Luke 4.38); that the leprosy patient was *covered* with leprosy (Luke 5.12 NEB); that the withered hand was the man's *right* hand (Luke 6.6); and that the young man of Nain was the *only* son of his mother, and she was a *widow* (Luke 7.12). This awareness of the significance of detail is a reflection and confirmation of Luke's medical training.

2. *Demon possession*

    A. With specific physical manifestations described.

1. Major epilepsy:
   The synagogue demoniac (Mark 1.26; Luke 4.35).
   The epileptic boy (Matthew 17.15; Mark 9.17-26; Luke 9.39).
2. Acute mania:
   The Gadarene demoniac (Matthew 8.28; Mark 5.2-7; Luke 8.29).
3. Mutism or an inability to speak:
   The dumb demoniac (Matthew 9.32-33).
4. Mutism accompanied by blindness:
   The blind and dumb demoniac (Matthew 12.22; Luke 11.14).
B. With no specific physical manifestations described.
   The Syrophoenician girl (Matthew 15.22; Mark 7.25).

The evidence that the demoniac healed in the synagogue at Capernaum suffered from major epilepsy is found in the words used to describe what happened when Jesus healed him. Mark tells us that the demon cried with a loud voice and produced a convulsion in the man (Mark 1.26). He uses the verb *sparassō*, to tear or rend, to describe the convulsion. Luke describes how the demon threw him down to the ground and uses the verb *riptō* which in Hippocrates is frequently used of convulsions (Luke 4.35).[4] This evidence convinced Alexander that this man had major epilepsy,[5] but Micklem was not so sure.[6] All that we can say is that although the evidence is not strong, it is suggestive of the diagnosis of epilepsy in this case. It is worth noting how Luke once again adds a significant detail when he records that although the man did fall to the ground in a convulsion, he was not injured.

It was suggested by Alexander that the Syrophoenician girl also suffered from major epilepsy, the result of demon possession. He calls her condition one of 'epileptic idiocy'.[7] The basis of this diagnosis is Mark's description of the girl's state when her mother returned home. Mark 7.30 describes the girl as *beblēmenos epi tēn klinēn* which the AV and the RV render as 'laid upon the bed', whilst the RSV and the NEB translate it as 'lying in bed'. The perfect participle *beblēmenos* comes from the verb *ballō*, to throw, and Alexander understands it to mean that the girl was hurled upon the bed by an epileptic convulsion before she was healed. However, the verb *ballō* may be used without any suggestion of violence about it, and the same participle is used to describe Peter's mother-in-law *lying* in bed with a fever in Matthew 8.14, and of the paralytic *lying* on his bed in Matthew 9.2. Mark's description therefore need not mean that the girl had had a convulsion before she was healed, and also it is unnecessary to regard her as suffering from epilepsy. It is equally unnecessary to suggest that she is suffering from idiocy in any form, for there is not a shred of evidence in the text to support this suggestion.

Demon possession is often regarded as a concept which has been rendered unnecessary by modern psychiatry. What ancient writers called demon possession is said to be mental disorder of the various types which are familiar to psychiatrists today. It is then argued that since modern psychiatry can explain the phenomena formerly attributed to demon possession we no longer need to believe in the existence or activity of demons. This is the thesis which is maintained by McCasland in his book *By the Finger of God*.[8] However, the matter is not as simple as this view would suggest, for the introduction of psychiatry by no means excludes the possibility of demon possession. Psychiatry is rarely able to *explain* mental disorder, but only to *describe* it as we can see from its terminology, which is almost entirely symptomatic or descriptive in character. It deals with descriptions more than causes although in a few cases it is able to identify specific causes of mental disorder. The term demon possession defines a cause of mental disease, and is in a different category from the descriptive terminology with which modern psychiatry works. In psychiatric terms we may diagnose the Gadarene demoniac of Mark 5.2-7 as suffering from a manic-depressive psychosis. At the time he met Jesus he was in a state of acute mania, and from his local reputation he appears to have been frequently in such a state. By calling his disease a manic-depressive psychosis we have simply described his condition as a disorder of his personality which manifests itself by the occurrence of attacks of either mania or depression, or of both states at different times in the same person. The diagnosis therefore is a purely descriptive one and tells us nothing about the cause. Psychiatry can tell us little about the cause of this disorder although it can describe various concomitant features of the condition such as its occurrence in other members of the patient's family, its association with a particular type of personality, and a possible correlation with biochemical changes in the nervous tissue at the base of the brain. It can also describe certain factors or states which are observed to precede the occurrence of the attacks, and which may therefore be held to precipitate their onset. However, nothing that psychiatry can tell us about manic-depressive psychosis can exclude demon possession as a possible cause of the condition. This is not to say that every case of this type of psychosis or of any type of mental disorder is always due to demon possession. We shall see this illustrated when we come to discuss the case of the epileptic boy in chapter seven. In epilepsy we can demonstrate the operation of specific causes such as a brain tumour or head injury in some cases, but in the majority of cases no physical cause is demonstrable and there is no reason why demon possession should not be the underlying cause of the convulsions in these cases. It is not true, therefore, that modern psychiatry excludes the possibility of demon possession as a cause of mental disease.

The diagnosis may not always be clear in these individual cases of disease which Jesus healed, but it is evident that they were almost all cases which the medical profession of his day had failed to cure. In the case of the woman with the flow of blood this failure by many physicians is explicitly stated in Mark 5.26, and admitted in Luke 8.43, and it must have been true for most of the other cases also. It is relevant to add that they are mostly examples of conditions which medical knowledge and skill are still not able to cure today.

IN THE HEALING OF GROUPS

The description of the diseases healed on the twelve occasions on which it is recorded that Jesus dealt with a group or a crowd of sick people is much more general than in the case of the healings of individual sick persons. Physical conditions predominate in these incidents and in only a third of the accounts is there a mention of demon possession. The terms which are used to describe the different conditions which were brought to Jesus for healing are set out in the following list.

Incident	Reference	English	Greek
1. In an unnamed city	Luke 5.15	infirmity	*astheneia*
2. In the Temple	Matthew 2.14	blindness	*tuphlos*
		lameness	*chōlos*
3. On a tour in Galilee	Matthew 9.35	disease	*nosos*
		illness	*malakia*
4. In answer to John the Baptist	Luke 7.21	disease	*nosos*
		plague	*mastix*
		evil spirits	*pneumata ponēra*
		blindness	*tuphlos*
5. At Gennesaret	Matthew 14.35	sickness	*kakōs echō*
6. In the hills	Matthew 15.30	lameness	*chōlos*
		lameness	*kullos*
		blindness	*tuphlos*
		mutism	*kōphos*
7. In Judaea	Matthew 19.2	no description given	
8. At Capernaum	Matthew 8.16	demon possession	*daimonizomai*
		sickness	*kakōs echō*
	Luke 4.40	sick with various diseases	*astheneō nosois poikilais*
9. On another tour in Galilee	Matthew 4.23-24	disease	*nosos*
		illness	*malakia*
		sickness	*kakōs echō*
		suffering from torture	*basanois echō*
		demon possession	*daimonizomai*
		epilepsy	*selēniazomai*
		paralysis	*paralutikos*
10. By the seaside	Mark 3.10	plague	*mastix*
		unclean spirits	*pneumata akatharta*
	Luke 6.17	disease	*nosos*
11. At Nazareth	Mark 6.5	sickness	*arrōstos*
12. After the return of the Twelve	Matthew 14.14	sickness	*arrōstos*

The terms used in this list of the incidents of group healings may be divided into two main groups. The first group consists of those which describe symptoms which are referable to a specific organ or system of the body. Examples of the terms which belong to this group are blindness, lameness, mutism and paralysis. They give no indication of the cause of the condition they describe, but the disability produced by these conditions would make those afflicted by them come to Jesus for healing.

The other group consists of terms which are much more general in meaning and give little assistance in the recognition of the condition they describe. In most languages the words used to denote illness are general in meaning like the terms in this group. In English the effect of sickness is to produce a state of dis-ease or discomfort; an illness makes a person feel ill (i.e. evil, of which the word ill is a contraction) or bad; and an ailment causes him to feel anguish or afflicted. These English words describe the effects of sickness rather than the nature of the sickness itself. A brief survey of the Greek terms used for sickness in the gospels and shown in the above list will show that this is true of them also.

1. *Astheneia* and its related verb *astheneō* are the commonest words used to describe sickness in the gospels. They denote weakness or a lack of strength (*sthenos*) which results from disease of all types, and are commonly translated by infirmity in the English versions. Of the four gospels it is Luke and John who use these words most frequently with Luke showing some preference for the noun, and John for the verb.

2. *Kakōs echontes* or some variant of it is the commonest phrase for sickness in the gospels. It means literally being in a bad way and is used in the papyri for sickness in both man and cattle. It is not used by John and is chiefly a Markan word and is used only once by Matthew and Luke apart from their parallel accounts to Mark.

3. *Nosos* is cognate with the Latin verb *noceo*, to harm or injure and is the common Hellenistic word for disease. Mark uses it only once (1.34) whilst Matthew and Luke both use it four times.

4. *Arrōstos* means literally powerless and is used of sickness three times by Mark (6.5 and 13; and 16.18) and once by Matthew (14.14). The noun *arrōstia* is the term used for disease in Modern Greek and *nosos* has dropped out of use except in compound words such as *nosokomeion*, hospital.

5. *Mastix* means a whip and is used to denote disease on four occasions when it is translated by the AV and RV as plague which is derived from the Greek *plēgē* meaning a blow or a stroke. It is used in Mark 3.10; 5.29; 5.34, and Luke 7.21.

6. *Malakia* is used only by Matthew and always in combination with *nosos* (Matthew 4.23; 9.35 and 10.1). It literally means softness and the adjective is used to describe soft rich clothing in Matthew 11.8. It therefore refers to the debility and weakness which disease produces.

7. *Basanos* is used of disease in Matthew 4.24. This word has an interesting history, for it originally meant the Lydian touchstone which was used to test the purity of a sample of gold. It then came to mean the torture applied in the examination of slaves and prisoners, and finally it was used to describe disease as that which tortured and tormented people. Most of the English versions understand the term to mean a painful disease. The cognate verb is used in Matthew 8.6 and 8.29 to describe the torments of disease and demon possession.

None of these terms appears to have a specific application to any disease although with the exception of *basanos* and its verb *basanizō* they all refer to physical disease and are distinguished from demon possession. It is therefore difficult to distinguish exactly between them in usage. Bruce has made the attractive suggestion that in Matthew 4.24 we may find the nearest approach to a classification of disease which we have in the New Testament.[9] This classification may be set out in the following way:

The sick (*hoi kakōs echontes*).
1. Those with specific diseases (*poikilais nosois*).
   These diseases are not listed, but Bruce suggests they might include fever, leprosy and blindness.
2. Those with tormenting diseases (*basanois*).
   a. Demon possession.
      The Gadarene demoniac asked Jesus not to torment him according to Mark 5.7 and parallels, and used the verb *basanizō*.
   b. Epilepsy
      Although the word *basanizō* is not used, the account of the epileptic boy in Mark 9.14-27 gives a vivid description of how the disease tormented him.
   c. Paralysis.
      In Matthew 8.6 the centurion describes his servant as lying paralysed and in terrible distress and uses the verb *basanizō*. The AV and RV both speak of him as grievously tormented.

However, even if we do accept the suggestion that this list is meant to be a classification of disease, it does not take us much nearer the precise identification of the diseases which Jesus healed when he was confronted with a crowd of sick people. In these cases we are not able to go much further than the distinction between acute and chronic diseases. The term *hoi kakōs echontes* means simply that the people so described are ill. Acute illness appears to be indicated by the use of the terms *nosos*, *mastix* and *basanos*, whilst chronic disease is described by the words *astheneia* with its verb *astheneō*, and *malakia*. These distinctions are not hard and fast as we can see from the use of the word *mastix* for the chronic debilitated condition of the woman with the flow of blood in Mark 5.29 and 34, in spite of the fact that the derivation of this word would appear to suggest an acute condition.

We conclude that, although it is possible to recognise a broad distinction between acute and chronic states of disease in the use of the words which describe the condition of the sick, the terms are essentially general in meaning and give little help in the precise recognition of the conditions to which they are applied. It is clear, therefore, that a study of the diseased conditions healed by Jesus in the crowds of sick people who came to him does not give us any more information than we have already obtained from our consideration of the case records of the individual cases he healed.

IV. THE WORDS FOR HEALING

The word *health* does not occur in the gospels in the English AV, RV or RSV, whilst the verb heal and its derivatives occur fifty-five times in the AV and fifty-eight times in the RSV. This fact illustrates how the gospels are more interested in describing healing than in defining health. The verbs used for healing in the gospels may be listed as follows in the order of their frequency of usage.

Verb	Matthew	Mark	Luke	John	Total
Therapeuō	16	6	14	1	37
Iaomai	4	1	12	3	20
Sōzō	3	6	4	0	13
Apokathistēmi	1	2	1	0	4
Diasōzō	1	0	1	0	2

This table takes no account of the usage of the words in parallel accounts. When we exclude the parallel usages we get the following figures for the absolute usage of the words:

Therapeuō is used 26 times and is commonest in Matthew, but Luke also is very fond of this word.

Iaomai occurs 19 times and is most frequent in Luke.

Sōzō is used eleven times and most frequently by Mark.

Apokathistēmi and *diasōzō* are both used twice.

The commonest word for healing in the gospels is therefore the verb *therapeuō*. In Classical Greek this word meant to serve or attend a person, with special emphasis on the willingness of the service rendered and on the personal relationship between the server and the served. This is well illustrated in Plato's *Euthyphrō* where, in the thirteenth chapter, Socrates and Euthyphro discuss the meaning of *therapeia* which is usually translated 'service' or 'attention' in the standard English translations. Plato gives several senses in which the word may be used and one of them is to denote the art of the physician in which the purpose of *therapeia* is to produce health (*hugieia*). It is in this sense that the verb *therapeuō* is used in the gospels where it is never used in the general sense of rendering service, but only in the sense of healing.

Out of the twenty-six times it occurs in the gospels, twice it refers to the work of physicians. The first reference is in the proverb quoted by Jesus in Luke 4.23, 'Physician, heal yourself', and the second is in the reference to the failure of the physicians to heal the woman with the flow of blood in Luke 8.43. On every other occasion the verb refers to non-medical healing or healing carried out by those who were not physicians. On one occasion it is used for this type of healing which was attempted unsuccessfully by the disciples on the epileptic boy in the absence of Jesus in Matthew 17.16. With these three exceptions the verb is always used of miraculous healing by Jesus. In the majority of cases it refers to the healing of physical disease, but it may also be used of exorcism as in Matthew 12.22; Luke 6.18; 7.21 and 8.2. It is most frequently used by the gospel narrator to describe the healing activity of Jesus, but the verb is also used by Jesus himself to describe his own healing activity in Matthew 8.7 and Luke 14.3. It is also used by Jesus to describe the kind of healing he commissioned his disciples to perform when he sent them out in Matthew 10.8 and Luke 10.9.

In the gospels the idea of willing personal service which the word embodied in Classical Greek usage is still present, but there is a great difference in the type of service rendered when the word is used of our Lord's healing work. It is no longer a service which demands the frequent attendance of the attendant to attain its object as in the care of dogs or horses, or the building of a house or ship, or in the worship of the gods as Plato describes in the *Euthyphrō*. These activities all need time for the attainment of their object, but in the gospels the art of healing by Jesus is the art of the immediate and complete restoration to health. The sick were willingly and personally attended to by him, but their cure was immediate and complete and their sickness needed no more attention. It is this immediacy of cure which characterises the use of the verb *therapeuō* in the gospels, and therefore it does not simply mean to treat medically as a physician treats his patients, except in the two passages already mentioned where it is used specifically of the activity of physicians.

The verb *iaomai* is the origin of the word *iatros* which is the Greek name for a physician. It is less frequent in the New Testament than *therapeuō*, whilst in the Greek Old Testament the reverse is true. In the gospels it is more commonly used by Luke than by the others, perhaps because Luke himself was a *iatros* or physician as we know from Colossians 4.14. The derivation of the verb is uncertain, but from its earliest appearance in Homer it is used in the medical sense of curing or healing. It is used almost exclusively of physical healing in the gospels, the only exception being in Luke 9.42 where it is used of the exorcism of the demon from the epileptic boy. This verse is an example of how Luke sometimes replaces the verb *therapeuō* used by Matthew by *iaomai* (cp. Matthew 17.16). Another example is the group healing described in Matthew 14.14 where *therapeuō* is used, but which Luke replaces by *iaomai* in his account in Luke 9.11. On several occasions Luke uses the two verbs synonymously in the same context. In Luke 9.1-2 he says first that Jesus gave the Twelve authority to heal (*therapeuō*), and then sent them out to heal (*iaomai*). Matthew had used *therapeuō* in both cases (Matthew 10.1 and 8). Shortly after that in 9.11 Luke speaks of Jesus healing (*iaomai*) those who had need of healing (*therapeuō*). In Luke 14.3-4 we have Jesus using *therapeuō* when speaking about healing, and Luke using *iaomai* to describe the healing which Jesus carried out on the man with the dropsy. Similarly in the fourth gospel, John appears to regard the two verbs as synonymous, for he uses both of them to describe the healed state of the paralysed man at the pool of Bethesda (John 5.10 and 13). It appears therefore that in their usage in the gospels these two verbs are regarded as synonymous. Amongst the four gospels, Luke used the verb *iaomai* most frequently and even on occasions preferred it to *therapeuō*. This may be because it was a more congenial word to a physician.

The occurrence of the verb *sōzō* amongst the words used for healing in the gospels is of great interest and potentially of great significance for the understanding of the New Testament concept of health and healing. We have already considered the use of the noun *sōtēria* as meaning health, and we now come to consider the verb *sōzō* as meaning to heal. Both words are derived from the adjective *sōs* which means safe. The verb originally meant to make safe and was used for deliverance from danger by an acute intervention of the gods or of men. It came to have a wide range of use in daily life and in religion, and this

broad spectrum of usage is reflected in the gospels where it may mean deliverance from danger, disease and death, both physical and spiritual.

$S\bar{o}z\bar{o}$ and its intensive form $dias\bar{o}z\bar{o}$ occur fifty-eight times in the gospels,
but when we exclude its use in parallel passages in the synoptic gospels this
figure is reduced to a total of thirty-eight. Of these thirty-eight occurrences
there are eleven in which the verb refers to physical healing or exorcism, and
most of these cases are translated by the RSV as 'made well'. These occurrences
are as follows given in the order of the gospels:

	Reference	Incident
1.	Matthew 9.21 = Mark 5.28.	The woman with the flow of blood.
2.	Matthew 9.22a = Mark 5.34 = Luke 8.48.	
3.	Matthew 9.22b.	
4.	Matthew 14.36 (*diasōzō*) = Mark 6.56 (*sōzō*).	The healings at Gennesaret.
5.	Mark 5.23. The request of Jairus.	The daughter of Jairus.
6.	Luke 8.50. The reassurance of Jesus.	
7.	Mark 10.52 = Luke 18.42.	Blind Bartimaeus.
8.	Luke 7.3 (*diasōzō*).	The centurion's servant.
9.	Luke 8.36 ('was healed' RSV).	The Gadarene demoniac.
10.	Luke 17.19.	The Samaritan leprosy patient.
11.	John 11.12 ('will recover' RSV).	The raising of Lazarus.

In addition to these eleven examples of the use of *sōzō* or *diasōzō* to describe
the healing of physical disease or exorcism, there are nine more occurrences of
the verb *sōzō* (or eighteen if we include the parallel references) in which the
word refers to deliverance from physical danger or death. These are as follows:

	Reference	Incident
I.	Deliverance from danger of drowning.	
1.	Matthew 8.25: *Save Lord; we are perishing.*	The stilling of the storm.
2.	Matthew 14.30: *Lord save me.*	Peter walking on the water.
II.	Deliverance from death.	
1.	Mark 3.4 = Luke 6.9: *To save life or to kill.*	The man with the withered hand.
2.	Matthew 16.25 = Mark 8.35 = Luke 9.24. *Whoever would save his life.*	Teaching on discipleship
3.	Matthew 27.40 = Mark 15.30 = Luke 23.37. *Save yourself.*	The crucifixion of Jesus.
4.	Matthew 27.42a = Mark 15.31a = Luke 23.35a. *He saved others.*	
5.	Matthew 27.42b = Mark 15.31b = Luke 23.35b. *He cannot save himself.*	
6.	Matthew 27.49: *Let us see whether Elijah will come to save him.*	
7.	Luke 23.39: *Save yourself and us.*	

The most significant of these nine occurrences of the verb *sōzō* is the double
use of the word in Matthew 27.42 where the taunt of the Jewish religious
leaders is quoted as: 'He saved others; he cannot save himself'. McNeile ex-

plains this as a sarcastic reference to Jesus' claim to be king implying that as Messiah he had not brought salvation to anyone,[10] but this does not do justice to the past tense of *sōzō* in this verse. It is more probable that the Jewish leaders are throwing in his teeth the fact that he had saved others from sickness, demons and death as Filson suggests,[11] and yet was now apparently unable to deliver himself from death on the Cross. In this remark they are admitting that he did heal disease and raise men from the dead, for they have little to lose by admitting this now that he is dying himself.

These twenty cases in which *sōzō* means deliverance from disease, demons or death make up over half the occurrences of the verb in the gospels. It is probable that in these twenty cases the reference is not only to physical deliverance, but includes the physical as part of the deliverance of the whole being of the one healed or delivered. Foerster goes so far as to say: 'In the healings of Jesus *sōzō* never refers to a single member of the body but always to the whole man'.[12] He supports this statement by drawing attention to the fact that Jesus addressed the phrase 'Your faith has saved (*sesōken*) you' equally to the woman with the flow of blood (Mark 5.34) and to the woman who was a great sinner and did not need physical healing (Luke 7.50). In the remaining eighteen occurrences of *sōzō* in the gospel it is mostly used in an unqualified sense. In these cases the physical part of man's being is not specifically in view, but that is not to say that it is excluded, for it is the whole man which is the object of salvation, and this includes all aspects of man's being. Green speaks of *sōzō* being used 'ambiguously' in the gospels to refer to both physical and spiritual healing,[13] but its use is comprehensive rather than ambiguous, for it includes both the physical and the spiritual, and all the other aspects of man's being in its scope. With a word of such comprehensive meaning as *sōzō* enjoys it is not always easy to define its primary meaning in any particular context. However, it is clear that its wide application in the gospels indicates that the Christian concept of healing and the Christian concept of salvation overlap to a degree which varies in different situations, but are never completely separable. Healing of the body is never purely physical, and the salvation of the soul is never purely spiritual, but both are combined in the total deliverance of the whole man, a deliverance which is foreshadowed and illustrated in the healing miracles of Jesus in the gospels.

The remaining verb used in the gospels for healing is *apokathistemi* which means to restore to a former condition of health. It is used of the restoration to its previous condition of soundness (*hugiēs*) of the withered hand of the man Jesus met in the synagogue (Matthew 12.13 and parallels). It was his right hand which was affected according to Luke 6.6 and Jerome tells us that according to the Gospel of the Hebrews the man was a stonemason to trade and therefore worked with his hands.[14] The atrophy of his right hand was, therefore, an economic tragedy for him and his family. The other medical use of the verb is in Mark 8.25 where its use of the restoration of sight to the blind man of Bethsaida implies that he had formerly been able to see and then had gone blind. This explains how he was able to describe men as trees walking for he could remember what trees looked like when he had been able to see, and men carrying burdens on their heads or on their backs looked much the same as trees had done. This miracle is unique in the gospels in that the physical healing of the man took place in two stages. In the first stage no verb of healing is used, but his visual appreciation of the shape and movement of objects returns. In the second stage full vision is restored and he is able to see all things at a distance clearly, and it is for this complete restoration of sight that the word *apokathistēmi* is used.

One of the most interesting accounts of a healing miracle from the point of view of the vocabulary used is that of the healing of the woman with the flow of blood. This miracle is recorded in all three synoptic gospels and the relationship of the different words used for healing can be seen from the following table.

Source	Matthew 9	Mark 5	Luke 8
Narrator	—	26. *ōpheleō*	43. *therapeuō*
Woman	21. *sōzō*	28. *sōzō*	—
Narrator	22b. *sōzō*	29. *iaomai*	—
Narrator (indirect speech for woman)		—	47. *iaomai*
Jesus	22a. *sōzō*	34. *sōzō*	48. *sōzō*
	—	*eirēnē*	*eirēnē*
	—	*hugiēs*	—

The first thing to notice in this story is Luke's defence of the physicians in Luke 8.43. Mark had accused them of taking all her money from her in fees, of causing her much suffering by their methods of treatment, and in the end of leaving her no better (*ōpheleō*) but actually becoming increasingly worse (Mark 5.26). According to the most probable reading in Luke 8.43,[15] Luke says simply that the woman 'could not be healed by anyone' and uses the verb *therapeuō* which we take to mean in this context 'heal by normal medical methods'. The next thing to note is how Matthew uses the verb *sōzō* throughout his account, and in one case he uses it as the synonym of *iaomai* which Mark had used (cp. Matthew 9.22b with Mark 5.29). Finally, it is noteworthy that when Jesus dismisses the woman he described her healed state using three different words according to Mark 5.34. First, he says that she is made well (so RSV) and uses the verb *sōzō* to describe this. Then he tells the woman to go in peace (*eirēnē*) which we must regard as more than the conventional formula of dismissal for she certainly did not come in peace but in distress and weakness with no peace of·body or of mind. Behind *eirēnē* lies the concept of *shalōm* and the idea of wholeness which it denotes. In the third place she was to be sound (*hugiēs*) or whole from the disease which had troubled her for so long. The story of this woman who was healed of a chronic gynaecological complaint provides a very vivid illustration both in event and in vocabulary of the comprehensive concept of healing which characterises the gospel record.

REFERENCES

1. F. W. Beare, *The Earliest Records of Jesus* (Blackwell, Oxford, 1962), p. 176.
2. R. Bultmann, *The History of the Synoptic Tradition* (Blackwell, Oxford, 1968), ET by John Marsh, p. 213.

3. The diagnosis in this case is fully discussed in chapter eight below.
4. W. K. Hobart, *The Medical Language of St Luke* (Dublin University Press, 1882), p. 2.
5. W. M. Alexander, *Demonic Possession in the New Testament* (T. & T. Clark, Edinburgh, 1902), pp. 67-68.
6. E. R. Micklem, *Miracles and the New Psychology* (Oxford University Press, 1922), p. 53.
7. W. M. Alexander, *Demonic Possession in the New Testament* (T. & T. Clark, Edinburgh, 1902), p. 88.
8. S. V. McCasland, *By the Finger of God. Demon Possession and Exorcism in Early Christianity in the Light of Modern Views of Mental Illness* (Macmillan, New York, 1951).
9. A. B. Bruce, *The Expositor's Greek Testament* (Hodder and Stoughton, London, 1901), vol. 1, p. 94.
10. A. H. McNeile, *The Gospel according to St Matthew* (Macmillan, London, 1915), p. 420.
11. F. V. Filson, *A Commentary on the Gospel according to St Matthew* (Black, London, 1960), p. 296.
12. W. Foerster in *Theological Dictionary of the New Testament*, edd. G. Kittel and G. Friedrich (Eerdmans, Grand Rapids, 1971), vol. 7, p. 990, s.v. *sōzō*.
13. E. M. B. Green, *The Meaning of Salvation* (Hodder and Stoughton, London, 1965), p. 218.
14. M. R. James, *The Apocryphal New Testament* (Oxford University Press, 1924), pp. 4-5.
15. Here we follow the RSV which relegates the clause 'and has spent all her living upon physicians' to the margin. The evidence for the omission of this clause from the text is divided, and whilst I. H. Marshall in his *International Greek Testament Commentary* on the *Gospel of Luke* (Paternoster Press, Exeter, 1978, p. 344) says that 'a clear-cut decision is impossible', B. M. Metzger in *A Textual Commentary on the Greek New Testament* (United Bible Societies, London, 1971, p. 145) regards the early and diversified evidence for its omission as 'well-nigh compelling'.

Chapter Five

THE APPROACH TO HEALING

I. THE INITIATIVE IN HEALING

The identity of the person who took the initiative which resulted in a miracle of healing performed by Jesus is not always clearly indicated in the gospel record. The writers of the gospels do not appear to have been particularly interested in this detail of the miracles. The result is that in some cases we are left in doubt about who it was who made the first move in bringing the sick to the attention of Jesus. The following list is an attempt to classify the narratives of the miracles of healing according to who it was who took the initiative in each case. In some cases the identification can only be regarded as probable.

1. *Those in which Jesus himself took the initiative:*

    1. The woman with a spirit of infirmity (Luke 13.12).
    2. The impotent man (John 5.6).
    3. The ear of Malchus (Luke 22.51).
    4. The widow's son at Nain (Luke 7.14).

2. *Those in which the sick took the initiative:*

    1. The two blind men (Matthew 9.27).
    2. The ten leprosy patients (Luke 17.13).
    3. The man full of leprosy (Mark 1.40).
    4. The woman with the flow of blood (Mark 5.27).
    5. Blind Bartimaeus (Mark 10.47).
    6. The synagogue demoniac (Mark 1.24).
    7. The Gadarene demoniac (Mark 5.6).

3. *Those in which others took the initiative:*

    1. The deaf mute (Mark 7.32). Persons not identified.
    2. The blind man of Bethsaida (Mark 8.22). Persons not identified.
    3. The nobleman's son (John 4.47). His father took the initiative.
    4. The man born blind (John 9.2). The disciples took the initiative.
    5. The centurion's servant (Matthew 8.5). His master took the initiative.
    6. Peter's mother-in-law (Mark 1.30). The disciples took the initiative.
    7. The paralytic man (Mark 2.3). His friends brought him.
    8. The dumb demoniac (Matthew 9.32). Persons not identified.

9. The blind and dumb demoniac (Matthew 12.22). Persons not identified.
10. The Syrophoenician girl (Mark 7.26). Her mother came to Jesus.
11. The epileptic boy (Mark 9.17). His father brought him to Jesus.
12. Lazarus (John 11.3). His sisters sent for Jesus.
13. Jairus' daughter (Mark 5.23). Her father came to Jesus.

4. *Those in which Jesus' enemies appear to have taken the initiative*:

1. The man with dropsy (Luke 14.1-3).
2. The man with the withered hand (Luke 6.6-7).

If we analyse the eight records of the occasions on which Jesus healed the multitude we find that on four occasions he took the initiative, on three occasions the sick did so, and on four occasions it was other people who took the initiative, whilst in one case it is not mentioned who did.

The fact that our Lord so seldom took the initiative in healing the sick comes as a surprise, but it is clearly and undeniably the impression given in the records of his healing ministry. The significance of this fact is that the healing of the sick, the casting out of demons and the raising of the dead were not his primary task during his earthly ministry. It is never recorded of him that he sought out the sick, but that he healed them when he saw them or when they were brought to him. The most interesting record of all in this connection is that of the healing of the impotent man by the pool of Bethesda in John 5.1-9. Around and between the twin pools of Bethesda King Herod the Great had built five porches to shelter the sick who gathered there because of the healing reputation of the waters. In these porches 'lay a multitude of invalids, blind, lame, paralysed' (v. 3). Jesus comes into their midst and chooses only one of the multitude for healing, and withdraws quietly and quickly after he has healed him. What an opportunity he missed if healing had been one of his primary tasks. The fact that he did not take advantage of the opportunity presented by the crowd of sick people at Bethesda shows clearly that physical healing was not one of the primary reasons why he had come into the world. He always taught the people, but he did not always heal the sick of their diseases.

The number of cases in which it is recorded that Jesus took the initiative is too few to draw any firm conclusions from, but there are several features which should be noted. It is Luke alone who records three of the cases and this may mean that he was particularly interested to know who took the initiative in the miracles of healing. In each case except that of Malchus a definite formula appears to introduce the miracle. This can be seen by comparing the three narratives:

The bent woman:
And when Jesus saw her, he called her and said to her . . . . . Luke 13.12.

The impotent man:
When Jesus saw him and knew that he had been lying there a long time, he said to him . . . . . John 5.6.

The widow of Nain:
And when the Lord saw her, he had compassion on her and said to her . . . . .
Luke 7.13.

In the case of the man born blind John tells us that Jesus saw him (John 9.1), but he goes on to tell of the disciples' question about the origin of his blindness and not of what Jesus said. For this reason we have suggested that the initiative here came from the disciples who took up his case, but it may be that this should be regarded as another incident in which Jesus took the initiative as Barrett suggests.[1] Jesus never took the initiative in any case of demon possession or in any case in which the sick belonged to a non-Jewish race.

The source of the initiative in the two cases which are at the end of the list above is uncertain. The fact that Jesus' enemies were present and were particularly concerned to know what he would do about healing the sick on the sabbath day makes it at least possible that they were responsible for arranging for the sick to be present on these occasions.

II. THE CONTEXT OF HEALING

When Jesus unrolled the scroll of Isaiah in the Nazareth synagogue on that sabbath morning at the beginning of his ministry he found the sixty-first chapter and from there he read out to the assembled congregation the terms of his own commission (Luke 4.16-19). This commission combined preaching or proclamation and healing, and Jesus combined these two activities throughout his ministry as this is recorded for us in the gospels. The most explicit mention of the combination occurs first in Matthew 4.23 where we read:

'And he went about all Galilee, teaching in their synagogues and
preaching the gospel of the kingdom and healing every disease and every
infirmity among the people.'

A similar statement to this occurs again in Matthew 9.35 and acts as a preface to the mission charge to the Twelve when Jesus sent them out to preach and to heal.

No precise distinction is made in the gospels between preaching and teaching. In general, preaching was the initial proclamation of the good news to all who would listen, whilst teaching was the more detailed explanation of the content of the good news. The words for preaching are commoner in the earlier part of the gospel record than in the later part, and the words for teaching are commoner in the later chapters than in the earlier. The Twelve were sent to preach with no mention of teaching. However, the distinction is not hard and fast and we do not need to analyse it further for our present purpose. It is clear that our Lord's ministry combined preaching, teaching and healing and that the relative proportions of these activities varied with the circumstances in which he found himself.

There are definite indications, however, that the emphasis in our Lord's ministry is on preaching and teaching rather than on healing. For instance, when Peter and the others interrupted Jesus at prayer above Capernaum with the news that everyone was looking for him, he replied, 'Let us go on to the next towns, that I may preach there also; for that is why I came out' (Mark 1.38). He had spent the previous evening healing all the sick and demon-possessed of Capernaum, and the thirty-ninth verse tells us that he went from there throughout Galilee preaching and casting out demons, but he did not mention healing in his reply to Peter, only preaching. This emphasis on preaching and teaching is seen in the amount of space devoted to them by the gospels in comparison to that given to the accounts of the healing activity of Jesus. We have already seen how the amount of space given to the record of our Lord's teaching varies from fifty per cent of Mark's gospel to seventy-five per cent of Matthew's gospel, whilst the amount of space devoted to healing ranges from nine per cent of Matthew's gospel to twenty per cent of Mark's gospel. The contrast is obvious and clearly indicates where the emphasis lies. This emphasis on preaching and teaching is also apparent when we examine the gospel accounts of our Lord's ministry more closely. There are three occasions where Matthew mentioned that healing was performed by Jesus, but where Mark in recording the same incident spoke only of teaching. We see this if we compare Matthew 9.35 with Mark 6.6; Matthew 14.14 with Mark 6.34; and Matthew 19.2 with Mark 10.1.

In general, therefore, it appears that healing is carried out in the context of preaching and teaching in the gospels rather than the other way round. In other words, healing as an activity of Jesus is practised in illustration of his preaching and teaching rather than as their text and occasion. There are, of course, exceptions to this general observation and it is of interest to note that they are found more often in the fourth gospel than in the synoptic gospels. The point remains, however, that physical healing was not the primary purpose for which Jesus came and it is for this reason that preaching and teaching receive the primary emphasis in the gospel records.

III. THE MOTIVE FOR HEALING

In fewer than half the accounts of the miracles of healing performed by Jesus is any indication of his motive given. In most cases it is implicit rather than explicit, and the following list is an attempt to identify and classify the motives which appear to underlie most of the healing incidents whether individual or multiple which are recorded in the gospels.

1. *An expression of compassion*
   a. The man full of leprosy (Mark 1.41).
   b. The dead son of the widow of Nain (Luke 7.13).
   c. Blind Bartimaeus and his friend (Matthew 20.34).
   d. Healing after the return of the Twelve (Matthew 14.14).

2. *A response to a cry for mercy*
   a. The two blind men (Matthew 9.27).
   b. Blind Bartimaeus (Mark 10.47 and parallels).
   c. The epileptic boy (Matthew 17.15 and Mark 9.22).
   d. The Syrophoenician girl (Matthew 15.22).
   e. The ten leprosy patients (Luke 17.13).

3. *An answer to faith*

   a. The centurion's servant (Matthew 8.10 and Luke 7.9).
   b. The paralysed man (Mark 2.5 and parallels).
   c. The two blind men (Matthew 9.28-29).
   d. The Syrophoenician girl (Matthew 15.28).
   e. The epileptic boy (Mark 9.24).
   f. Blind Bartimaeus (Mark 10.52 and Luke 18.42).

4. *A manifestation of glory*

   a. The nobleman's son (John 4.54 cp. 2.11).
   b. The man born blind (John 9.3).
   c. The raising of Lazarus (John 11.4).

5. *A fulfilment of Scripture*

   a. The evening healings at Capernaum (Matthew 8.16-17).
   b. The demonstration to the Baptist's disciples (Matthew 11.2-6 and Luke 7.18-23).
   c. The healings by the seaside (Matthew 12.15-21).

1. *An expression of compassion*

Since it is usual to attribute our Lord's healing miracles to his feeling of compassion for the sick, it is surprising to find that this is not frequently done in the gospels. There are only four cases in which it is done explicitly and the word used in each case is the verb *splanchnizomai* which is derived from the noun *splanchnon*. In the plural form *splanchna* this word is used to denote the inward parts of the body particularly the more noble organs such as the heart, lungs and liver in contrast to the *entera* or intestines. The verb means, therefore, to be moved in the inward parts, i.e. to feel sympathy, pity or compassion for a person. As Lightfoot suggested, it appears to have been a coinage of the Jewish dispersion, for, apart from an isolated occurrence in a fourth-century B.C. inscription from Cos it is unknown before its occurrence in Biblical Greek.[2] In the New Testament its use is confined to the synoptic gospels where it occurs twelve times including two occurrences in parallel accounts.

The compassion of Jesus was aroused by the presence of hunger (Matthew 15.32 and Mark 8.2), by the condition of leaderlessness (Matthew 9.36 and Mark 6.34), by the sight of mourning (Luke 7.13), and by sickness. In the four cases relating to sickness which are listed above, we are told that our Lord's compassion was directed to the relatives or friends of the sick. In the case of the widow of Nain it was the mother of the dead man who was the object of his compassion (Luke 7.13), and in the case of the group healing after the return of the Twelve from their mission we are told that Jesus had compassion on the crowd and healed their sick (Matthew 14.14). The only individuals on whom we are told that Jesus had compassion because of their sickness were the leprosy patient of Mark 1.40-41 and Blind Bartimaeus and his friend of Matthew 20.34. The case of the leprosy patient needs further consideration for there is some doubt about whether he was the object of the compassion of Jesus. The case is described in all three synoptic gospels, and Luke adds the clinical detail that he was a very advanced case of his disease. It is Mark alone who tells us that Jesus was moved with compassion (*splanchnistheis*, 1.41) and stretched out his hand to touch and heal him. There is a very impressive array of textual evidence for this reading of the original Greek text, but there is an alternative reading from the Western textual tradition which instead of speaking of Jesus' compassion speaks of his anger and reads *orgistheis*, being angry. Vincent Taylor and many other commentators on this verse accept this second reading on the well-established rule of textual criticism laid down by J. A. Bengel (1687-1752) that where there is a choice of readings the more difficult reading is likely to be the correct one.[3] It is certainly more difficult to understand why Jesus was angry when the leprosy patient came before him, than to understand why he felt compassion which would be much more natural in the circumstances. The standard Greek texts still retain the reference to compassion and put the reference to anger in the critical apparatus, and this is probably the correct procedure.[4] If we do accept the reference to anger as the correct text then we accept a reading for which no satisfactory explanation has yet been given. Any acceptable explanation for the anger is rendered only more difficult when we realise that the man's disease was not really leprosy as we know it today and therefore not as disfiguring as that disease can be, but some variety of skin disease which showed the features which made it ritually unclean according to the Levitical regulations.

2. A response to a cry for mercy

On three occasions sick people, and twice their close relatives, approached Jesus with the cry, '*Eleēson*, Have mercy!' This cry for mercy recognised Jesus' power to heal and assumed his willingness to heal. It was an appeal to his feeling of compassion which we have seen that he had towards the sick. When the gospels refer to this feeling of compassion on the part of Jesus they do not use the verb *eleeō*, to have mercy, which is used by the sick in their plea for healing. They use the verb *splanchnizomai* which refers to that inner feeling of compassion of which acts of mercy and of healing are the outward expression.

The cry for mercy is never used alone by those who seek healing from Jesus. It is always accompanied by a confession of faith in him which is a recognition of his power to heal. This confession and recognition is conveyed in the title by which Jesus is addressed along with the cry for help. These titles are five in number and none is identical with the others, although they are made up of only four basic titles. The five titles are as follows:

Lord, used by the father of the epileptic boy (Matthew 17.15).
Son of David, used by the two blind men (Matthew 9.27).
Lord, Son of David, used by the mother of the Syrophoenician girl
(Matthew 15.22).
Jesus, Son of David, used by Blind Bartimaeus (Mark 10.47 and Luke
18.38).
Jesus, Master (epistatēs), used by the ten leprosy patients (Luke 17.13).

These titles all acknowledge the authority of Jesus and express different aspects of it. The title Lord (kurios) applied to Jesus in the New Testament has been the centre of much discussion, but its use by the father of the epileptic boy must be more than that of a title of courtesy. He was expecting Jesus to do what his disciples had failed to, and this meant that he believed that he had more power than they had. As if to remove any doubt on this matter, both Mark and Luke substitute *Teacher* (*didaskalos*) for *Lord* although they omit the cry for mercy (Mark 9.17 and Luke 9.38). The title *Son of David* is Messianic and clearly expresses the belief in Jesus as the Messiah, and since the Messiah was to bring healing with him (Malachi 4.2) it was a very appropriate title on the lips of those who approached Jesus for healing, and it linked his healing activity with the expectations of the Old Testament. The name *Jesus* is the most frequently used name when our Lord is spoken of in the gospels, but it is used to address him on only four occasions and only by sick or demon-possessed persons. It is never used alone as the sole form of address. Twice it is used by possessed persons who were disturbed at our Lord's presence, but this usage was not associated with a plea for mercy or for help, for the demon-possessed never approached Jesus for healing on their own initiative. The synagogue demoniac addresses him as 'Jesus of Nazareth' and goes on to recognise him as the Holy One of God who has power to destroy demons (Mark 1.24 and Luke 4.34). In a similar manner, the Gadarene demoniac calls him 'Jesus, Son of the Most High God' (Mark 5.7 and Luke 8.28) which also implies that he has power and authority over demons. In the other two cases in which the name of Jesus is used it is associated with a cry for mercy. Blind Bartimaeus calls our Lord 'Jesus, Son of David' (Mark 10.47 and Luke 18.38), and the ten men afflicted with leprosy address him as 'Jesus, Master (*epistatēs*)' in Luke 17.13 using a word which describes one who has authority over others, but which apart from this occasion is only used by the disciples in addressing Jesus. Of these four basic titles or names used of our Lord, *Son of David* and *Master* are not used in the New Testament outside of the gospels and did not survive in Christian usage, although in certain circles of Anglo-Saxon Christianity in the nineteenth century the term *Master* was temporarily revived but not with a very precise meaning.[5] The other two, *Jesus* and *Lord*, did survive and are still in common use amongst us, now filled and enriched by centuries of Christian experience. In our present context all these four designations express the faith on the basis of which the sick approached our Lord with a cry for mercy and a plea for healing.

3. *An answer to faith*

The writers of the gospels are not as interested in the role played by faith in the healing miracles of Jesus as writers would be today. Modern authors are often very concerned to determine the place of faith in our Lord's healing activity in order to decide whether he can be regarded as a faith-healer or not. Out of the twenty-six accounts of individual healing miracles recorded in the gospels, there is mention of faith in only twelve, and amongst these there are only five cases in which it appears that Jesus healed as an answer to faith. In only one of these cases was it the faith of the sick themselves to which Jesus responded. This was the case of the two blind men in Matthew 9.27-31 where before he healed them by restoring their sight, Jesus asked them, 'Do you believe that I am able to do this?' In the other four cases it was the faith of the friends or relations of the sick which produced the healing response of Jesus. An exception to this may be present in the healing of the paralysed man where we read that he was healed 'when Jesus saw their faith' (Mark 2.5), for modern commentators usually understand this to refer to the faith of the sick man and his friends, rather than to the faith of the friends alone which was often the understanding of older commentators. The healing miracles in which there is no doubt that the faith referred to is that of the friends or relatives of the sick person are as follows:

1. The centurion's servant in Matthew 8.10 and Luke 7.9 where the faith is on the part of the centurion.
2. The Syrophoenician girl in Matthew 15.28 where the faith is that of the girl's mother.
3. The epileptic boy in Mark 9.24 where the faith is that of the boy's father.

The significance of this fact is that these cases cannot simply be labelled as psychoneurotic in nature and their cure as due to the mechanism of psychological suggestion. Furthermore, not only was the faith that of one other than the sick, but in two of the cases the sick person was not even present when Jesus was asked to heal them and so presumably was not aware of what was happening, and in the third case which is that of the epileptic boy, the sick person was present but was unconscious (Mark 9.26). This makes it all the more difficult to regard these cases as those of psychoneurotic conditions responding to suggestion.

The object of the faith to which Jesus responded by healing is not usually explicitly stated. The sick or their relations are exhorted to believe, but it is not commonly stated in what they are to believe, as we can see in such references as Mark 5.36; 9.23; John 4.48 etc. In the case of the two blind men Jesus directed their faith to his ability to heal them by his question already quoted above, 'Do you believe that I am able to do this?' (Matthew 9.28). Also, he sought to elicit Mary's faith in himself as able to restore her brother Lazarus to life before he actually did so (John 11.25-26). The faith which was answered by healing was faith in the power and ability of Jesus to heal. A faith which was sometimes expressed in the title by which Jesus was addressed by the sick as we saw in the last section, but more often was implied in the approach of the sick or their relatives to Jesus that they might be healed.

4. A manifestation of glory

Glory or *doxa* is another example of a Greek word whose meaning was completely transformed on its adoption into Biblical Greek and its use in the LXX translation of the Old Testament. It originally meant an opinion or a conjecture about something which may be true or false. Then it meant the honour and reputation of one about whom a good opinion was held, and in the Greek Old Testament it was used to denote the honour, majesty and visible splendour of the presence of God. In the New Testament when John spoke of the miracles or signs (*sēmeia*) which Jesus did as manifesting his glory (John 2.11) he meant that they revealed the presence and power of God in the person

and work of Jesus. This can be seen in such verses as John 9.3; 11.4 and 40, as
well as 4.54, with which should be compared 2.11 since this verse makes clear
that the function of a sign (*sēmeion*) was to manifest the glory of Jesus.[6] The
healing miracles are therefore a revelation of the deity of Jesus Christ, an indication that his presence and power is the presence and power of God. Although
this idea is most obviously present in the fourth gospel, it also occurs in the
synoptic gospels where the emphasis is not on the manifestation of our Lord's
glory, but on the recognition of that glory by those who saw and experienced
his healing power at work. We are frequently told by Luke that those who
were healed 'glorified God' which means they recognised and acknowledged
his presence and power at work (Luke 5.25; 13.13; 17.15; 18.43). Matthew and
Mark do not speak of the healed individuals glorifying God as Luke does, but
they record how the crowds who witnessed the healings did so (Matthew 9.8;
15.31 and Mark 2.12). It cannot be denied that there is an evidential aspect to
the healing miracles in the gospels for they do witness to the fact that Jesus is the
Christ, the Son of the living God. Their occurrence caused men to acknowledge that Jesus manifested the glory of God as he lived and walked amongst
them on earth.

5. A fulfilment of scripture

The earliest indication of a motive underlying his healing activity was
given by Jesus as he read and applied to himself the lesson from the book of the
prophet Isaiah in the synagogue at Nazareth at the outset of his ministry (Luke
4.16-21). He had come to fulfil the scripture which had been written of him.
On two other occasions Matthew quotes the book of the prophet Isaiah to
show how the healing miracles of Jesus fulfil what was written there about
him. When he spent an evening healing the sick and casting out demons,
Matthew records this with the comment, 'This was to fulfil what was spoken
by the prophet Isaiah, "He took our infirmities and bore our diseases"' (Matthew
8.17 quoting Isaiah 53.4). Again, after the healing of the man with the withered
hand Jesus healed many sick people and as Matthew records this he quotes
Isaiah 42.1-4 as the scripture fulfilled by this incident.

There is no doubt that Jesus himself saw his healing activity as a fulfilment
of Messianic prophecy in the Old Testament. This is shown by his reply to the
disciples of John the Baptist when they came from John after he had been
imprisoned by Herod Antipas, the tetrarch of Galilee. John had heard of all that
Jesus was doing and he sent two of his disciples to Jesus with the question, 'Are
you he who is to come, or shall we look for another?' (Matthew 11.3 and Luke
7.19). By the phrase 'He who is to come' the Baptist clearly meant the Messiah,
but this has been denied on the grounds that this term was not a recognised
Jewish title for the Messiah and was more appropriate as a description for Elijah
who was to come to prepare the way for the Messiah according to Malachi 4.5
(cp. Mark 9.11-13). However, this is not a valid reason for excluding a Messianic meaning of this phrase. The Baptist had already spoken of the one who
was to come after him (Mark 1.7 and Luke 3.16) by whom he meant the
Messiah, and there is no reason why he could not speak of him in similar terms
again. In response to the question from the Baptist, Luke tells that Jesus 'cured

many of diseases and plagues and evil spirits, and on many that were blind he bestowed sight'. Then he said to the two disciples, 'Go and tell John what you have seen and heard: the blind receive their sight, the lame walk, lepers are cleansed, and the deaf hear, the dead are raised up, the poor have good news preached to them' (Luke 7.21-22). The description of Jesus' healing activities which he asks the disciples to take back to John the Baptist is derived from a combination of such passages as Isaiah 29.18-19; 35.5-6 and 61.1 where the work of the Messiah is described. Jesus is clearly appealing to his fulfilment of these prophecies by his healing and preaching activity in order to reassure John that he is indeed the Messiah who is to come.

When we suggest that the fulfilment of scripture was a motive behind the healing activity of Jesus, we do not mean to imply that miracles were performed for the express purpose of fulfilling scripture. That would be too naïve and unimaginative a view. But it is evident that whatever the primary motive was for which they were performed, once they had been performed, it could be seen that they did in fact fulfil the scripture prophecies concerning the Messiah as Matthew in particular is anxious to point out to his readers. John also makes use of the healing miracles in this way and uses them as evidence of who Jesus was. John's word for miracle is *sēmeion* which means a sign, something which points beyond itself and which gives the sign its meaning. Four healing miracles are included amongst the eight *sēmeia* which John records, and at the end of his twentieth chapter he says that he has recorded these signs so that his readers may believe that Jesus is the Christ, the Messiah, the Son of God and that believing they might have life through his name (John 20.30-31). This evidential use of the healing miracles is not so popular today as it once was, but there is no doubt that it is a valid New Testament approach to their meaning and motive.

It is clear that in most cases of healing it is impossible to separate out one single motive. Any one healing miracle could be at one and the same time an expression of compassion, a response to faith or a cry for mercy, a manifestation of the glory of God, and a fulfilment of scripture.

It is also clear that the writers of the gospels are not at pains to spell out for their readers the motive underlying every incident of healing carried out by Jesus. We have already seen how compassion is mentioned in only four cases of healing by Jesus in the synoptic gospels and not at all in the fourth gospel. This does not mean that compassion was not also the motive in incidents in which it is not mentioned. Compassion is the expression of love, but love is mentioned even less frequently in the synoptic gospels, for only once are we told there that Jesus loved (Mark 10.21). In John's gospel however where compassion is not mentioned there are many references to the love of Jesus for his disciples. The motives of Jesus which underlay his healing activity cannot be examined statistically nor assessed clinically. They are basically the expression of his love for men manifest initially in the Incarnation and finally in the Atonement.

REFERENCES

1. C. K. Barrett, *The Gospel according to St John* (SPCK, London, 1962), p. 292. This is also the view of L. Morris, *The Gospel according to John* (Marshall, Morgan and Scott, London, 1972), p. 477.

2. J. B. Lightfoot, *Saint Paul's Epistle to the Philippians* (Macmillan, London, 1908), fourth edition, p. 86. See also Arndt and Gingrich, p. 770 s.v. *splanchnizomai*.

3. See Bruce M. Metzger, *A Textual Commentary on the Greek New Testament* (United Bible Societies, London, 1971) p. 76. Metzger indicates that a majority of the Committee which produced the *United Bible Societies' Greek New Testament* were in favour of the reading *splanchnistheis*, and he gives a brief statement of the basis of their opinion.

4. V. Taylor, *The Gospel according to St. Mark* (Macmillan, London, 1957), p. 187.

5. V. Taylor, *The Names of Jesus* (Macmillan, London, 1953), p. 14.

6. For a discussion of the Christological significance of the *sēmeia* see R. Schnackenburg, *The Gospel according to St John* (Burns and Oates, London, 1968), ET by Kevin Smyth, vol. 1, pp. 521-525.

Chapter Six

THE METHODS OF HEALING

The methods used by Jesus in his healing activity cannot fail to be of interest to anyone who is concerned with the art and science of healing. His methods were simple and they were effective. They achieved a cure which was beyond the capability of the medical skill available in his day in cases which were both acute and chronic in character. The results were dramatic and caused men to glorify God.

His methods were basically only two in number. He healed by word and by touch except in those cases in which the sick were some distance away. We may classify his methods as follows:

1. Healing by word.
2. Healing by touch.
3. Healing by both word and touch.
4. Healing involving the use of saliva.
5. Healing at a distance.

1. *Healing by word*

(a) *In exorcism.* In his healing of demon-possessed persons by exorcism Jesus addressed a word of command to the demon to leave the possessed person. This is the only method of exorcism recorded as used by him. He never laid hands on the demon-possessed. The words of command which he used are preserved in three cases:

   (1) The synagogue demoniac: *Be silent, and come out of him* (Mark 1.25 and Luke 4.35).
   (2) The Gadarene demoniac: *Come out of the man, you unclean spirit* (Mark 5.8).
   (3) The epileptic boy: *Come out of him, and never enter him again* (Mark 9.25).

In each case it is Mark who records the exact words used by Jesus in exorcising the demon, and in each case the command is addressed to the demon: *Come out!* In the case of the synagogue demoniac, the demon is also commanded to be silent, for he had been announcing publicly who Jesus was, the Holy One of God. Jesus never accepted the testimony of demons and always sought to silence them by exorcising them as we see in the two cases of the synagogue demoniac and the Gadarene demoniac. In the two cases of exorcism which do not come from the Markan tradition the details of the method used are not given. In the case of the blind and dumb demoniac Matthew says simply that Jesus healed him (12.22 where the verb *therapeuō* is used to describe the exorcism), and Luke says that he cast out the demon (11.14). In the case of the dumb demoniac Matthew tells us that the demon was cast out, after which the dumb man spoke (9.33). The remaining case of exorcism of the six which are recorded in detail is that of the Syrophoenician girl who was one of the people who were healed at a distance, and so no words could be spoken directly to the demon in her case (Matthew 15.24-28 and Mark 7.24-30).

The references to multiple healings by Jesus frequently mention that he cast out evil spirits, but only Matthew 8.16 gives any indication of the method used. Here we are told that 'they brought to him many who were possessed with demons; and he cast out the spirits with a word'. Exorcism by word or command appears to have been the method used by Jesus. This method implies the existence and personality of the demons whom he addressed in words. In the exorcisms carried out as part of the multiple healings we find that Jesus refused to allow the witness of the demons to himself and commanded them to be silent. This is stated explicitly in Luke 4.41 where we are told that 'demons also came out of many, crying, "You are the Son of God!" But he rebuked them, and would not allow them to speak, because they knew that he was the Christ.'

(b) *In physical healing.* In four cases of physical healing Jesus spoke a word of command to the sick persons themselves:

(1) The paralysed man: *Rise, take up your bed and go home* (Matthew 9.6; Mark 2.11 and Luke 5.24).

(2) The impotent man: *Rise, take up your bed, and walk* (John 5.8).

(3) The man with the withered hand: *Stretch out your hand* (Matthew 12.13; Mark 3.5 and Luke 6.10).

(4) The ten leprosy patients: *Go and show yourselves to the priests* (Luke 17.14).

In each case the command of Jesus was to do something of which the sick persons had been incapable of doing because of their sickness and its effects. They were commanded to move powerless limbs which were incapable of movement after long years of paralysis and disuse, or in the case of the ten leprosy patients they were bidden to present themselves to the priest to be declared clean when the signs of the skin disease which made them unclean were still florid upon them.

(c) *In raising the dead.* In two cases in which he raised the dead to life Jesus addressed a word of command to the dead person:

(1) The widow's son at Nain: *Young man, I say to you, arise* (Luke 7.14).

(2) Lazarus: *Lazarus, come out* (John 11.43).

It may seem odd that Jesus addressed words of command to the dead who could not be expected to hear them. John gives us the explanation of this in 11.42 where he records that Jesus prayed aloud so that the crowd might understand that his authority and power came from the Father. Similarly his word of command to the dead was spoken aloud to be heard by the crowd so that there would be no doubt that it was Jesus who raised the dead by a deliberate act of power.

In the case of the raising from the dead of the son of the widow of Nain in Luke 7.11-17 we are told that our Lord touched the bier on which the young man lay and then ordered him to get up. It has been suggested that our Lord's touch conveyed healing and revitalising power to the dead man through the bier, but this is unlikely. It is much more likely that he touched the bier to indicate to the bearers to stand still and set their burden on the ground, and when they had done this Jesus spoke to the young man and raised him from the dead. Touch played no part in the miracle in this case.

2. *Healing by touch*

(a) *At Jesus' own initiative.*
(1) The man with dropsy: *He took him and healed him* (Luke 14.4).
(2) Malchus' ear: *He touched his ear and healed him* (Luke 22.51).
(3) Healing at Nazareth: *He laid his hands upon a few sick folk and healed them* (Mark 6.5).
(4) Healing at evening: *He laid his hands on every one of them and healed them* (Luke 4.40).
(b) *At the initiative of the sick.*
(1) The woman with the flow of blood: *She touched the fringe of his garment and immediately her flow of blood ceased* (Luke 8.44).
(2) Healing by the seaside: *He had healed many, so that all who had diseases pressed upon him to touch him* (Mark 3.10 cp. Luke 6.19).
(3) Healing at Gennesaret: *As many as touched the fringe of his garment were made well* (Matthew 14.36 and Mark 6.56).

In the case of the man with dropsy we are given no details but simply told that he was *hudropikos* (Luke 14.2). The implication is that he suffered from *hudrops*, a word which lost its first syllable when it came into Middle English as dropsy. This word is no longer in common medical use, but it was used to describe the swelling of some part of the body due to the accumulation of watery fluid in its cavities or tissues usually the result of a chronic disease of the heart or kidneys. There is no reason why we should not accept this case as one of classical dropsy, but because dropsy is so difficult to cure, Micklem has suggested that this man really had what we call today angioneurotic oedema or giant urticaria.[1] This is a localised form of swelling of allergic origin which comes on more quickly than dropsy and passes off more rapidly. However, these two conditions are readily distinguished and it is unlikely that Luke would have regarded the disappearance of the swelling of angioneurotic oedema as worth recording as a miracle. The fact that he did record it means that he regarded it as a miracle, for even with modern treatment dropsy does not disappear·immediately as the use of the aorist tense of *iaomai* implies it did in this case. However, it is not unequivocally clear that Jesus did heal the man by touch. We are told that he took hold of the man and healed him (Luke 14.4). The verb used is *epilambanō* which in Mark 8.23 is used to describe how Jesus took hold of the blind man of Bethsaida by the hand and took him out of the village before spitting on his eyes and laying his hands on him to restore his sight. It is clear that Mark does not use the verb to describe healing and it may be that we should not understand it to indicate the method of healing in Luke. If this is so, then we do not know what method he used in this case.

3. *Healing by word and touch*

(1) Peter's mother-in-law: *He touched her hand and the fever left her* (Matthew 8.15 cp. Mark 1.31). *He rebuked the fever and it left her* (Luke 4.39).

(2) The advanced leprosy patient: *He stretched out his hand and touched him, saying, 'I will; be clean'* (Matthew 8.3; Mark 1.41 and Luke 5.13).

(3) Jairus' daughter: *Taking her by the hand he called, saying, 'Child, arise'* (Luke 8.54 and Mark 5.41).

(4) The two blind men: *He touched their eyes, saying, 'According to your faith be it done to you'* (Matthew 9.29).

(5) The bent woman: *He called her and said to her, 'Woman, you are freed from your infirmity.' And he laid his hands on her* (Luke 13.12-13).

(6) Blind Bartimaeus: In this case Matthew 20.34 records the touch but not the word, and Mark 10.52 and Luke 18.42 record the word but not the touch.

In the case of Peter's mother-in-law and of Blind Bartimaeus all three synoptic gospels do not record that healing was due to both word and touch. The case of Peter's mother-in-law is of particular interest. She had contracted a febrile disease which produced a high continuous temperature and which had prostrated her upon her bed (Luke 4.38). Luke calls the fever *puretos megas*, a great fever, which the Greek physicians recognised as a serious sign to be distinguished from the less serious *puretos mikros* or small fever.[2] Modern medicine still recognises the distinction of *hyperpyrexia* and *pyrexia* as fevers above and below 105° Fahrenheit or 40.5° Centigrade, and regards hyperpyrexia as a serious sign. Whatever the disease, it is obvious that Peter and the others were very concerned about her and asked Jesus to see her. Luke tells how he stood over her and rebuked the fever and it left her, and she got up and served them. In verse thirty-five Luke had used the same verb *epitimaō* in the same tense to describe how Jesus rebuked the unclean spirit which possessed the man he found in the synagogue and told him to be silent and come out of the man. Since the rebuke was expressed in words there, it is very probable that it was similarly expressed here and consequently this miracle is an example of healing by word and touch. The question remains, however, of what were the words in which the rebuke was expressed, and to whom or what was the rebuke addressed. The probability is that the words were a simple command to the fever to be gone. In view of the fact that the verb had previously been used to describe an exorcism it is sometimes suggested that here too Jesus' rebuke was directed to the demon causing the fever or even to Satan himself as its causal agent.[3] This need not necessarily be the case since the same verb in the same tense is used of Jesus rebuking the wind and the waves in the storm on the Sea of Galilee in Mark 4.39 and Luke 8.24. If it be maintained that in both cases Jesus was rebuking a demonic power behind the physical phenomenon, the problem remains of why he rebuked the phenomenon rather than its cause. In Mark 11.14 he spoke to the fig tree in terms which made it clear that he was speaking to the tree and not any spirit behind it, for a spirit could not bear fruit. As Taylor remarks, 'it is perverse to explain this language as a kind of primitive animism'.[4] It is rather an assertion of divine power and authority over the phenomena of physical nature, although it is undeniable that these phenomena may have a demonic cause on particular occasions. It appears therefore that when we take the three synoptic accounts together, the healing of Peter's mother-in-law was not an exorcism, but an example of the healing of physical disease by word and touch. Matthew and Mark record the healing touch and Luke implies the healing word.

In two of the cases he healed by word and touch Jesus would have contracted ceremonial or ritual uncleanness by touching the body of the one he sought to restore. In the case of the leprosy patient we are told by all the synoptic accounts that Jesus 'stretched out his hand and touched him' (Matthew 8.3; Mark 1.41 and Luke 5.13). The combination of the verbs *ekteinō*, stretch out and *haptomai*, touch found in these verses does not occur elsewhere in the New Testament and it conveys the impression of a very deliberate act of touching. After he had touched the leprosy patient, Jesus betrayed no consciousness of having contracted ritual uncleanness and does nothing to purify himself by seeking cleansing from a priest. This is in contrast to his instruction to the healed man to show himself to the priest and offer for his cleansing what the law of Moses required so that he could be pronounced clean (Mark 1.44). Only a priest could pronounce him clean and restore him to the life of the community and so add the social element to his healing. Jesus prefaced his instruction to the healed man about his cleansing with a stern warning not to say anything to anyone. Farrar suggested that this was because he 'desired to avoid the Levitical rites for uncleanness which the unspiritual ceremonialism of the Pharisees might have tried to force upon Him'.[5] This explanation is unlikely, for the warning is more naturally understood as one to avoid social intercourse with people before he had been declared clean by the priest. The other case was that of the daughter of Jairus, the ruler of the synagogue near Capernaum. Jesus took her hand before he restored her to life (Matthew 9.25; Mark 5.41 and Luke 8.54) and so was in contact with her body as it lay recently dead. Afterwards he took no steps to have himself cleansed from the resultant ritual uncleanness which according to Numbers 19.11-13 should last seven days and only be removed by the application of the water of purification. If this was not done then the unclean person was to be excluded from the community of Israel. The attitude of Jesus to ritual uncleanness illustrated by these two cases is in keeping with his teaching on what defiles a man in Matthew 15.1-20 and Mark 7.1-23. The medical interest of these accounts lies in the anatomical and physiological knowledge they reveal and which is based on the simple observation of the process of digestion. From these passages it is clear that for Jesus uncleanness or defilement is not physical in origin or nature, but is moral and spiritual. This explains why he did not concern himself with the failure of his disciples to wash their hands before meals which was a ritual requirement of the Jewish oral law which Mark calls 'the tradition of the elders' (Mark 7.3). It also explains his unconcern with the ritual uncleanness which might be derived from contact with a case of an unclean skin disease or with a dead body. Mark's remark on the significance of Jesus' teaching when he said, 'Thus he declared all foods clean' (Mark 7.19) is therefore very relevant and the principle which

Jesus enunciated applied to more than just food, for it applied to all physical things.

According to the gospel record, touch was the main method by which Jesus healed the sick, and for this reason it demands a fuller discussion than the other methods. Healing or restoration by touch was well recognised as an effective method in New Testament times. This is shown by the following requests made to Jesus by those who sought his healing for others.

(1) Jairus for his daughter: *Come and lay your hands on her, so that she may be made well, and live* (Mark 5.23).

(2) Friends of the deaf mute: *They besought him to lay his hand upon him* (Mark 7.32).

(3) Friends of the blind man of Bethsaida: (*They*) *begged him to touch him* (Mark 8.22).

As well as these specific requests for Jesus to touch the sick and heal them, we also find references to the sick people's belief that they could be healed by touching Jesus with or without his permission. The woman with the flow of blood touched him without his permission and was healed (Mark 5.27-29), whilst the friends of the sick by the Sea of Galilee sought Jesus' permission for the sick to touch 'even the fringe of his garment' (Mark 6.56) so that they might be healed. On a third occasion we are not told if permission was sought, but the sick pressed on Jesus to touch him to obtain healing (Mark 3.10 and Luke 6.19).

The commonest verb used to describe the act of touching which produced healing is *haptomai* which is the middle voice of *haptō*, touch. It means more than a light touch or an exploratory feeling of the surface with the pads of the fingers. It means a purposeful laying hold of something in order to modify or influence it in some way. It implies a touch which tends to hold and even sometimes to cling. It is used to describe the effective healing grasp of Jesus on the sick, and the earnest believing grasp of the sick on Jesus.

The next most common verb used for the healing touch is *epitithēmi* which when it is used for healing is always used in the phrase *epitithēmi tas cheiras*, put or lay hands upon. The phrase is used twice by those who approach Jesus with a request for healing (Mark 5.23 and 7.32), and five times to describe the action Jesus performed in healing (Mark 6.5; 8.23, 25; Luke 4.40 and 13.13). The phrase does not appear to have any technical application in the gospels such as it came to have in the history of the Church. It simply meant to touch a person in a deliberate and purposeful manner in blessing (as in Matthew 19.15) or more commonly in healing.

The least frequent phrase used of Jesus touching the sick is *krateō tēs cheiros*, take by the hand. This phrase is used of healing on only three occasions, but the verb is also used in the more violent sense of the arrest of a person and was used of Jesus' own arrest in Mark 14.1, 44, 46, and 49. When it is used of Jesus in the account of a healing miracle it is not always clear that it describes the method of healing, and not simply physical assistance given to the healed person to get up. The phrase would appear to have the latter sense in Mark 9.27 where Jesus helps the epileptic boy to his feet after the spirit had been cast out. However, in the case of Peter's mother-in-law (Mark 1.31) and the daughter of Jairus

(Matthew 9.25; Mark 5.51 and Luke 8.54) the phrase may also describe part of the healing method used by Jesus to restore the sick.

Although these three words or phrases are used separately for the touch of Jesus, there are occasions when they are used synonymously by the evangelists. The Markan usage of *haptomai* in 10.13 is changed by Matthew to *epitithēmi tas cheiras* in Matthew 19.13, and Mark's *krateō tēs cheiros* in 1.31 becomes *haptomai* in Matthew 8.15. It would appear that there is little to choose in meaning between these three words when they are used of the healing touch of Jesus.

The gospel record does not usually tell us what part of the body Jesus touched when he healed. It would be natural to assume that he touched the part which needed healing and certainly this was the case on the three occasions on which the part touched is specified. Jesus touched the eyes of Blind Bartimaeus (Matthew 20.34), the ears and tongue of the deaf mute (Mark 7.33), and the ear of the injured Malchus (Luke 22.51). In other cases in which the disease was localised we may imagine Jesus laying his hands on the place of the disease. For example, it is probable that in the case of the bent woman that he laid his hands on her spine (Luke 13.13). Where the disease was not localised he would lay his hands on a readily accessible part of the body such as the head or shoulder. However, the fact remains that in most cases we are not told where he laid his hands on the body of the sick, but merely that he touched them, and this suggests that the place he touched was not regarded as of sufficient importance to record. The important thing was that he touched the sick and those he wished to restore.

What happened when Jesus touched a sick person to heal him? This question is not answered explicitly, but only implicitly in the answer to the converse question of what happened when a sick person touched Jesus in search of healing. The most instructive case in this respect is that of the healing of the woman with the uterine haemorrhage which is recorded in its greatest detail in the fifth chapter of Mark. Her chronic loss of blood over a period of twelve years was most probably due to the presence of fibroid tumours or fibromyomata in the uterus which are the commonest tumours of the genital organs of the female. They are benign tumours in nature, but in about a quarter of the cases in which they are present they cause chronic abnormal uterine bleeding as in this woman's case. This type of bleeding would make her ritually unclean according to Leviticus 15.25, and her touch would render our Lord unclean, but as in the case of the man with the unclean skin disease whom Jesus touched (Mark 1.41 and parallels) there is no mention of his contracting ritual uncleanness in this way. The woman worked her way through the crowd and came up behind Jesus and touched his clothes. There was no actual physical contact with his skin. Although Mark says simply that she touched his cloak or *himation*, both Matthew and Luke tell us that it was the tassel or *kraspedon* of his cloak which she touched (Mark 5.27; Matthew 9.20 and Luke 8.44). The *himation* was a large rectangular garment worn as an outer cloak which had four corners and attached to each of these corners was a tassel in accordance with Numbers 15.37-39 and Deuteronomy 22.12. One end of the garment could be thrown over the shoulder in the manner of a Scots plaid which the *himation* resembled in form and use, and so the tassels would be readily accessible from behind. It was one of these which the woman touched. It seems unnecessary to suggest that a special virtue or power was thought to reside in the tassels in order to explain why people sought to touch them (Mark 6.56) when an adequate reason can be found in the fact that the tassels were the most readily accessible part of a person's clothes to touch. This woman's touch was different from all the contacts which Jesus had had with other members of the crowd as they pressed upon him from all sides (Mark 5.24 and 31). He was immediately conscious of her touch and knew that it came from behind, and so he turned around. Mark also tells us that he was conscious that power (*dunamis*) had gone out of him (5.30). Indeed it seems likely that it was his loss of power which made Jesus conscious of her touch rather than any sensation derived from his clothes. The woman on her part felt the constant trickle of blood dry up and her strength begin to return, and she knew that she was healed. Jesus insisted on her identifying herself, and when she had done so he told her that her faith had healed her, using the verb *sōzō*. Then he dismissed her to go in peace and to remain free of the disease which had been the scourge of her life for twelve years, as Jesus recognises by his use of the word *mastix* to describe it (Mark 5.34).

How then had she been healed? She had been healed by touching Jesus, as a result of which the power (*dunamis*) which produced healing proceeded from him and flowed into her body to stop the bleeding and to rid her of the tumours which were causing it. The power is spoken of in an unusual way which requires careful translation. Most recent commentators accept the RV rendering as the most appropriate one, 'And straightway Jesus, perceiving in himself that the power *proceeding* from him had gone forth, turned him about in the crowd' (Mark 5.30).[6] It is clear that the power went forth from Jesus himself and not from his clothes. No power resided in his clothes. Power to heal resided in him and was available to proceed from him as required, and it was this power which flowed out to this woman in response to her touch. Her healing was not by magic, nor was it independent of our Lord's will although the text appears to suggest that it may have been outside his knowledge until it was happening. The power which proceeded from Jesus was that of God himself and under God's control, and it was his will that the woman should be healed. To probe deeper is to become involved in suggestions derived from the internal relationships within the Trinity such as that which proposes that in this case the healing was carried out by God the Father without the direct intervention of God the Son.[7] Such suggestions do not seem either desirable or profitable in this case. The woman was healed by the power of God which was available in Jesus for healing. It was this power which Jesus used in every method he used for healing. Wherever he was, it could be said that the power of the Lord was present to heal (Luke 5.17).

The source of the healing power of Jesus becomes even more explicit in his casting out of demons. It was from the Spirit of God. Even his enemies had to admit that he needed spiritual power to exorcise evil spirits, but they attributed his power to the prince of demons and not to God. Jesus had little difficulty in demonstrating the inconsistency of their argument, for demons would hardly cast out demons. He pressed his argument home by turning it back on themselves and asking by whom did they think that their sons cast out demons if they maintained that he did this by the power of the prince of demons (Matthew 12.27 and Luke 11.19). This may mean that Jesus recognised that Jewish exorcists were really able to exorcise demons, but on the other hand it need not imply that Jewish exorcists had succeeded in casting out demons, but only that they were credited with no diabolical witchcraft in making the attempt. The question may mean no more than 'Judge me on the same principles as you would judge your own exorcists'. Whatever they may think, he has no doubt. He casts out demons by the finger of God (Luke 11.20), by the Spirit of God (Matthew 12.28).

Although we have now discussed the main methods by which Jesus healed the sick and the possessed, and restored the dead to life, there remain two groups of cases in which he healed the sick and in which the method of healing included a special feature. In the first group he added the application of saliva to his touch, and in the second group he healed in circumstances in which the use of word, touch or saliva was impossible for the healing was carried out in the absence of the patient.

4. *Healing involving the use of saliva*

(1) The deaf mute: *He put his fingers into his ears, and he spat and touched his tongue; and looking up to heaven, he sighed, and said to him, 'Ephphatha,' that is, 'Be opened'* (Mark 7.33-34).

(2) The blind man of Bethsaida: *He took the blind man by the hand, and led him out of the village; and when he had spit on his eyes and laid his hands upon him, he asked him, 'Do you see anything?' And he looked up and said, 'I see men; but they look like trees, walking.' Then again he laid his hands upon his eyes* (Mark 8.23-25).

(3) The man born blind: *He spat on the ground and made clay of the spittle and anointed the man's eyes with the clay, saying to him, 'Go wash in the pool of Siloam'* (John 9.6-7).

The first thing to notice about these three accounts is that the use of saliva was not the only method which Jesus used for the healing of the sick people concerned. In the case of the deaf mute, it is not even clear that he used saliva at all, for we are simply told that he spat. No indication is given of whether or in what way he used the saliva. Wharton has suggested that he spat to disperse the demonic forces but this suggestion finds no support in the gospel record either here or elsewhere.[8] One result of this uncertainty in the case of the deaf mute has been the production of a number of variant readings all of which are aimed at making the method of use of the saliva more explicit, but the very existence of these attempts at explanation only serves to make the common reading more probable.[9] Presumably Jesus went on to use the saliva and perhaps applied it to the deaf mute's tongue with his fingers. The important thing about the use of saliva along with other methods is that it excludes any suggestion that it was being used in any magical way in these cases. If it had been used magically then it would have been efficacious by itself, and would not have needed any other method to be used. At most it would have required some form of incantation, but it is very evident from the gospel record that no incantation formed any part of our Lord's healing practice.

The saliva was applied in different ways in the three cases. In the case of the deaf mute it was probably applied by the fingers (Mark 7.33). With the blind man of Bethesda Jesus spat directly on (*eis*) his eyes (Mark 8.23). In the case of the man born blind he spat on the ground and used the saliva to make a paste with the dust, and then applied this to the blind man's eyes (John 9.6). This absence of uniformity in the application of the saliva suggests that no ritual pattern was being followed or prescribed by Jesus.

The other healing procedures used by Jesus along with the application of saliva include some interesting features. In healing the deaf mute Jesus did no less than six things to produce healing. He first put his fingers into the man's ears which may suggest that the deafness had a physical cause, and if this is so, it is the only case of physical deafness amongst the individual healing miracles. Then he spat, and we presume that he used the saliva which resulted in some way in the healing. Possibly he spat on to his fingers in order to apply the saliva to the tongue when he touched it. Then we are told that Jesus did something which is only rarely recorded of him in his healing activities, he looked up to heaven which probably means that he prayed as the phrase clearly does in Mark 6.41. As well as raising his eyes to heaven, we are told that Jesus sighed which Taylor regards as 'a sign of his deep feeling and compassion for the sufferer'[10] and Swete comments that this sigh arises from his humanity.[11] The verb used is *stenazō* which is used for sighing as the expression of inward emotion, and according to Cranfield 'it indicates the strong emotion of Jesus as he wages war against the power of Satan, and has to seek divine aid in urgent prayer'.[12] Finally, he gives the command 'Be opened' which Mark preserves in the original Aramaic transliterated as *Ephphatha* (Mark 7.34). This command is not appropriate to an exorcism and seems to be addressed to the physical organs which are causing the sick man's disability. This disability could have been due to some form of conduction deafness by which the pathway of the sound waves from the outside to the sensitive inner ear was obstructed, and to the condition of tongue-tie in which the tongue was bound down by a congenitally short frenulum which is the band which binds the front of the tongue down to the floor of the mouth.[13] The fact that the man is described as speaking immediately after he was healed suggests that he had already learned to speak and so had not been born deaf, but had become deaf as the result of a childhood infection which affected both his ears.

The healing of the blind man of Bethsaida in Mark 8.22-26 is unique in the gospels, for it is the only case in which Jesus had to lay his hands on a sick person twice before he was healed. This healing took place in private away from any emotional effect which a large watching crowd might produce. Jesus took the man and spat on his eyes and laid his hands on him. We are not told where on his body Jesus laid his hands on this first occasion. He then goes on to ask the blind man a most unexpected question, one which he had never asked in any other case. The question was, 'Do you see anything?' (v. 23). The question reads as a request for information, but could be interpreted as implying doubt of whether the method of healing which Jesus had used was effective. The man looked up and said, 'I see men; but they look like trees, walking' (v. 24). His reply suggests that he had not been blind from birth, for he re-

membered what trees looked like, and men with burdens on their heads resembled trees to his newly returned but still blurred vision which allowed him
to recognise the gross outline of objects and their movement, but not the finer
detail of these objects. So Jesus laid his hands on him a second time, and this
time it was on his eyes. After this the man's vision was restored and he saw
clearly. This healing was not immediate, but took place in two stages. This fact
alone is an indication of the truth of the incident, for no one would invent a
story which suggested that Jesus had not healed a sick man completely the first
time he had tried.

The blindness of the man born blind was cured by a combination of three
procedures (John 9.1-7). First, Jesus spat on the ground and made a paste of the
saliva and the dust. Then he smeared this paste on the blind man's eyes, and told
him to go and wash in the pool of Siloam. He went and washed and his sight
returned.

The function of saliva in these three cases of healing is not easy to assess
because saliva has no recognised healing properties today. Suggestions that the
use of saliva made the cure more personal and individual do not seem to be
appropriate in this context. There are indications that in the ancient world
saliva was believed to possess healing power, but this was usually of a magical
nature which is not the case in the gospel record. Tacitus records how Vespasian
was credited with the restoration of a blind man's sight at Alexandria by the
use of his saliva,[14] but this can hardly be compared to the healing activity of a
humble Galilean peasant teacher. About a century later Galen, a famous Greek
physician, attributed the cure of certain skin diseases such as psoriasis to saliva,
and described how saliva which he calls *phlegma* could destroy venomous
animals such as scorpions.[15] References to its use are infrequent in Rabbinic
literature where its application is condemned principally because of the magical
practices which accompanied its use.[16] Whatever its significance in the healing
practice of Jesus, saliva was never used alone and certainly never with anything
resembling an incantation. Its use in healing did not persist in the healing practice of the Church, which indicates that it was not regarded as an essential
constituent of any healing procedure even though it had been practised by Jesus
himself.

5. *Healing at a distance*

(1) The nobleman's son: *Go; your son will live* (John 4.50).
(2) The centurion's servant: *Go; be it done for you as you have believed*
(Matthew 8.13).
(3) The Syrophoenician girl: *For this saying you may go your way; the demon
has left your daughter* (Mark 7.29).

Here we have three cases in which Jesus healed without touch or word. It
is not clear why he chose to heal from a distance in these cases, for there were
other cases in which he could have healed from a distance and did not do so.
When Jairus asked him to heal his daughter Jesus went with him to his house to
heal her (Luke 8.41-42). It may be that the distances involved in the three cases
in which Jesus did not go were greater than in the case of Jairus' daughter. In
each case, as we might expect, Jesus was asked by the one who came to him to

help them; none of the sick persons sent a message to him directly. In each case there is mention of faith, and the two cases in which this is mentioned most explicitly were concerned with persons of non-Jewish race. These were the Roman centurion whose faith was such that Jesus said he had never found any faith like it, not even in Israel amongst Jewish people (Luke 7.9); and the Syrophoenician woman whose faith he described as great (Matthew 15.28).

In these three cases there was no word of command to the sick or to a demon. There was no touch of sympathy or for the transfer of healing power. There was no special method at all, simply a command to the person who had come to seek help from Jesus that they should return, and an assurance that the sick one was well again. In the case of the nobleman's son we know from the record that the boy's fever left him at the very time that Jesus spoke the word of reassurance to his father. The fact that in none of these cases was a word of healing spoken has been used by some commentators to suggest that they are not examples of healing but of the possession by Jesus of special medical knowledge. In the case of the nobleman's son, for example, Bernard says that all that Jesus is represented as saying is, 'Your son will live' i.e. he will recover. He assumes that the father had described his son's symptoms to Jesus who diagnosed the disease and knew that it was not a fatal one, but that even at that moment the crisis had passed and he was getting better.[17] What Jesus did was not beyond human power to do at that time, although it may have been beyond human knowledge. This explanation is not a very satisfactory one in view of the use of the word *sēmeion* to describe this incident in John 4.54. It is unlikely that John would have included this event amongst the *sēmeia* if it was simply the display by Jesus of a superior knowledge of the nature and prognosis of the disease from which the boy was suffering. In all the other *sēmeia* there was a demonstration of supernatural power by Jesus, and this suggests that when Jesus spoke the word to the distraught father it was a word of healing power and not just a word of favourable prognosis such as any Jewish physician might give.

The suggestion is often made that the basis of the healing of the three sick people who were healed at a distance by Jesus is telepathy, but this suggestion does not shed much light on the method of healing which Jesus used. The word *telepathy* was introduced by F. W. H. Myers in 1882 and he defined its meaning as 'the communication of impressions of any kind from one mind to another independently of the recognised channels of sense'. This definition is quoted in the Oxford English Dictionary as the standard meaning of the word. Efforts to establish telepathy on a scientific basis and even to found a science of parapsychology based on extra-sensory perception or ESP have not succeeded in spite of the strenuous advocacy of Professor J. B. Rhine and his associates at Duke University at Durham in North Carolina.[18] Therefore to endeavour to explain our Lord's healing of the absent sick on the basis of telepathy or ESP is only to try and explain the unknown by the uncertain and leads nowhere. Furthermore, although investigators in this field have claimed to be able to transfer information from one mind to another, no one has reliably claimed to have cured cases of physical disease characterised by fever or paralysis, or cases of demon possession by methods which could be described as telepathic. To suggest that the method used by Jesus here was one of telepathy may give it a name, but does not help us to understand how it produced healing.

Over a century ago, Trench in his still valuable book *Notes on the Miracles of our Lord* (first published in 1846) likened the Syrophoenician mother to a living electric conductor transmitting the power of Christ to her sick daughter by offering in her faith a channel of communication between him and her distant daughter.[19] More recently, Weatherhead speaks of the cases of the centurion's servant and the nobleman's son (whom he regards as one and the same person) as cases in which 'at an unconscious level of the mind our Lord's mind actually made contact with that of the patient', and he goes on to say that 'it is attractive to think that in a sense Jesus did go to the patient . . . and that therapeutic forces in His mind flowed into the deep mind of the patient, achieving his recovery'.[20] Regretfully it has to be admitted that these attempts at understanding are but similes and do not advance our understanding of what happened in the cases of absent healing. However, there is no difficulty here if we believe in the fact and efficacy of prayer. In Christian experience throughout the ages the effect of prayer has never been limited by distance. What happened in the healing of the absent sick still occurs today when prayer for those who are absent from us is heard and answered. We may not understand how it happens, but we know that it does.

Our survey of the methods which Jesus used in healing men and women is now complete, and this concludes our general examination of healing in the gospels. In this examination we have looked at the records which describe the healing work of Jesus and the descriptions of this work which they contain. We have considered the context of his healing activity and sought to understand his motive for healing. Finally, in this present chapter we have discussed the methods by which he made men whole.

In the next two chapters we proceed to study in more detail two of the cases which he healed, both of which are described in some detail, and both of which present features of special interest.

REFERENCES

1. E. R. Micklem, *Miracles and the New Psychology* (Oxford University Press, 1922), p. 126.
2. Galen, *Opera omnia* (ed. C. G. Kühn, Leipzig, 1821-33), vol. 7, p. 275.
3. E. Langton, *Essentials of Demonology* (Epworth Press, London, 1949), p. 151, and L. Morris, *The Gospel according to St. Luke* (Inter-Varsity Press, London, 1974), p. 110.
4. V. Taylor, *Mark*, p. 275.
5. F. W. Farrar, *The Gospel according to St Luke* (Cambridge University Press, 1880), p. 116.
6. C. E. B. Cranfield, *The Gospel according to Saint Mark* (Cambridge University Press, 1959), p. 185.
7. D. W. Burdick in *The Wycliffe Bible Commentary* (Oliphants, London, 1963), p. 998.
8. J. A. Wharton, *Interpreter's Dictionary of the Bible* (Abingdon Press, Nashville, 1962), vol. 4, p. 437, art. 'Spit'.
9. V. Taylor, *Mark*, p. 354.
10. V. Taylor, *Mark*, p. 355.

11. H. B. Swete, *The Gospel according to St. Mark* (Macmillan, London, 1909), p. 161.

12. C. E. B. Cranfield, *Mark*, p. 252.

13. The rare word *mogilalos* is used in v. 32 to describe the man's speech difficulty. According to Arndt and Gingrich (p. 527) the ancient versions understood the word to mean 'dumb' (cp. Isaiah 35.6 LXX), but it may also mean 'having an impediment of speech'. This impediment could be due to tongue-tie since the fact that Jesus touched his tongue may suggest that it was there that the cause of his impediment lay.

14. Tacitus, *Histories*, 4, 81, cp. Suetonius, *Vespasian*, 7.

15. Galen, *On the Natural Faculties*, 3, 7 (Loeb edition, p. 252).

16. See references in C. K. Barrett, *The Gospel according to St John* (SPCK, London, 1962), p. 296.

17. J. H. Bernard, *International Critical Commentary on the Gospel according to St John* (T. & T. Clark, Edinburgh, 1928), vol. 1, p. clxxx.

18. J. B. Rhine, *The Reach of the Mind* (Penguin Books, London, 1954).

19. R. C. Trench, *Notes on the Miracles of our Lord* (Kegan Paul, Trench and Trübner, London, 1900), sixteenth edition, p. 371.

20. L. D. Weatherhead, *Psychology, Religion and Healing* (Hodder and Stoughton, London, 1952), second edition, p. 75.

Chapter Seven

THE CASE OF THE EPILEPTIC BOY[1]

An older generation of commentators spoke of this lad as 'the lunatic boy' taking their cue from the AV rendering of Matthew 17.15. The word used in this verse is *selēniazomai* which means literally 'to be moonstruck', and for which 'lunatic' is the literal translation which was adopted into English from the Latin Vulgate rendering *lunaticus est*. The RV, however, boldly labelled him 'the epileptic boy', and has been followed by most of the more recent English versions. The RV did not escape criticism for its new rendering. Creighton tells us that the Revisers justified it on the ground that 'epileptic' was a more scientific term than 'lunatic' and they quoted a seventh-century Greek medical writer in support of this.[2] However, Liddell and Scott give the gospel account of the healing of this boy as the earliest authority for their definition of the word *selēniazomai* as meaning 'to be epileptic'.[3] The literal meaning of the word is derived from the popular belief that the moon in certain of its phases, and especially when it is full, is injurious to human beings and produces disease of a paroxysmal nature such as epilepsy. This belief appears to be referred to in Psalm 121.6. We have no means of knowing whether this belief was still a living one in New Testament times, or whether by then the word was used for epilepsy without any reference to its derivation. In this chapter we are concerned to look at the justification for regarding this boy as epileptic, more particularly from a medical point of view.

I. THE CASE RECORD

The case of the epileptic boy is recorded in all three synoptic gospels. It is one of the few incidents where the narrative of Mark is much fuller than the narratives of Matthew and Luke. The wealth of detail given by Mark suggests its derivation from an eye-witness, and there can be no doubt that this account comes from the apostle Peter whose eye for detail and ear for the memorable word we know so well in the gospel of Mark who, as Papias tells us, was regarded by the early Church as Peter's interpreter (*hermeneutēs*) and faithful reporter.[4] The incident is told from the standpoint of one who has returned with Jesus from the Mount of the Transfiguration, rather than of one who was present with the disciples waiting below. This feature fits in with the traditional setting of the story as immediately following the Transfiguration, for we are told that Peter had gone with Jesus on that occasion along with James and John, while the rest of the disciples remained at the foot of the mountain.

Although this is a miracle of healing, it should be noted that the medical evangelist does not give the same detail of the miracle as Mark does, although his summary of the clinical features of the case in Luke 9.39 is a masterly example of compressed and relevant description. Matthew's summary of the case in 17.15 is much less medically informed, but his account gives us the *Kyrie eleison* which became the earliest and simplest form of litany used in liturgical worship.

We are fortunate in this case to have not only the father's description of what happened when the boy had a convulsion, but also a description of an actual fit as seen by an independent eye-witness. This is the kind of case record which a physician hopes for in epilepsy, but is not often able to obtain. Usually he is given a description of a fit by a relative of the patient, but rarely sees a fit or obtains an eye-witness account of one from an accurate and independent observer. It is this which makes this account of the epileptic boy so valuable and so convincing to a medical reader. To such a reader there is no need to dissect the account into two distinct narratives such as Bultmann proposes.[5] The suggestion of Taylor that we have two accounts of the same incident is much more acceptable,[6] for it is obvious that we have here intertwined the account of the father describing his son's fits in Mark 9.17-18 and 21-22, and the account of the eye-witness describing the two fits which the boy had in his presence (Mark 9.20 and 26-27)

II. THE HISTORY

In medical usage the *history* means the information about the disease, its onset, its progress and its present manifestations which is derived from questioning the patient or his relatives and friends. There are some diseases in which the history is very important for establishing the diagnosis, and epilepsy is one of these. Often in cases of epilepsy we can see no signs of the disease on the patient, and since he loses consciousness during a fit, he cannot be expected to help much in the description of what happens to him.

We are fortunate in having no fewer than seven descriptions of what happened to the boy when he had a fit, and each of these adds new detail to the picture. Four of these accounts are derived from the father's account of his son's seizures (Matthew 17.15; Mark 9.17-18 and 21-22, and Luke 9.39), and the other three derive their details from the eye-witness (Mark 9.20 and 26-27, and Luke 9.42). Beare comments on the exuberance of the story in Mark saying it is 'unusually full of detail, some of it repetitive, some irrelevant'.[7] No one who has listened to an anxious father describing the history of an afflicted son's illness could regard the repetitiveness as more than a true and natural characterisation of how this boy's father told his story to Jesus. Repetitive it may be, and that is understandable in the circumstances, but each repetition adds more detail to the picture none of which can be dismissed as irrelevant in describing a condition such as epilepsy.

We learn from the father that his son has suffered from fits since childhood (*ek paidiothen*, Mark 9.21). This must mean that they began very early in childhood for we are told that he was only a *pais* when he was brought to Jesus by his father (Matthew 17.18 and Luke 9.42), and this has commonly been taken to mean that he was about twelve years old as Jesus was when he was called a *pais* in Luke 2.43, but its New Testament usage is not always as precise as this.[8] Infancy is a well-recognised time for the onset of epileptic fits, and such an early onset is a mark of true epilepsy rather than of hysteria which occurs later in life.

The description of the condition makes it clear that it was paroxysmal or periodic in occurrence. A fit may seize him in any place (Mark 9.18), and had often cast him into the fire or into water endangering his life (Matthew 17.15 and Mark 9.22). We may add to these references the command of Jesus to the unclean spirit never to enter the boy again (Mark 9.25) which implies that he had been in the habit of entering him periodically. We are given no indication of the frequency of the convulsions. It is unlikely that the father's use of the verb *seleniazomai* was meant to indicate that they occurred monthly. Indeed, it is probable that he had convulsions more frequently than this, for his father told Jesus that his son suffered severely from the disease (*kakos echei*, Matthew 17.15).

The father makes clear that these attacks had occurred in dangerous situations, and had thrown the boy into the fire or into water (Mark 9.22). His body may have borne the scars of the burns he had suffered on some of these occasions. Because these incidents could have been fatal the boy has been described by some commentators as showing suicidal tendencies. However it is well recognised that epilepsy may endanger life if a convulsion occurs in a situation in which sudden unconsciousness may plunge its victim into fire or water. Death may then occur from severe burns or drowning, but this is not suicide, for the afflicted person is not in control of his actions during such a convulsion. The occurrence of accidents due to a loss of consciousness as described by the boy's father is another indication that we are not dealing with a case of hysterical fits in this boy.

As well as being accused of suicidal tendencies, this boy has also been described as mentally deficient. Some modern commentators have been very unkind to him and called him an epileptic idiot and a low grade moron. This is quite unjustified by the facts which are recorded. There is nothing in the history or description of this boy's illness which would suggest to a medical reader that he suffered from any degree of mental deficiency. It is true, of course, that mental subnormality may be accompanied by epilepsy, and also that severe epilepsy may eventually be accompanied by some degree of mental deterioration, but we owe it to this boy to make clear that neither of these situations is even hinted at in the gospel narrative.

III. THE CONVULSIONS

The evangelists do not give us an exact medical description of the convulsions from which this boy suffered such as we might find in a modern textbook of neurology, and we have no right to expect this from them. Even so, the details which are recorded and the words in which these details are described give us a very vivid picture of the seizures, and leave us in no doubt that this boy suffered from the major form of epilepsy or what the French neurologists of last century spoke of as *le grand mal*.

Before we examine the details set out in the gospel record let us briefly summarise the different stages of a major epileptic fit as we recognise them in modern medical practice. The following five stages are generally distinguished:

1. The premonitory stage.
2. The stage of unconsciousness.
3. The stage of muscular convulsion:
    a. The stage of muscular rigidity, or the *tonic* stage.
    b. The stage of muscular jerking, or the *clonic* stage.
4. The stage of flaccid unconsciousness.
5. The stage of recovery.

This scheme is useful for the purposes of description, but it is not entirely satis-factory because all the stages are not entirely distinct. Thus the second and third stages begin together at the same point of time, whilst the unconsciousness of the second stage continues through the third and fourth stages.

1. *The premonitory stage*

This stage does not occur in every case of epilepsy, but when it does occur it warns the afflicted person that an attack is about to commence. Sometimes this warning may precede the actual convulsion by hours or even days, but more commonly occurs only a few seconds before the fit begins. It consists of a brief subjective experience of some form of sensation and is usually called the *aura*. This term is the Greek word for a breeze and was first used to denote the premonitory symptoms of epilepsy by the Greek physician Galen since they may take the form of the sensation of a current of cold air rising from the body to the head.[9] This stage is only momentary in duration, but the patient is now so taken up with what is happening to him that he becomes unresponsive to his surroundings, and this becomes even more marked when he loses consciousness with the onset of the second stage. Here we have the explanation of the father's description of the spirit which seizes his son as dumb (Mark 9.17), and also why Jesus addresses the same spirit as dumb and deaf (Mark 9.25). The spirit was not deaf, for it heard and obeyed Jesus' command to come out of the boy, but it caused the boy to appear dumb and deaf as he went into an epileptic fit, and as he became incapable of speaking and hearing during the period of unconscious-ness. It is possible, of course, that the boy was a deaf mute, but the narrative connects his dumbness and deafness with the occasions when the spirit seizes him (Mark 9.17-18) rather than suggesting that they describe a permanent state. Also, the boy was brought to Jesus not as a deaf mute, but as an epileptic.

2. *The stage of unconsciousness*

The loss of consciousness in epilepsy is sudden and complete, and the affected person falls rigid to the ground as he loses consciousness. This is de-scribed in the accounts in two ways. He is said to fall (Matthew 17.15 and Mark

9.20), and also he is said to be seized by the spirit and dashed to the ground (Mark 9.18 and Luke 9.42). We still speak of epileptic fits as seizures, and the term epilepsy is derived from the Greek verb *lambanō*, to take hold of, which is used of the spirit seizing the boy in Mark 9.18 and Luke 9.38.

3. *The stage of muscular convulsion*

The onset of this stage coincides with the loss of consciousness. It may be divided into two separate stages according to the condition of the muscles affected.

a. *The stage of muscular rigidity.* For the first thirty seconds or so of the convulsion the muscles are contracted and the body held rigid. This stage of muscular rigidity does not appear to have been recognised in any of the seven descriptions of the fit, and this is not surprising in view of the short duration of the muscle spasm. However we know that this stage did occur in this boy's case because one result of the sudden spasm of the muscles is a loud weird guttural cry which may be suddenly emitted by a person at this stage of a fit. This cry is due to the forced expiration of air through the narrowed opening between the vocal cords which results from the spasm of the muscles of the larynx. This cry is referred to by the father in Luke 9.39 and by the eye witness in Mark 9.26. The verb used to describe the cry is *krazō* which originally was used as an echoism for the croak of the raven and so came to be used for any inarticulate cry. Its later use is illustrated by the articulate cry for help by the boy's father which this same word describes in Mark 9.26.

b. *The stage of muscular jerking.* The most striking stage of the fit is that in which contractions of the muscles of a part or the whole of the body produce strong jerking movements for a period of one to two minutes. This stage is described by the verb *sparassō* in Mark 9.26 and Luke 9.39, and by its intensive form *susparassō* in Mark 9.20 and Luke 9.42. During this stage the patient may roll about as the result of the irregular unco-ordinated movements of the trunk and limb muscles, and this is described by the eye-witness in Mark 9.20 where his use of the appropriate verb in the imperfect tense suggests that he kept on rolling about on the ground. In a fit the patient may also gnash his teeth as this boy did according to his father in Mark 9.18, and if the tongue happens to be protruded between the teeth it may be bitten. Froth may appear on the lips from the churning up of air and saliva in the mouth by the jerking movements of the muscles of the mouth and the jaw, and the appearance of froth is described by the father in Mark 9.18 and Luke 9.39, and by the eye-witness in Mark 9.20. As a result of his uncontrolled movements during this stage the patient may knock against objects in his vicinity and so bruise himself as this boy did in his fits according to his father's account in Luke 9.39 where the verb *suntribō* should be translated 'bruises' rather than 'shatters' (RSV). In many cases the afflicted person ends this stage lying face downwards and he may easily drown in quite a shallow depth of water.

4. *The stage of flaccid unconsciousness*

When the muscular convulsions are past, the patient remains limp and unconscious and a casual spectator may readily regard him as dead as we are told most of the crowd did when his last fit reached this stage (Mark 9.26). The word used by the father in Mark 9.18 to describe this stage of flaccid unconsciousness is the verb *xērainō* and this word has given rise to some difficulty in translation. It commonly means to waste or to wither away, and is used in Mark 3.1 to describe the withered state of the hand of the man who had probably suffered from acute anterior poliomyelitis in his youth, and also in Mark 4.6 to denote the dried up condition of the seed which fell on stony ground. The meaning of wasting or withering is inappropriate here, for epilepsy does not interfere with the nutrition of its victims. Arndt and Gingrich (p. 550) propose 'becomes stiff' as the translation, and the RSV renders the word as 'becomes rigid'. However, it seems preferable to extend the meaning to include the result of the wasting, namely, lack of movement, and so understand the father to mean that at the end of the fit his son is completely exhausted and motionless. This is the view of Cranfield who translates the word as 'becomes exhausted',[10] and of Taylor who suggests that it describes 'the pallor of complete exhaustion',[11] whilst Bruce speaks of 'the final stage of motionless stupor graphically described as withering'.[12]

5. *The stage of recovery*

When consciousness returns after an epileptic fit, the person is usually dazed and confused, and commonly goes off into a deep sleep for several hours. The fit seems reluctant to leave him, and this explains the remark of the father that the spirit left his son only with difficulty (Luke 9.39). It was during this stage that Jesus took the boy by the hand and raised him up (Mark 9.27) and gave him back to his father (Luke 9.42).

IV. THE DIAGNOSIS

Our examination of the case record of this boy has left no doubt that he suffered from the major form of epilepsy, and therefore the RV and all the English versions which followed its lead were fully justified in calling him *epileptic* rather than *lunatic*. However, there are a number of recent and reputable commentators on this story who still suggest that he might have been a case of hysteria rather than one of epilepsy, and so a short discussion of the differentiation of hysterical fits from those of epilepsy will serve to make the diagnosis even more secure in this boy's case. The relevant points of distinction between the two types of convulsion are set out below and compared with the description given of the features of this boy's condition.

Hysterical fit	*Epileptic fit*	*The boy's fit*
1. Onset in adolescence or early adulthood.	Onset in infancy or childhood.	Onset in childhood (Mark 9.21).
2. Fit begins slowly.	Fit begins suddenly.	Fit begins suddenly (Mark 9.20).
3. No loss of consciousness.	Consciousness lost.	Boy became unresponsive.
4. Injury does not occur.	Injury frequent.	Injured himself in fire and water (Matthew 17.15).
5. Patient normal after fit.	Patient drowsy and exhausted after fit.	Boy exhausted (Mark 9.26).

Once the features are set out in a table like this, the distinction between hysterical and epileptic fits becomes quite clear, and when we compare the features described in the boy's fits there can be no doubt that he suffered from fits which were epileptic in character and not hysterical. We conclude, therefore, that not only is there no evidence that this boy suffered from mental deficiency, there is also no evidence that he suffered from neurosis in the form of hysteria. The fits with which he was afflicted were epileptic in nature.

V. HIPPOCRATES ON EPILEPSY

Now that it is clear that we are dealing with a case of epilepsy in this boy, it is of interest to recall the classic description of this disease which has come down to us from the antiquity which preceded the Christian era. Hippocrates of Cos (460-355 B.C.) wrote a book on epilepsy which he entitled *Peri hierēs nousou*, On the Sacred Disease. In this book he denies that it is a sacred disease due to a divine visitation, but a disease which has its origin in the brain. In the course of the book he describes the features of an epileptic fit and this description is worth quoting in order to compare it with that of the fits which we have been considering in the gospels exhibited by the epileptic boy. According to Hippocrates the features of an epileptic fit are 'dumbness, choking, frothing at the mouth, gnashing of the teeth and convulsive movements of the hands; the eyes become fixed and the patient loses consciousness, and in some cases passes a stool'.[13] He then proceeds to discuss each feature in detail and to explain how it might be caused, but the passage is too long to quote and does not add much to the description already given. In this description Hippocrates gives eight separate signs which are obviously the result of acute observation of persons seen during an epileptic fit. Of these eight signs only five are noted in gospel account of the boy's fits. Those which are omitted are choking, fixation of the eyes and the possible passage of a stool. Conversely, of the ten features of an epileptic fit recorded in the gospels only six are included by Hippocrates in his description of the disease. Those omitted by him are the history of previous injury during fits, the occurrence of a cry at the onset of a fit, the fact that the patient falls to the ground as he loses consciousness, and his rolling about on the ground in the clonic stage of the fit. We need to combine both accounts to obtain a complete picture of an epileptic fit as a modern medical textbook would describe it, for both omit features which are enquired for when a diagnosis of epilepsy is being considered today. If we go further and compare the vocabulary used by Hippocrates with that used in the gospel accounts, a very interesting fact emerges. The only words which are common to the two descriptions are the nouns for froth and teeth. Luke uses the former word in 9.39 and Mark the latter in 9.18, but even Luke's word may be derived from Mark since Mark uses the verb in 9.18 and 20 from which the noun for froth is derived. This means that the Hippocratic description of the disease of epilepsy has not influenced Luke's description of the boy's epileptic fit at all. We know from Paul's reference to him as 'the beloved physician' in Colossians 4.14 that

Luke was a doctor. It is commonly assumed that he received his medical training in Tarsus, the chief city of Cilicia, but we do not know this for certain.
Since it would be reasonable to assume that his medical training would influence his use of words in the description of attacks of disease, the fact that this
did not appear to happen in this boy's case would suggest that Luke was not
trained in the Hippocratic tradition in the practice of medicine, but in some
other tradition of Greek medicine.

VI. THE CAUSE

The diagnosis of this boy's illness is not yet complete. Epilepsy is not a disease,
but a symptom which results from the sudden discharge of energy by nerve
cells in the brain. This discharge of energy may have many causes, and some
medical writers have preferred to speak of the epilepsies rather than of epilepsy.
Having satisfied ourselves that this boy was afflicted by epileptic convulsions,
we must now seek to determine their cause or we leave the diagnosis only half
made. This means that to arrive at the diagnosis of epilepsy in this boy's case
does not automatically exclude demon possession as the cause of his disease as
some of the commentators suggest.

If we investigate the causes of epilepsy we find that there is one group of
patients in whom an organic physical cause for the convulsions can be identified
and in some cases removed. Into this group fall those who suffer from certain
brain tumours or various acute or chronic infections of the brain, as well as the
after-results of head injury. These patients are said to suffer from *secondary* or
symptomatic epilepsy. When these cases have been separated out there remains a
much larger group of patients in whom the cause cannot be determined, and
these are said to suffer from *idiopathic epilepsy* which means epilepsy whose cause
is unknown. If demon possession is a fact, there is no reason why it could not be
a cause of some cases of epilepsy. We do not know enough about the spirit
world and the activity of demons to disprove demon possession, nor enough
about epilepsy to deny that it may be caused by such possession.

Demon possession is usually denied on dogmatic grounds, but it would
seem to be much more dogmatically congruous to recognise the existence of
demons and the possibility of possession than to deny them. The Christian
believes in the existence of the Holy Spirit and the possibility of his possessing
the believer, and has thereby already admitted the possibility of spirit possession. If evil spirits exist, and no one can deny that there is much evidence in
the modern world that they do, may they not also possess and influence men?
However, we do not wish to embark on the large subject of demon possession
at this time, but merely to insist that to conclude that this boy suffered from
epilepsy is not thereby to exclude the possibility that his illness was due to
demon possession.

VII. THE CURE

Modern medicine knows no cure for idiopathic epilepsy. There are drugs
which will control the convulsions by depressing the activity of the nerve cells

of the brain, but there is no method of treatment which will cure an epileptic immediately and permanently. Fits may cease with the passage of time, but of no patient can we say with confidence that he will never have another fit. This is why the instantaneous cure of this boy by Jesus is so striking from a medical point of view. Jesus told the spirit to enter the boy again (Mark 9.25), and Matthew records that he was cured from that very hour (Matthew 17.18). There were plenty of eye-witnesses still alive at the time that Matthew wrote to contradict this statement if it were not true. Even modern medicine cannot cure epilepsy like that. Here indeed was the finger of God.

REFERENCES

1. Matthew 17.14-21; Mark 9.14-29 and Luke 9.37-48.
2. C. Creighton, *Encyclopaedia Biblica* (A. and C. Black, London, 1914), column 2833, art. 'Lunatic'.
3. H. G. Liddell and R. Scott, *A Greeek-English Lexicon* (Oxford University Press, 1925-40), revised edition, pp. 1590, s.v. *sēlemazō*.
4. Eusebius, *The Ecclesiastical History* III, 39, 15.
5. R. Bultmann, *The History of the Synoptic Tradition* (Blackwell, Oxford, 1968), ET by J. Marsh, p. 225.
6. V. Taylor, *Mark*, p. 396.
7. F. W. Beare, *The Earliest Records of Jesus* (Blackwell, Oxford, 1962), p. 144.
8. According to Hippocrates, *Peri hebdomadōn*, 5, *pais* commonly meant a boy of eight to fourteen years of age in Classical Greek.
9. Galen, *Opera omnia* (ed. C. G. Kühn, Leipzig, 1921-33), vol. 10, p. 94.
10. C. E. B. Cranfield, *Mark*, p. 301.
11. V. Taylor, *Mark*, p. 398.
12. A. B. Bruce, *The Expositor's Greek Testament* (Hodder and Stoughton, London, 1901), second edition, vol. 1, p. 402.
13. Hippocrates, *On the Sacred Disease*, 10, lines 3-7 (Loeb edition, vol. 2, p. 158).

Chapter Eight

THE CASE OF THE BENT WOMAN[1]

Jesus was on his last journey up to Jerusalem. He was passing through the tetrarchy of Herod Antipas which embraced Galilee and Peraea. On the Sabbath day he attended the service of worship in a local synagogue, but we do not know where this synagogue was. Some believe that he was still in Galilee, and others say that he had crossed into Peraea, but we do not know for certain. We do know, however, that this was the last occasion on which he was allowed to enter and teach in a synagogue. It is possible that already many synagogues were closed to him and their elders would not allow him to preach in view of the fact that the Jewish hierarchy had become so hostile to him. This may in part explain the reaction of the ruler of the synagogue to our Lord's act of healing. The ruler's anger at the breaking of the Jewish law of the Sabbath by Jesus may have been intensified by his feeling of apprehension that he had unwittingly become a party to it by allowing Jesus to preach in his synagogue, an act which many other synagogue rulers would not have allowed in their synagogues at this stage of our Lord's ministry.

As he taught in the synagogue, Jesus noticed in the women's section of the congregation a woman with a spinal deformity, and he called her to him and healed her. The account of the healing of this woman is peculiar to the gospel of Luke, and contains some special features which merit a closer examination than they usually receive in the commentaries. Most commentators regard this incident as primarily an illustration of the attitude of Jesus towards the law of the Sabbath, and they spend more time and space on the attitude of the ruler of the synagogue to the fact of the healing than on the nature of the healing. When it is considered at all, there is no general agreement amongst the commentators on the nature of her condition, whether it was one of physical disease or of demon possession. Nor is much said about the meaning of the reference to the activity of Satan in her case, apart from the suggestion that this probably implies that her disease was due to her sinful life.

It is our purpose here to examine these problems more closely, and more especially from a medical point of view, and to endeavour to establish whether this healing of the bent woman was an exorcism or not.

We need not doubt the historicity of the story. Its atmosphere is wholly Jewish and its detail rings true to life. The deformed woman resigned to her deformity, the pharisaic attitude of the ruler of the synagogue, our Lord's logical refutation of his objection, and the crowd's delight in the discomfiture of his opponents and in his glorious works are all set out clearly in the narrative and make it come to life in a very vivid way. Also, it is no valid objection to the truth of this story that it is recorded by Luke alone, for its medical interest would explain this, and also its illustration of the conflict between the need of healing and man-made restrictions about the observance of the Sabbath. It is Luke alone who records all five of the Sabbath healings and the controversy they aroused which occur in the synoptic gospel tradition. Matthew records only two, and Mark only three, whilst John adds a further two from his own experience making a total of seven for the four gospels.

I. THE HISTORY

The woman was an Israelite, a daughter of Abraham (v. 16). We know that there are some diseases to which people of Jewish race are more prone than those of other races, but none of these diseases produces the spinal deformity which this woman displayed. It is unlikely therefore that the reference to her race had any medical significance.

We are given no clue to her age other than that she is called an adult woman (*gunē*, v. 11). She had been incapacitated for eighteen years (v. 11), but was still able to attend synagogue worship on the Sabbath, and so was not bedridden or completely crippled.

The only possible indication that we are given of the rapidity of onset of her disease is in the use of aorist indicative *edēse*, bound, in verse sixteen. Here Jesus speaks of the woman as being bound by Satan for eighteen years. The aorist tense normally means that the action denoted by the verb took place at a specific point in the past. Its use in this context, therefore, suggests two possibilities. Either the spinal deformity suddenly appeared at a definite point in time eighteen years previously, or the disease began then and its progressive development produced her spinal deformity. From a medical point of view, the latter interpretation is to be preferred as the only cause of the sudden appearance of an abnormal spinal deformity in the absence of pre-existing disease would be an injury which produced a crush fracture of one or more spinal vertebrae. This is a possible cause of such a deformity in this woman, of course, but we would not expect it to be described as being bound by Satan when everyone knew that it was the result of an accident. Hysteria may also produce the sudden onset of deformity, but this deformity would not in the first instance be outside the range of the normal movement or position of the spine, although later when physical changes had occurred due to disuse of the part, the deformity might well become abnormal and permanent.

II. THE DIAGNOSIS

The condition of the woman is described as one of *astheneia* in verses eleven and twelve. Most English versions translate this as 'weakness' or 'infirmity'. It is the common word for sickness in the New Testament, and presumably came to be applied to the state of sickness because sickness usually causes physical weakness. We need, therefore, to look for more specific terms to give us a clue to the nature of the disease in the case of this woman.

More specific information is given in verse eleven where we are told that the woman was 'bent double' (NEB). The verb used is *sunkuptō* which is used here only in the New Testament. It is used in the LXX version of Ecclesiasticus of being crouched down in humility (12.11), or in mourning (19.26), and therefore must mean being in a state of increased curvature of the spine in a forward direction. The cognate verb *anakuptō* is also used in verse eleven where the woman is described as unable to straighten herself up and stand upright. Such a state is called *kyphosis* in modern medical terminology, and this word is derived from the verb *kuptō*, although its modern medical meaning is not necessarily the same as that of its ancient usage. It would seem that the deformity from which this woman suffered was a markedly increased curvature of the spine because of which the upper part of her body was bent forwards on the lower. To quote the description of George Macdonald in his book on *The Miracles of our Lord*, she was 'bowed earthwards, the necessary blank of her eye the ground and not the horizon, the form divine deformed towards that of the four-footed animals . . . supported, I presume, by the staff which yet more assimilated her to the lower animals'.[2]

The degree of fixation of her spine is not clear as there is a grammatical ambiguity in verse eleven. Whether we understand her inability to straighten herself up to be partial or complete depends on which verb we decide to modify with the adverbial equivalent *eis to panteles*. The Latin Vulgate attached the phrase to the participle *mē dunamenē* and translated it by *nec omnino poterat sursum respicere*. Most English translations, e.g. AV, RV, NEB and TEV, have followed the Vulgate and have made the spinal rigidity complete so that the woman could not straighten herself up at all. In the words of the TEV, she 'was bent over and could not straighten up at all'. A few other versions including the RSV have with more probability attached the phrase to the infinitive *anakupsai* and translated the clause to mean that 'she could not fully straighten herself up'. In other words, she had some spinal movement left although it was not complete.[3]

From the description of the woman as 'bent double' we may assume that the site of her disease was the spine or vertebral column. Since she could not stand erect, the disease must have affected the bones, joints, ligaments or muscles of the spine. The two physical signs of spinal deformity and decreased spinal mobility narrow down our diagnostic field considerably.

Before we come to discuss specifically spinal diseases in our endeavour to reach a diagnosis in this woman's case, we must first consider the suggestion that her condition was one of hysteria as this diagnosis has been accepted by some authors. In his book *Psychology, Religion and Healing*, Weatherhead suggests a diagnosis of 'hysterical paraplegia' mainly on the grounds of her immediate cure.[4] Paraplegia would mean that she would have paralysis of both lower limbs, but there is no suggestion of this in the narrative which implies that she was able to attend synagogue worship and that her trouble lay in her back and not in her lower limbs. It is unlikely that she had a paraplegia. Did she, however, have hysteria? It is possible that her condition may have begun as a hysterical manifestation which showed itself in some disturbance of the position or function of the spine. Although this could explain the onset of her condition, after eighteen years of disuse there would be physical changes in the muscles, bones and joints of the spine resulting in a state of atrophy or wasting of the muscles, stiffness of the joints, and demineralisation of the bones. The result would be that whilst in the early stages the condition would be easily reversible, once atrophy and the other changes had set in, it would no longer be immediately reversible, and certainly not after so long a period as eighteen years. Her healing, therefore, was not just the making of a hysterical woman do what she was perfectly well able to do, namely, to stand erect. After eighteen years the physical changes which had occurred would prevent an instantaneous cure by ordinary natural means. It is on facts like these that the psychoneurotic theory of the nature of the healing miracles of Jesus breaks down, and we see no reason to suggest that the case of this woman was simply one of hysteria.

Although we do not have enough clinical detail to allow us to arrive at a diagnosis with absolute certainty, it would seem to be most probable that the disease was one which affected the spine. We may list the main diseases which produce kyphosis or an increased curvature of the spine causing a person to be bent forwards as follows:

I. Infective diseases:
1. Tuberculosis of the spine.
2. Spondylitis ankylopoietica or ankylosing spondylitis.

II. Degenerative diseases:
1. Osteoarthritis of the spine.
2. Osteoporosis of the spine.

Some authors use the term *spondylitis deformans* for the diagnosis in this woman's case.[5] However, this term simply means an affection of the spine which produces deformity, and it is applied to a number of different conditions some of which are not very well defined. It is often used as a synonym for ankylosing spondylitis, but in view of the ambiguity which surrounds the usage of the term it is best to avoid it altogether. It is one of those descriptive terms which have survived from older medical usage, and have not found a specific application to any particular disease in present-day usage in spite of the clearer differentiation of diseases in modern medicine. Consequently we have not used the term in our table above.

In general we may say that infective disease of the spine affects younger persons, and degenerative disease affects older persons. Hence the importance of a knowledge of the age of this woman, but this is unfortunately not possible as it is not included in the narrative. Since, however, the effects of the disease had already lasted eighteen years when she met Jesus, it seems reasonable to suppose that she was in the younger age group when the disease began. The shorter expectation of life in ancient society would also support this suggestion. If this is accepted then it would appear more probable that her condition was due to an infective rather than to a degenerative disease.

Tuberculosis of the spine is a possible diagnosis in this case. We know that tuberculosis of bones and joints existed in the ancient Near East, although most of the evidence has come from Egyptian mummies. This disease destroys the front part or body of one or more adjacent vertebrae of the spine, so that the vertebrae collapse in front and this collapse produces a local acute backward angulation of the spine in the area where the disease has developed. This acute angular deformity produced by tuberculosis in the spine is possibly greater than is implied in the verb *kuptō* and its cognates which are used to describe the condition of this woman. Elsewhere in the New Testament these words are used to describe the act of stooping down, or in the case of *anakuptō* the act of standing up straight or looking up as in Luke 21.28. They therefore appear to refer to a deformity which is less abnormal than the acute angulation of the spine backwards which tuberculosis usually produces. In verse eleven of our passage the woman is said not to be able to stand up straight or look up (*anakupsai*) as well as being bent double. Since she could neither straighten her spine nor lift her head up, it is unlikely that her disease was tuberculosis. Tuberculosis does not usually develop in two parts of the spine at the same time in the same person. Consequently if she suffered from tuberculosis and could not straighten her back, she would be able to lift up her head. If, therefore, she had a spinal deformity which affected both the thoracic and the cervical spine, as she appears to have had, then the probability is that it was not due to tuberculosis.

The other disease which may affect the younger age group is ankylosing spondylitis. This name is the English form of spondylitis ankylopoietica and it describes an affection of the spine which produces fusion or ankylosis of its joints. It is used for a well-defined disease of the spine whose exact cause is unknown, but whose features suggest that it is related to infection by some agent at present unidentified. Its incidence in the ancient world is unknown, but the closely related rheumatoid arthritis is known to have afflicted both palaeolithic and neolithic man, and to have occurred in ancient Egypt.[6]

This disease as we know it today begins in early adult life and although it is more common in the male sex, it does affect women too. It begins in the lower part of the vertebral column where it produces a progressively straight and rigid spine. To compensate for this straightness and immobility, the upper part of the spine assumes an increased forward curvature which eventually becomes fixed and rigid. Later, as a complication, a further increase in forward bending may occur and the patient assumes a permanent stooping position from which he cannot raise himself. This position is more like that of normal stooping than the acute angulation of the spine produced by tuberculosis, and so is more appropriately described by the verb *kuptō* and its derivatives. Also, since the rigidity affects the whole spine, the patient is unable to straighten himself up or raise up his head. It appears that this disease fits the scanty details recorded in this woman's case better than any other, and that ankylosing spondylitis is the most probable diagnosis in her case.

The degenerative diseases are less likely to have been the cause of the woman's bent condition than the infective ones because they begin later in life. Osteoarthritis of the spine is a disease of middle and old age. Its main effect is limitation of the movement of the spine, though it may also produce some degree of kyphosis. A more marked degree of kyphosis is produced by osteoporosis of the vertebrae in which their bony tissues become thin and decalcified, and may be compressed vertically to produce what is known as senile kyphosis or 'the dowager's stoop'. The true nature of this condition has only been recognised in recent years, although Macalister described this woman's case as one of senile kyphosis in 1900.[7] However, in terms of the medical knowledge of his day he understood this condition to be due to spinal osteoarthritis or 'chronic osteitis of the vertebrae' as he calls it, and not to senile osteoporosis.

We have now completed our consideration of the possible diagnosis of the disease in this woman's case. The relevant details provided by the narrative are scanty, and the author's main interest in recording the incident is not medical. Nevertheless it seems reasonable to suppose that the disease from which the woman suffered was that which today we call ankylosing spondylitis or spondylitis ankylopoietica.

III. THE QUESTION OF DEMON POSSESSION

The second problem which is raised by the case of the bent woman still divides commentators on the third gospel. It is the question of whether or not the basis of her physical condition was demon possession. This question perplexes not only commentators, but also translators, some of whom render the original of Luke 13.11 in a way which suggests that the woman was demon-possessed, in spite of the fact that all the original says is that she 'had a spirit of weakness for eighteen years'. Versions which understand this clause to mean demon possession include *The Twentieth Century New Testament* (1904), *The Jerusalem Bible* (1966), *The New English Bible* (1970), and *The Good News Bible* (1976).

We begin our discussion of this problem by outlining the case in favour of the presence of demon possession in this woman.

I. THE CASE IN FAVOUR OF THE PRESENCE OF DEMON POSSESSION

The case for the occurrence of demon possession as the basis of this woman's physical disease rests entirely on the interpretation of two phrases which are used to describe her condition in the narrative.

1. The *first* phrase speaks of the woman 'having a spirit of weakness' and is used by Luke in his initial description of her in verse eleven.

2. The *second* phrase was used by Jesus himself when he referred to her as 'this woman . . . whom Satan bound for eighteen years' as recorded in verse sixteen.

We propose, however, to postpone further discussion of the meaning of these two phrases, and in particular the question of whether they can be interpreted only in the sense of demon possession, until we have examined the case against the view that this woman was possessed by a demon.

II. THE CASE AGAINST THE DIAGNOSIS OF DEMON POSSESSION

1. The narrative does not employ the vocabulary of demon possession. There are six cases of individual exorcism described in the synoptic gospels, and

if we examine their vocabulary we find that the following words are characteristic of these descriptions.[8]

Greek	English	Occurrence
daimonion	demon	in all six cases
daimonizomai	be demon-possessed	in four cases
pneuma akathartos	unclean spirit	in four cases
ekballō	cast out	in five cases
exerchomai	come out	in five cases

It is significant that none of these words occurs in the account of the healing
of the bent woman. In all four of the undoubted exorcisms which are recorded
by Luke, the agent of possession is always called a *demon*. The absence of this
word from the present narrative suggests that Luke wishes to avoid describing
this woman as having a demon or being demon-possessed. It is true that he
speaks of her as 'having a spirit', but he does not call the spirit an *unclean* spirit
as he does in the three cases of exorcism in which he calls the agent of possession
a spirit (see Luke 4.33; 8.29 and 9.42). It is unfortunate that a number of English
versions including Barclay, Moffatt and the TEV have qualified the word spirit
and translated it as 'evil spirit'.

2. The method of treatment used by Jesus was not that of exorcism. In this
case he spoke directly to the woman and told her of her cure. In exorcism he
always spoke directly to the demon and commanded it to leave the possessed
person. Also, on this occasion Jesus laid his hands on the woman in order to
heal her. This was a procedure which he never used in exorcism in order to
cure a demon-possessed person. Even if it were clear that he laid hands on the
woman after the demon had left her it still remains true that he never did this in
any case of undoubted exorcism, and therefore it could not be used as an argument in favour of exorcism here.

3. The description of the cure is not like that of an exorcism, Jesus described her cure as being loosed or freed from her weakness. The verb he used
was *luō* which is never used of exorcism and is only used of disease here in the
whole New Testament. It is too mild a term to denote the casting out of
demons. In any case, it is important to notice that she was loosed from her
weakness and not from a spirit (v. 12). Then there is no dramatic description of
a spirit or demon coming out of the woman as we normally find in the accounts
of exorcism in the synoptic gospels.

4. The presence of a recognised and well-known demon-possessed person
in a synagogue service is unlikely. It is true that we are told of a demon-
possessed man in the synagogue at Capernaum in Mark 1.23 and Luke 4.33, but
he was presumably normal in appearance whilst this woman had an easily
recognised deformity. If this deformity was generally believed to indicate that
she was demon-possessed it is unlikely that she would be allowed to worship in
the local synagogue. The fact that she was allowed to worship there suggests
that she was not regarded as demon-possessed by the people of the community
in which she lived.

5. The account of the healing of the bent woman is included amongst the
narrative material which is peculiar to the gospel of Luke. This material does

not contain any description of an exorcism although it does contain the accounts of five healing miracles including that of the bent woman. When, therefore, no description of an exorcism is included in the material which comes from the same source as the account of the healing of the bent woman, and when this account does not conform to the usual description and vocabulary of an exorcism as recorded in the synoptic gospels, then we feel that these two facts provide an argument against the healing of this woman being regarded as an exorcism which should be given its due weight. That weight is against the occurrence of demon possession in this woman.

Equally, of course, the fact that no case of exorcism is recorded in the special Lukan material means that we do not know what form or vocabulary would have been used by this author if he had recorded a case of exorcism.

There is, however, no evidence that Luke has his own special vocabulary for exorcism narratives. When he includes in his gospel narrative the account of an exorcism from Mark or the source Q, he uses the same or a similar vocabulary as that used by the other evangelists. It may be presumed therefore that if he had described an exorcism from his own special source it would have been in similar terms to those used by the other evangelists.

We have now considered the evidence for and against the presence of demon possession in this woman. It is obvious that the evidence against demon possession is much stronger than that in favour of it, and would warrant the conclusion that this woman was not the subject of demon possession. However, before we come to a final conclusion let us re-examine the argument in favour of the diagnosis of demon possession, and look again at the two phrases in the narrative on which this argument rests.

IV. THE SPIRIT OF WEAKNESS

The phrase 'a spirit of weakness' in verse eleven is the phrase more than any other in this passage which has given rise to the idea that this woman was demon-possessed. In view of this the usage of the phrase in its context needs closer examination.

The first thing to notice is that the word 'spirit' occurs only once in this whole passage, and that is in this phrase. Furthermore it is not qualified by the adjective akathartos meaning 'unclean', nor does the word 'demon' appear as a synonym for it in the passage. This is in marked contrast to the usage in the narratives of the six undoubted cases of exorcism recorded in the first three gospels. In all three cases the word 'demon' is used of the agent of possession, and where the word 'spirit' is used it is always made clear that it is an *unclean* spirit which is being described. When the word 'spirit' is used alone it does not imply an evil spirit or the presence of demon possession.

This conclusion is supported by the construction used in Luke 4.33. In this verse Luke described the demoniac in the synagogue at Capernaum as 'a man having a spirit of an unclean demon'. Luke derives this story from the Markan tradition where he is spoken of as 'a man with an unclean spirit' (Mark 1.23).

Luke's construction here is therefore his own, and may be regarded as providing a parallel to the phrase we are considering. From this construction it appears that when Luke uses the phrase 'to have a spirit of' he does not mean to imply that the person described is demon-possessed. What he means is described by the noun in the genitive case which follows the phrase. In the example of the synagogue demoniac, the man was in fact demon-possessed, and so the noun in the genitive described the spirit as that of an unclean demon. In the case of the bent woman, however, the noun in the genitive case defined her state as one of weakness without any reference to demon possession.

These considerations suggest that when Luke uses the word 'spirit' in this phrase he does not refer to a spiritual being such as a demon, but to a state of mind or of the human spirit produced by the condition defined by the noun which follows it. This condition may be demon possession or it may not. In this woman's case it was weakness, and therefore we interpret the phrase 'a spirit of weakness' as meaning that it was the weakness which produced the spirit, and not the spirit which produced the weakness. In more modern terms, we may say that the result of the long years of physical weakness was a state of profound mental depression. This is not to say that her disease was purely psychological as Phillips suggests by his rendering that the woman 'had been ill from some psychological cause'. Ronald Knox also in his note on this phrase suggests that the spirit may have been 'a morbid attitude of hysteria, which kept the woman a cripple, although she suffered from no organic disability'.[9] The record makes clear that she had a real organic disability which had affected her for eighteen years and produced her state of weakness. Superimposed on her physical disability was a state of mental depression, and it is this which Luke describes as the spirit which resulted from her weakness.

We conclude, therefore, that the use of the phrase 'a spirit of weakness' by Luke in his description of this woman does not require us to believe that he was describing her as the subject of demon possession.

V. THE BOND OF SATAN

In verse sixteen Jesus described this woman as bound by Satan. This description has been taken along with Luke's characterisation of her as having a spirit of weakness and made the basis of a diagnosis of demon possession. We have just seen that Luke's phrase need not carry this implication. What are we to say of our Lord's reference to the bond of Satan?

Nowhere else in the New Testament do we read of anyone who was bound by Satan, and so we must seek the meaning of the phrase within its present context. Certainly we find that Paul speaks of delivering men to Satan in 1 Corinthians 5.5 and 1 Timothy 1.20 and uses the verb *paradidōmi* which may mean handing a person over to bondage, but this usage is of Church discipline and is not relevant here.

His healing of the bent woman had involved Jesus in an argument with the president of the synagogue about Sabbath observance. Jesus replied to him using an *a fortiori* argument. If on the Sabbath day you untie the bond which has confined your animals, in order to allow them to drink, how much more is it necessary to untie the bond of this woman who has been bound by Satan for eighteen years? The use of the words 'bound' and 'bond' by Jesus is therefore explained by the parallel which he draws for the purpose of his argument.

It is relevant to remark also that from a descriptive point of view the use of the word 'bound' is very appropriate to disease of the locomotor system of the body. This type of disease interferes with joint and bodily movement, and in many cases the most apt description is that the affected person appears to have his joints partly or wholly bound so that their movement is restricted.

There is a further implication in the usage of the word 'bound' which is significant for the interpretation of the phrase we are considering. Bonds are put on from without, and not from within. This fact would argue against the condition being demon possession for this affects the personality and the body of the possessed from within, not from without.

We come to the conclusion, therefore, that Jesus' reference to the bond of Satan does not mean that this woman was demon-possessed. What it does mean is that her condition is due to the activity of Satan as the primary cause of sin and disease. This idea appears elsewhere in the New Testament, notably in the case of Paul's 'thorn in the flesh' which we shall consider in a later chapter. In both cases, Paul and this woman suffered from a recognisable physical disease which may have had a discoverable physical cause, but nevertheless the origin of their disease is traced back to the activity of Satan.

VI. CONCLUSION AND SUMMARY

We have now completed our consideration of the two problems presented by the case of the bent woman when it is considered from a medical point of view.

The first problem was the identity of the disease which produced her bent condition. The data are scanty and the conclusion cannot be certain, but the most probable diagnosis is spondylitis ankylopoietica or ankylosing spondylitis. If this diagnosis is correct, it is the only case of a rheumatic disease which is identifiable in the Bible.

The second problem was the cause of her condition and the nature of her healing. Was the cause that of demon possession, and her healing a case of exorcism? We suggest that the evidence is in favour of physical disease, and against the presence of demon possession and the occurrence of exorcism in her case.

The main contribution which this account of the healing of the bent woman makes to the Biblical view of health and disease is its clear implication that disease is due to the activity of Satan. The cure of disease is therefore an illustration of the power of God over evil and over Satan which is revealed and expressed in the Life, Death and Resurrection of Jesus Christ.

REFERENCES

1. Luke 13.10-17.
2. George Macdonald, *The Miracles of our Lord* (Longmans, Green, London, 1886), p. 44.
3. I. H. Marshall in his recent commentary on the *Gospel of Luke* in *The New International Greek Testament Commentary* series (Paternoster Press, Exeter, 1978) prefers the interpretation of complete spinal immobility on the grounds that this stresses the severity of the complaint (see p. 558).
4. L. D. Weatherhead, *Psychology, Religion and Healing* (Hodder and Stoughton, London, 1951), p. 59.
5. See, for example, R. K. Harrison, *The Interpreter's Dictionary of the Bible* (Abingdon Press, Nashville, 1962), vol. 1, p. 852, art. 'Disease'.
6. Radiological features suggestive of spondylitis ankylopoietica have been found in bones from ancient Egypt, from which it appears that this disease occurred there although it was not common. See D. Brothwell and A. T. Sandison (edd.), *Diseases in Antiquity* (Chas. C. Thomas, Springfield, Illinois, 1967), pp. 357-360.
7. A. Macalister in *Hastings' Dictionary of the Bible* (T. & T. Clark, Edinburgh, 1900), vol. 3, p. 328, art 'Medicine'.
8. See p. 21 above for the relevant references.
9. R. A. Knox, *A New Testament Commentary for English Readers* (Burns Oates and Washbourne, London, 1956), vol. 1, p. 161.

Part Three

HEALING IN THE APOSTOLIC CHURCH

THE CLIMAX of the gospel story of Jesus was reached in his Death, Resurrection and Ascension. These events were unique in the history of mankind, and revealed at one and the same time the reason why Jesus had come and the source of the power by which he had healed men of disease and brought them forgiveness of sin.

After the gospels, the rest of the New Testament is concerned with the apostolic Church. If we ask when it was that this Church or ekklēsia came into being, then the evidence clearly points to the time after the Death and Resurrection of Jesus. All the early Christian writers use the word ekklēsia only for those Christian communities which came into existence after the close of the events which are recorded in the gospels. It was never used for the band of disciples which Jesus gathered around him and which frequently figured in the gospel narrative. It is true that Jesus used the word ekklēsia twice, but in Matthew 16.18 he spoke in the future tense of its foundation, and in Matthew 18.17 he speaks also of the future Church as the subsequent verses reveal.[1] Verse eighteen finds its parallel in Matthew 16.19 where the power of binding and loosing is said to be a future gift to Peter, and now is here extended to all the Twelve. Verse twenty contains Jesus' promise to be in their midst when two or three disciples gather together in his name. This promise could only be fulfilled after his Ascension and the coming of the Holy Spirit. Jesus, therefore, does not use ekklēsia of the original Twelve nor of any group of his disciples during his earthly ministry, but only of the future Christian community which was to be established after his Death and Resurrection.[2]

The question remains of when the Church (ekklēsia) came into being. Jesus spoke of it only in the future tense, but at what point in the future was it established? It seems most natural to identify this point with the day of Pentecost for it was on this day, which was the Jewish Feast of Weeks, that the Holy Spirit came upon the disciples, now called apostles, so that Jesus' presence could now be with them wherever they met in his name. It was on this day that the apostles, whose qualification for their office was that they were witnesses of the Resurrection (Acts 1.22), were invested with power (dunamis) from on high when the Holy Spirit came upon them (Luke 24.29 and Acts 1.8).

The word power or dunamis is used in the synoptic gospels to describe the works of healing which Jesus performed. These works were the outward expression of his power which came from God. The question which now arises is whether the power with which the apostles were invested when the apostolic Church was established included the authority and the ability to heal. It is to this question that we address ourselves in Part Three of this book, and seek to answer it by a consideration of the healing activity of the apostolic Church as described in the book of the Acts of the Apostles and in the epistles written by Paul and by James.

REFERENCES

1. There is no need to interpret this second use of *ekklēsia* as a reference to the synagogue under-stood as the Jewish community as K. L. Schmidt does in Kittel's *Theological Dictionary of the New Testament* (Eerdmans, Grand Rapids, 1966), vol. 3, p. 526, s.v. *ekklēsia*.
2. O. Cullmann, *The Early Church* (SCM Press, London, 1956), p. 118.

Chapter Nine

HEALING IN THE ACTS OF
THE APOSTLES

The training of the Twelve is over. Their Teacher has been put to death on a cross outside Jerusalem, and has been raised from the dead by the power of God. The book of Acts opens with an account of his Ascension to the right hand of God. Before his Ascension he gives to them his final commission. They had been given one commission already midway through their training. They had been sent out as miniature apostles or apprentice missionaries to use the terms which Bruce uses of them.[1] The content of that first commission was a threefold imperative bidding them to go, to preach and to heal (Matthew 10.5-8) and to equip them for their task they were given authority to cast out demons and to heal disease (v. 1). In view of this specific command to heal given in the first commission it is important to examine the terms of the final commission.

There is no common tradition of this commission. There are in fact no less than five different versions which were not all given on the same occasion. Together they compose the final commission which Jesus gave to his disciples after his Resurrection and before his Ascension. Their content according to the four gospel traditions is as follows.

'All authority in heaven and on earth has been given to me. Go therefore and make disciples of all nations, baptising them in the name of the Father and of the Son and of the Holy Spirit, teaching them to observe all that I have commanded you' (Matthew 28.18-20).

'Go into all the world and preach the gospel to the whole creation. He who believes and is baptised will be saved; but he who does not believe will be condemned' (Mark 16.15-16, i.e. The longer ending).

'Then he opened their minds to understand the scriptures and said to them, "Thus it is written, that the Christ should suffer and on the third day rise from the dead, and that repentance and forgiveness of sins should be preached in his name to all nations, beginning from Jerusalem. You are witnesses of these things. And behold, I send the promise of my Father upon you; but stay in the city, until you are clothed with power from on high."' (Luke 24.45-49).

'You shall receive power when the Holy Spirit has come upon you; and you shall be my witnesses in Jerusalem and in all Judaea and Samaria and to the end of the earth' (Acts 1.8).

'Jesus said to them again, "Peace be with you. As the Father has sent me, even so I send you." And when he had said this, he breathed on them, and said to them, "'Receive the Holy Spirit. If you forgive the sins of any, they are forgiven; if, you retain the sins of any, they are retained.'" (John 20.21-23).

It is clear from these versions of the final commission of Jesus to his disciples that they were to be empowered by the Holy Spirit to go out into all the world to preach the gospel of repentance and the forgiveness of sins. Those who accepted the gospel and believed were to be baptised and were to be instructed in the Christian way of life. It is equally clear that there is no mention of any healing command in these versions of the final commission. Preaching and teaching which formed the context of Jesus' healing activity are both present in the final commission, but there is no mention of healing the sick. This is in explicit contrast to the mission charge to the Twelve when Jesus sent them to preach and heal (Matthew 10.5-8 and Luke 9.2), and to the commission to the Seventy in Luke 10.9. The only mention of healing in relation to the final commission is in the longer ending of Mark where in verses 17 and 18 it is anticipated that those who believe as the result of the preaching of the gospel by the disciples will exorcise demons and lay hands on the sick to heal them. This is not a command to heal the sick but only a prophecy that those who believe will heal the sick as a sign which testifies to their faith. If this longer ending belongs to a later time than the rest of the gospel of Mark the omission of a command to heal is even more significant than if it belonged to the original text of the gospel. According to the original gospel tradition Jesus had not included a command to heal in his final commission to his disciples. If the longer ending of Mark was added to the gospel at a later time this was an opportunity to add such a command if Jesus had ever given it, and for the Church to record it, if the Church felt the need to have his authority for its healing activity. The fact that such a command was not included indicates that Jesus never gave it in explicit terms, but only commanded his disciples to preach and to witness as Peter said in Acts 10.42.

The significance of the mention of exorcism and healing of the sick in the longer ending of the gospel of Mark must however not be lost sight of, even though it cannot be construed as part of the final commission to the disciples. The Church at that early time was continuing the healing ministry of Jesus and regarded it as a legitimate activity of those who believed in him and a sign of the presence and reality of their Christian faith.

It is from a study of the book of the Acts that we can discover how the disciples interpreted their commission and used the power with which they had been endued by Jesus as he ascended to heaven and sent the Holy Spirit to be with them. From such a study we should be able to understand the place which healing occupied in the mission and ministry of the apostolic Church. There is no doubt that healing was a recognised activity of that early Church and is recorded for us by the author of the Acts whose records are made more significant by the fact that he was himself professionally trained in the art of healing.

I. THE NARRATIVES OF HEALING

The space devoted to accounts of healing in the book of Acts is much less than in any of the gospels. It amounts to only 4.5 per cent of the total in terms of verses.

If we now classify the healing narratives in the same way as we did for the gospels the result is as follows.

THE HEALING OF INDIVIDUALS

1. *Accounts of physical healing*

1.	The lame man at the gate of the Temple.	By Peter.	Acts 3.1-10.
2.	Paul's recovery of sight.	By Ananias.	Acts 9.17-19.
3.	Aeneas healed of paralysis.	By Peter.	Acts 9.32-35.
4.	Cripple healed at Lystra.	By Paul.	Acts 14.8-11.
5.	Cure of father of Publius.	By Paul.	Acts 28.8.

2. *Accounts of the exorcism of demons*

6.	The Philippian slave-girl.	By Paul.	Acts 16.16-18.

3. *Accounts of the raising of the dead*

7.	Tabitha (Dorcas) at Joppa.	By Peter.	Acts 9.36-41.
8.	Eutychus at Troas.	By Paul.	Acts 20.9-12.

THE HEALING OF GROUPS

1.	The sick in the streets of Jerusalem.	By Peter.	Acts 5.15-16.
2.	The sick in Samaria.	By Philip.	Acts 8.6-7.
3.	The sick at Ephesus.	By Paul.	Acts 19.11-12.
4.	The sick at Malta.	By Paul.	Acts 28.9.

OTHER POSSIBLE REFERENCES

1.	Wonders and signs in Jerusalem.	By all the apostles	Acts 2.43.
2.	More wonders and signs in Jerusalem.	By all.	Acts 5.12.
3.	More wonders and signs in Jerusalem.	By Stephen.	Acts 6.8.
4.	Signs and wonders in Iconium.	By Paul and Barnabas.	Acts 14.3.

II. THE DISEASES HEALED

It is possible to classify the narratives of healing miracles on the basis of the diseases whose healing they describe. In so far as the diseases can be identified we may classify them as follows:

Physical Disease

   I. Acute diseases:
      1. Acute blindness: Paul in Acts 9.8.

2. Acute fatal head injury: Eutychus in Acts 20.9.
3. Acute bacillary dysentery: Father of Publius in Acts 28.8.
4. Acute fatal disease of unknown nature: Tabitha in Acts 9.37.

II. Chronic diseases:

   1. Lameness or locomotor disability:
      a. The man at the gate of the Temple in Acts 3.2.
      b. The cripple at Lystra in Acts 14.8.
   2. Paralysis due to neurological disorder: Aeneas in Acts 9.33.
      In Acts 8.7 there is a reference to 'many who were paralysed or lame' who were healed by Philip.

Demon Possession

   1. The Philippian slave-girl of Acts 16.16.

These accounts of acute and chronic diseases in the Acts include details and features which are of great interest from a medical point of view.

We begin our consideration of these features with the sudden blindness which overtook Paul (or Saul as he was called then) on the road near to Damascus. It has been common to regard this blindness as psychosomatic in origin. Jung took this view and went on to say that 'psychogenetic blindness is according to my experience always due to an unwillingness to see, that is to understand and to realise something that is incompatible with the conscious attitude'.[2] In other words, Paul's physical blindness was due to his unwillingness to see in the person of Jesus the one who was the Christ of Israel. This view would seem to be just playing with words, and just too simple to be true. Even if it were true in cases of psychoneurotic illness, we cannot claim that Paul was such a case. Other writers have not followed Jung in his simple correlation of physical and psychological blindness, but have attributed the blindness to more complex psychological influences. Harrison in his article on blindness in the *Interpreter's Dictionary of the Bible* attributes the sudden onset of Paul's blindness to 'a state of profound psychic conflict' and 'intense emotional strain' resulting from 'the fundamental reorientation of his spiritual values involved in his conversion'.[3] However, it seems unnecessary to seek a psychological cause when Paul himself mentions what could have caused its sudden onset. In Acts 22.11 he is speaking to the Jerusalem mob from the steps of the Roman fortress of Antonia which connected it with the northern part of the outer court of the Temple. He tells them of his experience on the road to Damascus and how he lost his sight because of the brightness of the light that shone around him. On another occasion when he was speaking before Herod Agrippa he adds the significant detail that its brightness was greater than that of the midday sun (Acts 26.13). We know that looking into bright light can produce a condition called photo-retinitis or retinitis due to bright light, of which a good example is what is known as eclipse blindness due to looking directly at the sun during a partial eclipse.[4] The resulting blindness may be temporary, but more often is permanent due to an actual burn of the retina due to the infra-red rays of the light. It seems to be very probable that Paul suffered from temporary retinal damage due to exposure to bright light and this was responsible for his blindness. He saw the great light which shone about him and heard a voice which made him look into the light in order to try and discern the speaker. His companions too saw the light, but they did not hear the voice (Acts 22.9) and so did not look into the light to see whence the voice came and so their eyes were not affected in the same way as Paul's were. When his sight returned Luke tells us that 'immediately something like scales (*hōs lepides*) fell from his eyes' (Acts 9.18). The Greek phrase need not mean more than that the return of his sight felt to Paul as if scales had fallen off his eyes, but if it does mean more then the scales may have been the crusts of dried secretion which would have accumulated in and around his eyes during the three days of his blindness. These would break and fall away as he opened his eyes to see once more.

Attempts have been made to connect this experience which Paul had on the Damascus road with the thorn in the flesh which affected him later and is described in 2 Corinthians 12.7. These attempts either regard both conditions as psychogenic in origin or assume that the blindness left some weakness of the eyes which formed the basis of the condition of the eyes which troubled Paul later. We shall discuss the identity of the thorn in the flesh later in this book, and so content ourselves at this stage with the remark that it is unlikely that there was any connection between Paul's blindness and his thorn in the flesh.

Eutychus was a victim of poor illumination and bad ventilation, to say nothing of the effects of overcrowding. He had gone to attend Paul's farewell service at Troas at the end of his week-long visit (Acts 20.6-9). The service began after sunset on the Sunday evening for the lamps were already lit.[5] Many lamps were needed, for each gave only a restricted light. They were, in fact, torches producing as much heat as light, and the smoke and hot air they produced eventually found their way out of the room through the small window opening in which Eutychus sat listening to Paul's long sermon. The warmth of the air combined with the lateness of the hour to make him sleepy. The verb tenses which Luke uses reflect Eutychus' struggle to keep awake but which ended in his falling into a deep sleep (v. 9). As he relaxed into a deep sleep he lost his hold on the window-sill and fell to his death out of the third storey window. The most probable cause of his death was some form of head injury since he would land on his head as he fell backwards out from the window.

In the case of the father of Publius who was the chief man of Malta there can be no doubt that he suffered from an attack of acute bacillary dysentery. He had fever and since the word translated fever is in the plural we should probably speak of attacks of fever rather than a continued type of fever. Along with fever he had *dusenterion* (Acts 28.8) which Wyclif in his English version of 1380 translated 'a blodie flux', a term which persisted in later versions until the RV supplied 'dysentery' in its place in 1881. Lake and Cadbury in their commentary mention Malta fever as a possible diagnosis in this case,[6] but this is excluded by the use of the term dysentery which clearly means that an intestinal disorder with pain and diarrhoea was present. These symptoms do not occur in Malta fever which is now called brucellosis since its cause was demonstrated in 1887 by Sir David Bruce. The disease in this case is clearly acute bacillary dysentery with fever and diarrhoea with blood and mucus in the stool which resulted from the consumption of infected food.

Luke appears to have had a particular interest in chronic disease. This is suggested by the higher proportion of records of this type of disease included in the Acts when compared with the gospels. This impression is further deepened by the fact that he alone of the four evangelists recorded two cases of the healing of chronic disease, namely that of the bent woman (Luke 13.11-17) and that of the man with the dropsy (Luke 14.1-6). The number of case records is so small in both the gospels and the Acts that any conclusion drawn from them can only be suggestive and not significant of Luke's interest in chronic disabling conditions. Nevertheless such an interest does harmonise with what we know of Luke's warm sympathetic personality from his gospel where he is seen as one who is concerned for the disadvantaged members of society.[7]

All three of the cases of chronic sickness which Luke describes are unable to walk, and he recognises two causes of this condition, lameness and paralysis (cp. Acts 8.7). The lameness is due to some disability of the locomotor system composed of the bones and the joints, whilst the paralysis seen in the case of Aeneas (Acts 9.33) is probably neurological and due to some disease or injury of the central nervous system. Lameness is described by the term *chōlos* which like its English equivalent means disabled in the lower limbs. Both cases of lameness recorded by Luke in the Acts are said to have been lame from birth or literally from their mothers' womb (*ek koilias mētros*, Acts 3.2 and 14.8), and therefore their disability could not have been due to any infectious cause such as infantile paralysis or acute anterior poliomyelitis. The cause of their lameness must have been either a developmental abnormality arising in the foetus before birth or an injury to the feet and ankles occurring during the process of birth. It is difficult to see how a birth injury would produce local injury to the feet of a degree which would result in complete inability to walk, and so a developmental abnormality seems to be the more likely diagnosis in these cases. A probable diagnosis is a severe degree of clubfoot or what is known medically as congenital talipes equino-varus. In the case of the man at the gate of the Temple this suggestion is made more probable by the clear indication of Acts 3.7 that the disability was in the use of the feet and ankle bones. The cripple at Lystra on the other hand had never stood upright on his feet or walked (Acts 14.8) and there is no mention of a local disability, but the fact that he had survived to adulthood would exclude such congenital conditions as spina bifida as the cause of his lameness. In the condition of spina bifida the arches of the lower vertebrae fail to close over the spinal cord and there may be associated muscular paralysis of the lower limbs, but few cases of this condition reach their fifth birthday. In the case of Aeneas of Lydda in Acts 9.33 our data are very scanty. He was an adult male who was paralysed and had been bed-ridden for eight years. Luke describes him as *paralelumenos* which is the correct medical term according to Hobart, as distinct from *paralutikos* which is the commoner and popular term.[8] The paralysis obviously affected the lower limbs since he was confined to bed, and in an adult man could have been due to an infection such as tuberculosis of the vertebrae or have resulted from an accident in which the spine was fractured and the spinal cord damaged. However, we have no clue to the cause and are told simply that he was paralysed, and so apart from saying that his condition was due to some disease or damage to the spinal cord we have no knowledge of the cause.

The Philippian slave-girl was possessed by a spirit of divination whose ability to foretell the future was exploited by her masters for financial gain (Acts 16.16). Luke was with Paul when he met the girl as we know from the occurrence of the incident in the first of the 'we-sections' of the Acts where Luke writes in the first person plural to indicate that he was accompanying Paul on this occasion. He describes the girl as having 'a spirit, a python'. This name derives from the python which used to guard the Delphic oracle and was killed by Apollo who succeeded to the snake's oracular power. The spirit of the python was then thought to indwell the priestess of Apollo at the oracle who was then called the Pythoness and was believed to have the faculty of divination or prediction of the future. Later the term was used for a spirit of divination possessed by anyone. In this girl's case it is usual to offer the alternatives of fraud or insanity as the basis of her soothsaying. Most authors choose the alternative of insanity and regard her as a case of mental illness. This diagnosis is not supported by the account of the incident. There are no indications of mental illness mentioned in the account such as we find in some cases of demon possession in the gospels. This girl must therefore be a case of demon possession which was not manifested by any physical or mental illness, but by the gift of divination or second sight. Once she came into contact with Paul and his companions it became obvious what was the source of her faculty of prediction. This is the only case of demon possession recorded in the Acts and it demonstrates the same reaction of irritation shown by the demon which was so vividly described in the gospels when Jesus met the demon-possessed.

III. THE WORDS FOR HEALING

The three verbs which were commonly used to describe healing in the gospels are the most frequently used words to describe healing in the Acts. These are as follows:

Therapeuō which occurs in Acts 4.14; 5.16; 8.7; and 28.9.

Iaomai in Acts 9.34; 10.38; 28.8 and 27.

Sōzō in Acts 4.9 and 14.9.

The verb *therapeuō* is always used in the passive voice in Acts and is never used of our Lord's healing, in contrast to the gospels where it is always used in the active voice and of his healing activity. In Acts 17.25 Luke uses the verb in the only non-medical sense which occurs in the New Testament when he employs it to mean service given to a god. In our study of the vocabulary of healing in the gospels we found cause to regard the verbs *therapeuō* and *iaomai* as synonymous, and there seems to be no reason why this should not be true of the Acts too. However, Harnack suggested that this was not true in the account of Paul's enforced sojourn in Malta recorded in Acts 28.1-10. He would distinguish Paul's healing of the father of Publius by prayer and the laying on of hands for which the verb *iaomai* was used (v. 8) from what he suggests was Luke's medical healing of the rest of the sick on the island for which the verb *therapeuō* was used (v. 9).[9] Harnack finds support for this suggestion in the fact that the gifts (*timais*) were given to both Paul and Luke according to the 'us' in verse ten, and that the word *timais* may also mean fees paid for medical attention. This explanation is unconvincing for several reasons. If Luke meant to record what Harnack suggests why did he not do so more explicitly? Why should the verb *therapeuō* mean to provide medical attention in this context when in every other case in which it describes acts of healing by Jesus or his disciples it means to heal by non-medical means? In no other place are we told that Luke practised healing by medical means and when we find that the verb *therapeuō* in the same voice, mood and tense is used of healing by Peter by non-medical means (Acts 5.16), it appears more reasonable to regard it as describing non-medical healing by Paul in 28.9 rather than medical healing by Luke. We may agree with Lake and Cadbury who commented that Harnack's suggestion was ingenious but not convincing.[10]

When the medical author of the Acts was free of the constraints imposed by the use of written sources such as he used in writing his gospel, it was to be expected that he would reveal that he commanded a more extensive vocabulary for the description of healing than was evident in that gospel. Even in the gospel he showed some dissatisfaction with the usage of his sources which can be seen in the three occasions in chapter nine of the gospel where he prefers the verb *iaomai* to the *therapeuō* which Matthew accepts for the corresponding passages in his gospel.[11]

In the Acts we find several words for healing which are not used by any other New Testament author in a medical sense but only by Luke. These may be listed as follows:

   Stereoō which occurs in Acts 3.7 and 16, and also in a non-medical sense
      in 16.5

   Apallassō in Acts 19.12 and in the Western text of 5.15. This verb is used
      in a non-medical sense in Luke 12.58 and Hebrews 2.15

   Iasis in Acts 4.22 and 30. This word also occurs in a medical sense in
      Luke 13.32.

The verb *stereoō* means make firm, solid or strong. Hobart notes that the word was in medical usage applied to the bones in particular.[12] In Acts 3.7 it is used of the feet and ankles being made firm or strong. In Acts 16.5 it is used of the churches being strengthened in the faith. The second verb *apallassō* means set free or release and according to Hobart is one of the words most frequently used of the cure of disease in the Greek medical writers and he quotes a number of instances of its use by Hippocrates and Galen.[13] The Western text attributes a further two medical usages of this word to Luke. One is in Luke 9.40 where the reference is to the exorcism of the epileptic boy, and the other is in Acts 5.15 to which the codex Bezae adds a clause to say that the sick 'were being set free from every sickness'. Whether these additional usages are significant will depend on the value we place on the Western text, but they are at least interesting in our present context. The third word is the noun *iasis* which Hobart calls 'the great medical word' although it is used in non-medical writers as well.[14] Luke's use of it may reflect his fondness for the verb *iaomai* which we have already noted, and which is illustrated by the fact that out of the twenty-eight times it occurs in the New Testament, seventeen are found in his writings.

To complete our review of Luke's medical vocabulary for healing in the Acts we should mention two words which he uses to describe the state to which healing restored. The first is the adjective *hugiēs* which he uses in Acts 4.10 of the cure of the lame man at the gate of the Temple. We considered this word in an earlier chapter when we reviewed the words used for the concept of health in the New Testament.[15] We concluded from its usage that it usually meant a state of physical soundness which was produced by healing. Although the verb *hugiainō* is regularly used by the Greek medical authors for being in sound health, the adjective appears to be much commoner in non-medical writings than in medical and it is not even commented on by Hobart. The other word which Luke uses is the noun *holoklēria* which occurs in Acts 3.16 where it is a *hapax legomenon*, i.e. its only use in the New Testament. The word means wholeness or soundness of an object in all its parts, and Hobart was unable to find any instance of its usage in the medical writers who however frequently employ the adjective *holoklēros* in both a general and a medical sense.[16]

A convenient summary of the words used for health and healing in the Acts is to be found in the account of the lame beggar at the Beautiful gate of the Temple in chapters three and four. In this account every word used by Luke in the Acts with this meaning is given with the exception of the verb *apallassō*, and also the verb *iaomai* unless we follow the Textus Receptus which gives *iaomai* in Acts 3.11. The occurrence of the words for health and healing is as follows:

Acts 3.7:   *Immediately his feet and ankles were made strong* (stereoō).

3.16:   *His name . . . has made this man strong* (stereoō).

Faith . . . has given the man this perfect health (holoklēria).

4.9:   *By what means this man has been healed* (sōzō).

4.10:   *By him this man is standing before you well* (hugiēs).

4.14:   *The man that had been healed* (therapeuō).

4.22:   *This sign of healing* (iasis).

4.30:   *Thou stretchest out thy hand to heal* (iasis).

The conclusion seems inescapable that since these words all describe the same state they must be regarded as synonymous, or at least they must overlap each other in meaning in a large measure. It is clear, for instance, that *sōzō* in 4.9 must mean physical healing. It is used in the perfect tense *sesōstai* indicating that he had been healed and remained healed. This is said to be the result of a good deed (*euergesia*) which suggests it was a physical act of healing. This physical nature of the act of healing described by *sōzō* is further supported by the use of *hugiēs* to describe the state to which he was restored. In view of this it is of great interest that Peter goes on in 4.12 to use the verb *sōzō* in a much more comprehensive sense, and this would suggest that both physical healing and spiritual salvation are both included in the *sōtēria* which is available only in the name of Jesus Christ of Nazareth. We take this also to mean that this man found more than merely physical healing in Jesus Christ, but also a soundness and salvation which permeated his whole being.

IV. THE INITIATIVE IN HEALING

If we exclude the healing of Paul's blindness which is a special case from which no conclusions can be drawn for our present purpose, we are left with seven cases of healing which are described individually. In these cases the initiative in the production of healing was mostly taken by persons other than those who were sick. This is shown by the following analysis of the cases recorded in the Acts:

    I. *Those in which the sick person took the initiative*:
        1. The lame man at the gate of the Temple (Acts 3.3).
   II. *Those in which friends took the initiative*:
        1. The raising of Tabitha (Acts 9.38).
  III. *Those in which an apostle took the initiative*:
        1. Aeneas at Lydda (Acts 9.34). Initiative by Peter.
        2. The cripple at Lystra (Acts 14.9). Initiative by Paul.
        3. The Philippian slave-girl (Acts 16.18). Initiative by Paul.
        4. Eutychus (Acts 20.10). Initiative by Paul.
        5. The father of Publius (Acts 28.8). Initiative by Paul.

In the case of the group healings which are recorded in the Acts it was usually the friends or relatives of the sick who took the initiative (see Acts 5.16 and 19.12), except in the case of the sick who were healed by Paul in Malta after he had healed the father of Publius where it appears that the sick took the initiative and came to him according to Acts 28.9

The number of cases recorded in Acts is too small to allow any significant conclusions to be drawn from them, but certain comments appear to be justified. In general the narratives give the impression that healing occurred on a casual basis. Cases of sickness were dealt with as they arose or were met with. Healing did not play any part in a strategy of evangelism and was not used to attract an audience for the preaching. This is not to say that the opportunity to witness was not taken when it arose from a healing incident. The healing of the lame man at the gate of the Temple in the third chapter of the Acts provides an excellent example of how the apostles could use such an incident as a means of witness to both the people and the religious authorities when the opportunity arose.

It is noteworthy how much more frequently the apostles appear to have taken the initiative in healing than Jesus did in proportion to the total number who were healed. However, the numbers healed in the Acts are fewer than those in the gospels, and so no significant comparison can be made.

V. THE CONTEXT OF HEALING

In the gospels, healing not infrequently occurs in the context of the preaching and teaching of Jesus. When we come to the Acts we find that this connection is not as obvious as it was in the case of the gospels, but it is still present.

It appears in the teaching of the apostolic Church which recognised that preaching and healing were combined in the earthly ministry of Jesus. When Peter spoke to the company assembled in the house of the Roman centurion Cornelius at Caesarea he reminded them of how Jesus preached the good news of peace and went about doing good and healing all that were oppressed by the devil (Acts 10.36-38). It occurs too in the prayer of the Church for Peter and John after the Jewish authorities had forbidden them to speak or teach in the name of Jesus. They prayed that the two apostles might have boldness to speak the word of God, while God stretched out his hand to heal (Acts 4.29-30).

This same combination of preaching and healing appears in the practice of the apostolic Church leaders. As a result of the persecution of the Church which followed the death of Stephen, the great missionary expansion of the Christian community began. Philip the evangelist went north to a city of Samaria and we are told that the people listened eagerly to his preaching when they heard his words and saw the signs (*sēmeia*) which he did (Acts 8.6). These signs are described as the exorcism of unclean spirits and the healing of many who were paralysed and crippled (v. 7). Two other instances in which preaching and healing go together occur in the evangelistic activity of Paul. As he preaches at Lystra, a man lame from his birth listens to his words, and when Paul finds that he has the faith to be healed he calls on him to stand up and he is healed and able to walk normally (Acts 14.8-10). Later when Paul spent over two years in Ephesus proclaiming the word of God we are told that God worked healing miracles through him of an unusual kind by which evil spirits were cast out and sick persons rid of their diseases (Acts 19.10-12).

However, it must be remarked that the connection of preaching and healing in the Acts is neither as frequent nor as definite as it was in the gospels. After Philip had preached and healed in Samaria, he went on a tour of the coastal towns between Azotus (Ashdod) and Caesarea and whilst we are told that he preached in all these towns, there is no mention of any healing activity (Acts 8.40). Also, a closer examination of the prayer of the Church for Peter and John in Acts 4.29-30 appears to suggest some separation between preaching and healing in the thought of the Church. The Church prays that Peter and John might be given boldness to speak the word of God whilst God stretches out his hand to heal. It is true that the two apostles had only been forbidden to speak and teach in the name of Jesus (v. 18), and there had been no mention of a ban on healing. Nevertheless it cannot be without some significance that the Church appears to regard preaching as the main activity of the apostles, with healing coming from the hand of God.

We conclude, therefore, that although there is some evidence in the Acts of the occurrence together of preaching and healing, it is true to say that healing does not occur in the context of preaching in the same way or to the same degree as it did in the gospels.

VI. THE MOTIVE OF HEALING

The accounts of the healing miracles in the Acts are not always as specific or clear-cut in their indication of the underlying motive as those of the healing activity of Jesus in the gospels. In about half the cases no indication of a motive is provided, and we are left to guess at its nature.

Those cases in which some indication of a motive is given may be classified as follows in terms of the motive which they suggest.

1. *A response to a request*

    a. Of the sick man: The lame man at the gate of the Temple (Acts 3.2).
    b. Of friends: Tabitha at Joppa (9.38).

2. *A response to need*

    a. Aeneas the paralysed (9.33).
    b. Eutychus at Troas (20.10).
    c. The father of Publius (28.8).
    d. The sick on Malta (28.9).

3. *A response to faith*

    a. The cripple at Lystra (14.9).

4. *A reaction to vexation*

    a. The Philippian slave-girl (16.18).

5. *A witness to the gospel*

    a. The healing of the sick in Samaria (8.5-7).

There are some significant differences between this list of motives and the list we compiled from the gospel record of healing. There is no mention of compassion, and indeed the words for compassion and for mercy do not occur in the Acts in any context. It is not recorded of anyone that they cried to the apostles for mercy as they did to Jesus. The lame man asked for alms which is money given out of a feeling of mercy or compassion for the poor (Acts 3.3-6), and not healing out of a feeling of compassion for the sick. Nor is healing represented as being performed in fulfilment of Scripture as it was particularly in the gospel of Matthew in the case of Jesus. Faith is by no means as prominent a feature in the records of healing in the Acts as it is in the gospels, and neither is the presentation of healing as a manifestation of the glory of Jesus Christ the Son of God.

Although what we have just said is true, the differences between the Acts and the gospels in this matter are not absolute. It is true, for instance, that there is no mention of compassion in the Acts as a motive for healing, but in so far as compassion is the response of Christian love to need we cannot exclude compassion as the motive underlying healing in the four cases described as a response to need in the list given above. Also, it is clear that in some of the healing miracles in the Acts as in the gospels more than one motive may be discerned. Whilst the healing of the cripple at Lystra by Paul is stated to have been when Paul saw that he had faith to be made well and responded to it (Acts 14.9), it could also be regarded in the light of what followed as a witness to the power of the gospel which Paul preached. It undoubtedly played an important part in the planting of the Church in Lystra, and may even have played some part in the conversion of Timothy who lived there (Acts 16.1). It is also important to notice that Luke uses the word *sēmeion* not uncommonly of the miracles of healing in the Acts, whilst this word is not used specifically of any miracles of healing in his gospel.[17] A *sēmeion* is a sign which points to something beyond itself. In this context it points to him in whose name and by whose power the miracles of healing were performed.

The outstanding example of a healing miracle in which more than one motive was present is that involving the lame man at the Beautiful gate of the Temple recorded in the third chapter of the Acts. Luke first gives an account of the miracle and portrays it as a response by Peter to a request for alms by the man (Acts 3.3). If the record had stopped there then we would be justified in identifying the motive as the response to a request for help and nothing more. However, the record continues and sets out the events which followed this act of healing and incidentally uncovers several other possible motives which lay behind the response of Peter. It provides a salutary reminder that motives may underlie any of the healing miracles which are not indicated in the brief narratives in which many of them are described.

If we now examine the narrative of the healing of the lame man and the events which flowed from it as recorded in the third and fourth chapters of the Acts we shall discover no less than six descriptions of the healing miracle and its results which may be regarded as possible motives behind it. This is not to say that they were all explicitly and consciously present as such when the miracle was performed. The healing miracle is presented by Luke in his own record or in the words of the principal participants as the following:

1. A response to a request (3.3).
2. A response to faith (3.16).
3. An opportunity to witness:
    a. To the people (3.12-16).
    b. To the religious authorities (4.5-12).
4. A sign pointing to the power of the name of Jesus (4.16, 22, 30).
5. An authentication of the preaching of the word (4.29-30).
6. A cause for men to glorify God (3.8-10; 4.21).

There remains one unexpected and surprising motive to be considered. In the case of the Philippian slave girl (Acts 16.16-18) we are told that she developed the habit of following the apostolic party as they went each day to the place of prayer by the river Gangites at Philippi. As she followed close behind them she shouted out for all to hear that they were servants of the Most High God announcing how men were to be saved. Paul bore with her behaviour for many days, but finally was so vexed with her unsolicited testimony that he turned round on her and exorcised the spirit which possessed her. The verb which expresses Paul's feeling of vexation is *diaponeō* and the fact that it is used in Acts 4.2 and nowhere else in the New Testament (except in the Western text of Mark 14.4) gives us the clue to its meaning here. In 4.2 the word describes the reaction of the Sadducees to the preaching of the resurrection by Peter and John in Jerusalem. The Sadducees did not believe in the resurrection of the body as we learn from Matthew 22.23; Mark 12.18 and Acts 23.8, and they were annoyed at the apostles for teaching it to the people. Their annoyance was not petty or trivial, but arose from their firmly held denial of the possibility of a resurrection of the body. In a similar manner Paul's annoyance arose from his enmity towards all that was evil. It was directed not at the girl but at the spirit which possessed her. Like Jesus in the gospels, Paul was unwilling to accept the testimony of evil spirits even though this might help forwards the task of preaching the gospel of salvation. The only answer the New Testament knows to demon possession is confrontation with Jesus Christ and a demand based on his authority that the demon come out of the person whose personality he has possessed. That is what occurred here. Paul was annoyed at the spirit for his possession of the girl and his daily use of her to make his presence and purpose known in the way that he did. It was this annoyance which prompted him to exorcise the spirit and release the girl from his domination.

VII. THE METHODS OF HEALING

The methods of healing used by the apostles and others in the Acts are similar to those used by Jesus in the gospels. The principal methods were by word and by touch, and they may be classified as follows:

1. Healing by word.
2. Healing by touch.
3. Healing by word and touch combined.
4. Healing by other means.

1. *Healing by word*

(a) *In exorcism.* The only case of exorcism documented in the Acts is that of the slave girl at Philippi. In her case Paul said to the spirit, 'I charge you in the name of Jesus Christ to come out of her' (Acts 16.18). In Luke 8.29 Jesus had addressed the Gadarene demoniac in similar terms, and Paul invoked the authority of the name of Jesus here. In his command to the spirit he used the verb *parangellō*, charge, in what is usually interpreted as the aoristic present meaning that the spirit must come out at that very instant.[18]

There were other cases of exorcism in the apostolic Church which are not recorded in detail, but only mentioned incidentally in Acts 5.16; 8.7 and 19.12. We may assume that these cases too were dealt with by a word of command addressed to the spirit. Some confirmation of this is provided by the account which Luke gives of the itinerant Jewish exorcists at Ephesus in Acts 19.13-20, and who appeared to regard Paul as one of their own profession. He instances the seven sons of Sceva, an otherwise unknown Jewish high priest if he had any claim to this title and it was not merely assumed as that of professor is often assumed by magicians and astrologers today. These men were exorcists of the itinerant kind and two of them, or possibly all of them together according to how we translate the word *amphoterōn* in verse sixteen, attempted to exorcise a demon using the name of Jesus. Their attempt failed and they were attacked and routed by the possessed man. They failed because they used the name of Jesus simply as a magical or theurgic formula relying on the pronouncing of the name itself as magic strong enough to overcome the demon. But it was the person and the authority which lay behind the name which was the important factor in exorcism. This can be seen in the evil spirit's reply. He knew Jesus and Paul as persons who had authority over him, but these men had no faith in Jesus as a person nor any commission from him as their authority, and so he refused to obey them. The fact that they attempted exorcism by word alone suggests that this was the usual method in New Testament times.

(b) *In physical healing*. Two cases are described in the Acts in which physical healing was performed by the use of word alone:

(1) Aeneas: And Peter said to him, *Aeneas, Jesus Christ heals you; rise and make your bed* (Acts 9.34).

(2) The cripple at Lystra: Paul said in a loud voice, *Stand upright on your feet* (Acts 14.10).

As in the gospels, the sick are commanded to do what their sickness had rendered them incapable of doing. In both cases their incapacity arose from a physical cause and cannot be explained on the basis of hysteria or other mental condition. The cripple had never been able to stand upright and walk, and Aeneas had been paralysed for eight years.

In the case of Aeneas the word was more than a simple command. Peter first calls the sick man by his name and then makes the statement, 'Jesus Christ heals you'. His name is thoroughly Greek, but the statement implies that he knew the name of Jesus Christ and had heard of his ability to heal. We are not told that he was a Christian, but at least he was familiar with Christian teaching. Peter tells him that he is healed that very moment, for the tense of the verb *iaomai*, heal, is another example of the aoristic present.[19] Having told Aeneas that he was healed, Peter goes on to order him to stand upright on his feet immediately and make his bed (Acts 9.34). The exact meaning of the second part of this order is uncertain, for the verb *strōnnumi* may be applied either to making a bed on which to lie and sleep, or to preparing a couch on which to recline and eat at table. Aeneas had been able to do neither for the past eight years, and so his doing either now would be a significant demonstration of his cure. The making of his bed seems to be the more probable meaning, but Bruce points out that the alternative meaning would accord well with the interest which Luke shows in nourishment for convalescents (cp. Luke 8.55 and Acts 9.19).[20] However, there is no suggestion in the narrative that Aeneas had suffered from any lack of nourishment.

The cripple at Lystra was unable to stand or walk, and he had been brought each day to listen to Paul preaching. On one of these days Paul saw that he had faith to be made well (*sōzō*) and fixing him with his eye said in a loud voice for all to hear, 'Stand upright on your feet'. The Western text prefaces this order with a reference to the name of the Lord Jesus Christ, but this may safely be ignored as an assimilation to the account of Peter's healing of the lame man in Acts 3.6. The result was that the man leaped up in a single bound and began and continued to walk about as the tenses used describe. There are several touches in this record which suggest that it is based on the testimony of an eye-witness, and it may be that this eye-witness was Timothy who described the incident to Luke who recorded it. The implication of the record of the miracle is that the man's feet were restored to their normal structure and function and for the first time in his life he was able to stand upright and walk.

(c) *In raising the dead.* Tabitha was a Christian and when she died at Joppa the disciples sent for Peter, but there is no suggestion that this was for more than to be present at the funeral ceremony. When he came and was shown the body all laid out for burial, he put everyone outside the room and after prayer he turned to the body and spoke two words. He first called Tabitha by her name, and then he ordered her to get up using the same verb and form as he had addressed to Aeneas at Lydda. After she had returned to life Peter then took her by the hand and helped her to stand up (Acts 9.41). This unexpected restoration to life of Tabitha had a profound effect in Joppa, for when it became known we are told that many believed in the Lord (9.42).

2. *Healing by touch*

The only case in which touch alone was used in healing amongst those which are described in any detail in the Acts was that of the father of Publius, the chief man of Malta. Here we are told that Paul laid his hands on him and healed him (Acts 28.8).

There are also three general references which appear to describe healing by touch alone. These are as follows:

> Acts 5.12: Many signs and wonders (*sēmeia kai terata*) were done among the people by the hands of the apostles.
>
> Acts 14.3: At Iconium . . . the Lord . . . bore witness to the word of his grace, granting signs and wonders (*sēmeia kai terata*) to be done by their hands.
>
> Acts 19.11: God did extraordinary miracles (*dunameis*) by the hands of Paul.

In each case the phrase *dia tōn cheirōn*, by the hands, is used and this may mean literally by the use of the hands in touching the sick, or it may be a Semitism for 'by the agency of', and not necessarily involving the hands at all.[21] However, there is no real reason why the phrase should not be understood literally to refer to healing by means of touch, especially when we recall that healing by touch was the commonest method employed by Jesus in the gospels.

3. *Healing by word and touch*

There are two incidents of healing in the Acts in which word and touch are combined. The first is the cure of the lame man at the gate of the Temple in Acts 3.1-10. Peter first asked him to fix his attention on John and himself, and then ordered him in the name of Jesus Christ of Nazareth to walk. At the same time he took the man by the right hand and raised him up, and as he did so the man's feet and ankles were made strong and he was healed. The second incident is the restoration of Paul's sight in Acts 9.17-19. In this incident Ananias, acting on instructions received in a vision, seeks out Paul (or Saul as he then was called) and lays his hands on him saying that he has been sent by the Lord Jesus to restore his sight. The result of this combination of word and touch is the restoration of Paul's sight.

4. *Healing by other means*

We have now considered the methods which were used in most of the cases of healing in the Acts of which we have any detail. It has become evident that most cases were healed by word or by touch, or by a combination of these, and it appears that as in the gospels the main method used was by touch. There remain, however, three incidents of healing in which the methods used do not appear to fit into the classification of word and touch which we have used so far. These are the following:

(1) The restoration of Eutychus (Acts 20.9-12).
(2) The effect of Peter's shadow (Acts 5.15).
(3) The healing by cloths from Paul's body (Acts 19.12).

We begin by looking at the account of the restoration to life of Eutychus by means which appear to resemble modern methods of resuscitation. Eutychus fell from the upper storey of the house where the Christian community of Troas was met together to hear Paul preach his final sermon before he left them never to return. The young man was taken up dead, and Paul went down, bent over him and embraced him and life returned to his body (Acts 20.10). Paul's words, 'His life (*psuchē*) is in him' have been taken to mean that he was not dead, but Luke states quite clearly that he was taken up dead in verse nine. By quoting Paul's words, 'Luke intends us to understand that his life returned to him when Paul embraced him'.[22] We are told that Paul fell on Eutychus as he lay on the ground and threw his arms around him, and since both verbs are used in the aorist tense this would suggest that the action they describe was performed once only. This means that the method Paul used was not artificial respiration as it is practised today since to describe this the imperfect tense would be used. Neither was it the same as the method of resuscitation used by the prophet Elijah in 1 Kings 17.21 or by Elisha in 2 Kings 4.34-35 with which it is often compared. The method used by Elisha appears to resemble the modern kiss of life method of resuscitation, but there is no suggestion that Paul used any similar method to restore Eutychus. That it was a miraculous and not a medical restoration to life is borne out by the fact that although Luke was present in the meeting at Troas, he was not called down to attend him and did not go down with Paul when he went to attend him. That Luke was present at the meeting in the upper room is shown first by the fact that he tells us so himself in verse seven, and second by the vivid eye-witness description of how Eutychus came to fall out of the window. Luke describes how as the result of long exposure to the smoke and fumes of the many lights in the room, Eutychus began to feel sleepy and doze off and then wake again. He fought against his sleepiness, but finally sleep overcame him, and he relaxed his hold and fell backwards out of the window. Having used the first person in describing events in the room, Luke then uses the third person to describe what happened outside when Eutychus was taken up and Paul restored him to life. In other words he took no part in the healing at all, which may be regarded as unusual behaviour for a doctor. The explanation may lie in verse thirteen where we are told that Luke went with the advance party to the ship in order to bring round Cape Lectum to pick up Paul at Assos and so give him a longer time with the

Christians at Troas. This would mean that Luke may not have been present when Eutychus fell to his death since he had already left the meeting for the ship. If this were so, then the eye-witness details of how the young man finally lapsed into a deep sleep came not from Luke, but from another member of the party who stayed on, probably Paul himself.

We now turn to consider the effect of Peter's shadow and its significance. After the healing of the lame man at the gate of the Temple the apostles stayed in Jerusalem and we are told that many signs and wonders (*sēmeia kai terata*) were wrought by their hands (Acts 5.12). Not suprisingly it was Peter who had the greatest reputation in this respect, for it was he who had been instrumental in healing the lame man. The result was that the people laid their sick on mattresses and camp beds in the street 'that as Peter came by at least his shadow might fall on some of them' (5.15). The Western textual tradition adds the words 'for they were all set free from every sickness which each of them had'. Our difficulty lies in the sparse detail which Luke gives us and which led Ramsay to remark that Luke 'as a rule, carries brevity to the verge of obscurity'.[23] He does not say that Peter's shadow was the means of healing the sick and even the Western textual addition does not state this explicitly. Why then is Peter's shadow mentioned? First, to show how near to Peter the people brought their sick. They were near enough for his shadow to fall on some of them as he passed by. Second, to reflect the people's superstition that healing was to be found in the shadow of an apostle. But the shadow fell only on some of them and we are told that all were healed (5.16). The explanation lies in verse twelve where we are told that the healing was performed by the hands of the apostles, and not by the shadow of any one of them. This record is therefore another account of healing by touch, by the hands of the apostles.

In Acts 19.11-12 we are told that God did extraordinary miracles (*dunameis ou tas tuchousas*) by the hands of Paul. Luke uses the figure of speech called litotes not infrequently in the Acts and here he employs it to describe the miracles that God did through Paul at Ephesus and he tells us that they were not of the ordinary kind. He is clear, however, that they were done by Paul's hands and Bruce notes that the phrase *dia tōn cheirōn*, by the hands of, indicates not merely the agency of Paul but his personal activity and his contact with the sick.[24] As the result of the extraordinary miracles performed by his hands, the people came to regard anything which had been in contact with his skin as potentially able to heal the sick. So they took his sweat rags or *soudaria*, the cloths which he wore round his head to keep the sweat out of his eyes as he worked, and his aprons or *simikinthia* which he would wear to protect his clothes as he worked at tent-making with Aquila and Priscilla at Ephesus (cp. Acts 18.3 and 19). The fact that he would not have had a great number of these items suggests that they were not in fact the means of healing the sick. The first clause of verse twelve describes not the method by which the sick were healed, but the result of the healing by which the people took away cloths which had been worn by Paul in the superstitious belief that they would convey healing to the sick equally with his hands. Luke does not in fact tell us what effect they had on the sick.[25]

Our consideration of the three accounts of healing in which means other

than a word or touch appeared to have been used shows that the method of
healing in these cases was really one of touch. In the case of Eutychus the touch
was applied in a special way and was not simply by laying on of hands. In the
other two cases we are specifically told that healing was effected by the hands
of the apostles (Acts 5.12 and 19.11). We do not therefore need to classify these
accounts in a separate category but only to include them along with other cases
in which healing was by touch.

At the beginning of this chapter we noted that much less space was devoted
by the author of Acts to accounts of healing in comparison with the space taken
up by such accounts in the gospels. As we conclude our study of healing in the
Acts of the Apostles it is appropriate to comment on the significance of this
difference between the gospels and the Acts.

The first consequence of the difference is, of course, that we have much less
material available for our present study of healing in the apostolic Church as
recorded in the book of Acts. This means that any conclusions which we may
draw from this material are less certain than any which we have drawn from
our study of the gospels.

The second observation which we may make on the difference is that it
means that the author of Acts felt under no obligation to collect together a
great number of stories of the miraculous in order to impress his readers with
the case for Christianity. This appears first of all in the fact that the healing
miracles of the Acts were not represented as a primary means of evangelism
performed in order to impress their spectators and to persuade them to embrace
the new religion. It is also reflected in the small number of miracles chosen for
detailed recounting when we know from incidental references that many more
were performed. This suggests that the author's purpose in writing the Acts
was more historical than theological.

Finally, the difference in the amount of space allowed for healing in the
gospels and in the Acts must mean that physical healing was not a major interest
in the apostolic Church. In order to investigate this matter further we proceed
in the next chapter to examine the other source of information about the
apostolic Church which is found in the epistles of Paul and the other apostolic
men whose writings are included in the New Testament.

REFERENCES

1. A. B. Bruce, *The Training of the Twelve* (T. & T. Clark, Edinburgh, 1888), pp. 96-97.
2. C. G. Jung, 'The Psychological Foundation of Belief in Spirits' in the *Proceedings of the Society for Psychical Research* for May, 1920, quoted by R. H. Thouless, *Introduction to the Psychology of Religion* (Cambridge University Press, 1936), second edition, p. 190.
3. R. K. Harrison, *Interpreter's Dictionary of the Bible* (Abingdon Press, Nashville, 1962), vol. 1, p. 449, art. 'Blindness'.
4. S. Duke-Elder, *Parsons' Diseases of the Eye* (J. & A. Churchill Ltd., London, 1964), fourteenth edition, p. 330.
5. We assume that Luke was using the Greek measurement of time by which the day began at dawn rather than at sunset according to Jewish custom. Verse eleven appears to imply the Greek method rather than the Jewish.

6. F. J. F. Jackson and K. Lake, *The Beginnings of Christianity* (Macmillan, London, 1933), Part I, Vol. 4, p. 343.

7. A convenient review of what the third gospel reveals about Luke's interests and personality is given in William Barclay, *The Gospels and Acts* (SCM Press, London, 1976), vol. 1, pp. 216-221.

8. W. K. Hobart, *The Medical Language of St Luke* (Dublin University Press, 1882), p. 6. Cp. also E. Haenchen, *The Acts of the Apostles: A Commentary* (Blackwell, Oxford, 1971), ET, p. 302.

9. A. Harnack, *Luke the Physician* (Williams and Norgate, London, 1906), ET by J. R. Wilkinson, p. 16.

10. Jackson and Lake, *Beginnings of Christianity*, vol. 4, p. 343. This view is shared by E. Haenchen, *The Acts of the Apostles*, p. 715.

11. This can be seen by comparing Luke 9.2 with Matthew 10.8; Luke 9.11 with Matthew 14.14, and Luke 9.18 with Matthew 9.24.

12. Hobart, *Medical Language of St Luke*, p. 35.

13. Ibidem, p. 47.

14. Ibidem, p. 23.

15. See above, p. 9.

16. Hobart, *Medical Language of St Luke*, p. 193.

17. In his gospel, Luke in common with the other synoptic gospels uses the word *dunamis* to describe the healing miracles of Jesus.

18. F. F. Bruce, *The Acts of the Apostles: The Greek Text* (Tyndale Press, London, 1952), second edition, p. 316.

19. F. Blass and A. Debrunner, *A Greek Grammar of the New Testament* (Cambridge University Press, 1961), ET by R. W. Funk, p. 167, para 320.

20. F. F. Bruce, *Acts (Greek text)*, p. 211. E. Haenchen, however, regards this latter translation as 'misconceived' in his *Acts of the Apostles*, p. 338, n. 9.

21. Both Lake and Cadbury in the *Beginnings of Christianity* (vol. 4, p. 239) and Haenchen in his *Acts of the Apostles* (p. 51) decide against interpreting the phrase as a Semitism and understand it to refer to the actual use of the hands in healing.

22. F. F. Bruce, *Acts (Greek text)*, p. 373.

23. Sir William Ramsay, *St Paul the Traveller and the Roman Citizen* (Hodder and Stoughton, London, 1902), sixth edition, p. 115.

24. F. F. Bruce, *Acts (Greek text)*, p. 357. Cp. our previous note on p. 98 above.

25. See the discussion of this topic by Haenchen, *Acts of the Apostles*, pp. 561-563.

Chapter Ten

HEALING IN THE EPISTLES

The book of the Acts of the Apostles is an account of the spread of the gospel outwards from Jerusalem through Judaea and Samaria, Asia Minor and Greece to the capital of the Roman Empire. In its progress from country to country there came into being local Churches or Christian communities. These Churches were at first minority groups in a pagan Hellenistic world and they faced problems of faith and practice for which they needed advice and guidance. Sometimes such advice and guidance could be given by word of mouth, but at other times it was given by letter, and some of the letters have survived and are included in the New Testament. They give a unique and fascinating glimpse into the life and work of the apostolic Church. By their very nature, however, these letters rarely give us a complete picture of any situation, and they often produce more difficulties than they resolve. What these letters have to say about the healing activity of the Church in the early years of its existence forms no exception to this general statement. There are only a few tantalising references to sickness and healing which are scattered quite incidentally throughout the epistles, with no indication of whether these references describe only local situations or practices, or such as are general throughout the Church. There is no complete description or discussion of attitudes to sickness or methods of healing, so that we can never be certain that we have the whole picture before us. Nevertheless we can gain some valuable glimpses and insights into the thought and practice of the apostolic Church from a consideration of these scattered references.

The paucity of specific references to health and healing in the epistles is of great interest in view of the fact that these writings form over a third of the bulk of the New Testament. Some of them are contemporaneous with events recorded in the Acts, whilst others are not, and it cannot be denied that they reflect a lessened interest in health and healing when compared with that book, as that book in turn reflects a lessened interest in healing when compared with the gospels. It can be argued that the character of a letter does not lend itself to the mention of incidents of healing in the same way as a chronicle of events such as we have in the Acts. However, the Pauline letters frequently deal with problems on which the local Christian communities have sought his advice and since healing is only referred to in passing in them we can only presume that healing was not a problem. Also, when we find that there are references in these same letters to illness which was left to the natural processes of recovery and not one reference to healing by supernatural means, it is only reasonable to conclude that there is a lessened interest in supernatural healing when the epistles are compared with the gospels, and even with the Acts.

When we look more closely at those references to healing which do occur in the epistles we find that there are some striking differences between them and those which occur in the gospels and the Acts. The vocabulary used in the epistles is much more limited than it was even in the Acts. There is no reference to demon possession and exorcism, and no mention of raising the dead. Healing appears to be confined to within the Christian community unlike that recorded in the gospels and the Acts, and there is mention of gifts of healing which are not mentioned elsewhere in the New Testament. Finally, we hear of Church leaders who are sick and yet nothing is done to heal them. Some of these points will be discussed in this chapter, but we reserve for fuller treatment in later chapters the two topics of Paul's experience of his thorn in the flesh, and James' instructions to those who became sick in the Christian community.

I. THE WORDS FOR HEALTH AND HEALING

The words which express the different aspects of health in the New Testament all occur in the epistles although they frequently have a different emphasis and application from that found in the gospels. The verb *hugiainō* occurs in 3 John 2 with its literal meaning of being sound in health, but with this exception, its use is confined to the Pastoral Epistles where it is used metaphorically to describe sound doctrine.[1] This has been interpreted as meaning doctrine which makes whole, whose goal is the health of the soul, but it is more probably doctrine which is sound because it conforms to apostolic teaching. The word *eirēnē* occurs frequently in the epistles and describes that aspect of health which consists of a right relationship to God, and the serenity of mind and heart which flows from that relationship. The adjective *teleios* is used by Paul to express the idea of man's complete maturity which he covets for his readers in such verses as I Corinthians 14.20; Ephesians 4.13 and Philippians 3.15. The example and standard of this maturity is Jesus Christ himself. The noun *sōtēria* is frequent in the sense of deliverance and salvation, and is usually unqualified, but in 1 Peter 1.9 the outcome of man's faith is described as the salvation of his soul (*psuchē*). In no place in the epistles is it applied specifically to the healing of the body, but that is not to say that the salvation of the whole man does not include his body, for Paul speaks explicitly of the redemption of the body (*apolutrōsis tou sōmatos*) in Romans 8.23.

The common verb for healing in the gospels is *therapeuō*, but this verb does not occur in the epistles. The verb *sōzō* is used only in James 5.15 in a sense which clearly includes the healing of the sick. On the few occasions on which a word is required for healing in the epistles, the verb *iaomai* or one of its derivatives is used. These occasions are in 1 Corinthians 12.9, 28, 30; Hebrews 12.13; James 5.16 and 1 Peter 2.24.

II. PAUL AND THE BODY

The question now arises of Paul's view of the body and physical health. It might appear from the last section that he had very little to say about the body, and yet Robinson in his essay entitled *The Body* gives his opinion that 'one could say without exaggeration that the concept of the body forms the keystone of Paul's theology'.[2] This arises from the fact that *sōma*, which is the common Greek word for the body, may mean both the physical body and the whole person, and may be understood individually and collectively. It is the collective sense which predominates in Robinson's own study. In the Pauline epistles, Stacey distinguishes no less than five different senses in which the word *sōma* is used. 'There is the body as flesh, the body as the whole man, the body as the principle of redeemable humanity, the body as the means of resurrection, and the Body of Christ meaning the Church.'[3] Clearly we must also distinguish between literal and metaphorical uses of the word. For our present purpose we are concerned with the literal meaning and the question of what Paul has to say about the physical body of man.

1. *The body has needs and functions*

The first thing we learn from Paul's epistles is that the body has physical needs. It needs food and drink or it will experience hunger and thirst (Romans 12.20; 1 Corinthians 6.13; 11.21 and 34). Paul had himself experienced hunger and thirst in the service of the gospel (1 Corinthians 4.11; 2 Corinthians 6.5; 11.27; Philippians 4.12). The body also needs clothes, shelter and sleep (Romans 8.35 and 2 Corinthians 11.27). The body also needs exercise as Paul recognises in 1 Timothy 4.8, although the AV translation of this verse has often been used to justify lack of exercise. The body is composed of different members and organs which each has its own function. These include the foot for walking, the eye for seeing, the ear for hearing, the sense of smell for smelling (1 Corinthians 12.14-26), and the joints for movement (Ephesians 4.16 and Colossians 2.19). The body is also the agent of sex for the procreation of life (Romans 4.19; 1 Corinthians 6.15-18 and 7.1-8).

2. *The body is subject to disease, decay and death*

We learn too that the body is subject to disease from the experience of Paul with his thorn in the flesh, and from his mention of the illness of three of his colleagues (2 Corinthians 12.7; Philippians 2.25-30; 1 Timothy 5.23 and 2 Timothy 4.20). The body is described as perishable and mortal, subject to decay and death in Romans 6.12; 8.11, 21; 1 Corinthians 15.42, 54; 2 Corinthians 4.16; 5.4 and Philippians 1.20.

3. *The body is the servant of the spirit and both were intended to serve the Lord*

In 1 Corinthians 9.27 Paul speaks of his attitude to his body and uses the rare verb *doulagōgeō* to describe it. The verb means 'to treat as a slave (*doulos*)'. The body is therefore the slave of the spirit and does its bidding whether this is to righteousness or unrighteousness. The classic passage on this subject is Romans

6.12-23. The body carries out the will of the spirit whether this is righteous or unrighteous, as the slave carries out the will of his master. The body therefore shares in the dedication to God to which Paul exhorts the Roman Christians in Romans 12.1-2. It is also the subject of possession by the Holy Spirit and is described as the dwelling place or temple of the Holy Spirit in 1 Corinthians 3.16 and 6.19. Like the whole man, the body was created to be dedicated to God and properly belongs to the Lord (1 Corinthians 6.13). We are therefore to honour and glorify God with our bodies (1 Corinthians 6.20 and Philippians 1.20).

4. *The body shares in the redemption of the whole man*

Paul in Romans 8.18-25 describes the present suffering and future glory of Christians, and how they and the whole creation are waiting for their final and complete adoption and the redemption of their bodies (vv. 22-23). In his previous paragraph Paul had reminded his readers that they were already adopted into the family of God (vv. 14-16), but the full realisation of their adoption and the completion of their redemption will only occur with the resurrection of the body. In 1 Corinthians 15.42-59 he describes the resurrection as a change from a *sōma psuchikon* or a natural physical body to a *sōma pneumatikon* or a spiritual body. The spiritual body is imperishable, glorious, strong, immortal and life-giving in contrast to the natural body we now possess which is perishable, dishonoured, weak, mortal and merely living. The spiritual body is not subject to disease, decay or death. It is not a body of flesh and blood, for blood is only necessary to a body that is subject to decay where the tissues require to be provided with materials for defence against disease, for the repair of damage due to injury or disease, or for the maintenance of normal growth and activity. In the natural body once the supply of blood to a part is cut off that part decays and dies, but the spiritual body does not decay and therefore needs no blood to maintain it. It is not without significance that when Jesus described his resurrection body to his disciples·he said that a spirit did not have flesh and bones as they could see he had (Luke 24.39). The natural phrase would have been flesh and blood, but his body did not now contain blood. His resurrection body is the only example we have of a spiritual body, and from the description given in the gospels it is clear that it resembled his previous natural body in form and could be recognised by those who had known him before death. It bore the signs of wounds inflicted before death and could be touched and handled (John 20.25-27). It was capable of intelligible speech and of taking food (Luke 24.41-43), but the food was not for nourishment, for nourishment implies mortality. As Cyril of Alexandria said long ago, Jesus took food not to nourish his body but the faith of his disciples.[4] His body bore a new relation to matter and could vanish and appear in a room at will even though the doors were shut (Luke 24.31, John 20.19 and 26).

The attitude of Paul to the body is an indication of how, alone amongst the spiritual religions of the world, Christianity takes the body seriously. This serious and realistic view of the body is the implication of the Incarnation of the Son of God in human flesh, the Atonement made in his body (1 Peter 2.24) and the Resurrection of his body from the dead, and is an essential element in the Christian Faith.

III. THE GIFT OF HEALING

The New Testament epistles contain six lists of what Paul calls the gifts (*charismata*) of the Lord to the Church. Five of them occur in Paul's own writings and one in the First Epistle of Peter, and they may be classified as follows:

1. Those which describe the gifts in terms of function (prophecy, teaching, healing, etc.).

    Romans 12.6-8.
    I Corinthians 12.8-10.
    I Peter 4.10-11.

2. Those which describe the gifts in terms of office (apostle, prophet, teacher, etc.).

    I Corinthians 12.28.
    Ephesians 4.11.

3. Those which describe the gifts in mixed terms of office and function (apostle, healing, etc.).

    I Corinthians 12.29-30.

The word used for the gifts is *charismata* which in the singular *charisma* means a gift freely given, a gift which results from grace (*charis*). The word is rare in Hellenistic Greek and apart from its use in I Peter 4.10, occurs only in Paul's writings in the New Testament. He uses it in a general sense when he speaks of God's gift to man of eternal life in Romans 5.15-16 and 6.23. It is used also in a special sense in the Pastoral Epistles to describe the particular gift of ministry given to Timothy by the laying on of Paul's and the elders' hands in I Timothy 4.14 and 2 Timothy 1.6. The gift in Timothy's case appears to have been for the ministry of the word if we are to judge from the context of the first reference, However, the most common usage of the word *charisma* by Paul is to denote a gift given to individual Christians by the Holy Spirit and through them to the whole Christian community. Such a gift is an individual endowment for the service of the community and so may be described in terms of a function such as teaching, or in terms of an office such as that of a teacher. When these gifts are described by Paul and Peter both are careful to say that they were given not for the glory of the individual but for the good of the Church (I Corinthians 12.7; Ephesians 4.12 and I Peter 4.10).

About twenty different gifts are included in the six lists, and there is no suggestion that these lists are exhaustive. The lists are not said to be in any order of priority, but in I Corinthians 12.31 there is a reference to 'the higher or greater gifts' which may mean those which are placed at the top of the lists given earlier in the chapter. That prophecy is amongst these and is to be preferred to speaking in tongues is made clear in I Corinthians 14.1. The gifts are described in terms of both offices and functions, and it is not always possible to equate office and function. It is easy to equate teacher and teaching, but no function is given corresponding to the office of apostle, and no office corresponds to generous giving (Romans 12.8).

The question which now arises concerns the nature of a *charisma*. As we approach this question, Bittlinger, who has been described as the most competent theologian of the charismatic movement in Germany, has a useful warning for us. He warns us to beware of a two-fold misunderstanding of the *charismata*. The first is the *enthusiastic* misunderstanding which regards them as purely supernatural and miraculous, and therefore an unnecessary addition to normal Christian life. The second is the *activist* misunderstanding which treats the *charismata* as purely natural in character, consisting of the normal activities and capabilities of man, so that a *charisma* is exercised whenever a Christian does anything within the Church. The first type of misunderstanding does not give man his true dignity as created by God, whilst the second ignores the result of his Fall. The truth must be that *charismata* are both natural and supernatural. To quote Bittlinger's definition, we may say that a *charisma* is a gracious 'manifestation of the Holy Spirit, working in and through, but going beyond, the believer's natural ability for the common good of the people of God'.[5] The Holy Spirit does not work independently of a man as he was created by God, and the individual does not exercise a *charisma* except as a member of the Church which is the body of Christ. If we are to be faithful to the context of Paul's teaching on the *charismata*, we may only speak of a *charisma* if the words are spoken or the deeds performed in dependence on Jesus as Lord (1 Corinthians 12.3), in accordance with the measure of faith given by God (Romans 12.3), and as the expression and realisation of love (1 Corinthians 12.31 and 14.1).

One of the *charismata* which is mentioned in all three lists in the Corinthian epistles, but in none of the others, is the gift of healing. Literally it is the gifts of healings, for both nouns are in the plural. This is usually interpreted as meaning that there is specialisation amongst the gifts of healing with different gifts for different diseases, and that no one person could heal all diseases.[6] A gift of healing was not given to all, but only to some as we learn from 1 Corinthians 12.30. Also, the gift of healing is always described as a function and is not confined to an office, in so far as we may speak of an office and officers in these early days of the Church. The evidence for the exercise of the gift of healing in the apostolic Church is very scanty in the New Testament apart from the apostles themselves, and when Paul refers to his healing activity he includes it amongst the *sēmeia* or signs of an apostle (2 Corinthians 12.12, cp. Romans 15.19). There is no mention of a special gift of healing in the Epistle of James where it appears that the elders heal by virtue of their office and prayer (James 5.14-15), and even ordinary Church members can be agents of healing as they pray for the sick (v. 16). The gift of healing is not mentioned in the lists of the *charismata* given in the Epistles to the Romans and to the Ephesians, and it is of interest to note that two of Paul's colleagues who were sick and were not healed by charismatic means were sick in Rome and Ephesus. These were Epaphroditus (Philippians 2.27) and Timothy (1 Timothy 5.23). Does this mean that the Church in Rome and in Ephesus knew nothing of the gift of healing? If they did know, then this means that the gift was not always used when an obvious case for its use occurred.

What, then, was the nature of the gift of healing? Presumably the Christians at Corinth knew, for Paul did not describe it in any detail, and even Calvin can say that 'everyone knows what is meant by the *gift of healings*', and feel that he need make no further comment.[7] Today there is great interest in the gift of healing combined with a lack of understanding of its nature. If the definition proposed by Bittlinger and quoted above is correct then we must look for the basis of the gift of healing in the nature of man as created by God and endowed by him with certain aptitudes and capabilities. It is a matter of common experience that some people are better at healing than others by virtue of their natural attributes of sympathy and compassion. This is one reason why some people make better doctors and nurses than others do. When a man or woman with these natural gifts acknowledges that 'Jesus is Lord' and so becomes a Christian and is incorporated into the body of Christ which is the Church, then the Holy Spirit enhances and intensifies these gifts and places them at the disposal of the Church. A consideration of the other *charismata* will show that what we are suggesting as the nature of the gift of healing is true also of some of the other gifts mentioned by Paul. It is a matter of common experience that God has bestowed on some people gifts of preaching and teaching, of leadership and administration, of helpfulness and generosity, and these are all mentioned by Paul in the lists of *charismata* which he gives. When an individual with one or more of these natural gifts becomes a Christian his gifts are taken by the Holy Spirit and used in the ministry and work of the Church. In 1 Corinthians 12.27 Paul sums the matter up by saying that Christians collectively are the body of Christ and individually are members (*melē*) of that body. As members they may be limbs, organs or other bodily parts each with their own gifts and function. Each one brings his own gifts and all are integrated into the body by God so that these gifts are exercised within the organism of the body which is the Church. Included amongst these gifts are the gifts of healing.

What was the content of the gift of healing? Was it a special acquisition of knowledge about disease and its cure, or of special skill in surgical manipulation or procedures? The probable answer is that it was neither of these, but consisted of a natural gift of sympathy or empathy combined with a capacity of knowing the right thing to do in any individual situation and with any individual patient. This intuitive knowledge was sharpened and made more sensitive by the operation of the Holy Spirit on the mind of the healer, and had no necessary connection with medical knowledge or surgical training.

How was the gift of healing practised? Paul gives us no guidance on this matter, but if we are to judge from what we are told of his own practice in the Book of Acts and from what is described in the Epistle of James, then it is clear that the gift was used in the context of prayer.

There is much more that we would like to know about the gift of healing, but we are left with many of our questions unanswered. Why is the gift mentioned only in connection with the Church at Corinth and not elsewhere? Why are those who healed the sick in the Acts not said to have a special gift of healing? Why is there no mention of such a gift in the Epistle of James? Why, when such a gift existed, were leaders of the Christian community including the apostle Paul himself allowed to go unhealed? The existence of so many unanswered questions suggests that an understanding of the nature of the gift of healing is not necessary for the practice of healing. When we add to this the obscurity with which the gift of healing is described, and the fact that it is never associated with any act of healing in the New Testament record, and is not mentioned in the explicit description of the Church's practice of healing given by James, it suggests that the gift of healing consists essentially of the application of earnest prayer and the enhanced natural endowments of the members of the Christian community.

IV. THE FOUR WHO WERE NOT HEALED

One of the most significant facts about healing in the epistles is the occurrence of four cases in the apostolic Church who were not healed by the methods which Jesus used in the gospels and the apostles used in the Acts.

The first case is that of the apostle Paul whose thorn in the flesh was most probably some form of sickness, and who asked God on three occasions that it should be removed only to have his request refused each time. This experience of Paul's is considered in detail in the next chapter.

The second case is that of Epaphroditus who was a leader in the Church at Philippi and had brought gifts from that Church to cheer Paul in prison at Rome, or alternatively at Ephesus as some believe. He stayed on to serve Paul and the cause of the gospel in Rome, and contracted an acute infection which was almost fatal. When he recovered he became homesick for Philippi and was very concerned that the Christians there had heard about his illness. As he proposes to return home Paul takes the opportunity to write a letter for him to take to the Philippian Church, and so we owe the existence of the Epistle to the Philippians to the illness of Epaphroditus. The nature of the illness is unknown although it may have been some form of enteric fever. The interesting fact for our present purpose about the case of Epaphroditus is that there was no suggestion that any special means of healing should be used. The disease was allowed to run its course and even to bring him very close to death. This appears from Paul's description in Philippians 2.25-30 where he says that Epaphroditus' illness very nearly proved fatal.

Timothy is the third case. In 1 Timothy 5.23 he is advised by Paul to take a little wine for the sake of his stomach and his frequent sicknesses (*astheneiai*). Timothy was a young man but appears to have been ill frequently. In modern terms we might diagnose his condition as a chronic achlorhydric dyspepsia. However, the problem is why was he allowed to continue to suffer from frequent disabling attacks of dyspepsia? Why was he not healed by someone who had the gift of healing?

Finally, we come to the case of Trophimus, a Gentile Christian of Ephesus, who was a travelling companion of Paul's on his third missionary journey (Acts 20.4) and was with him in Jerusalem where he became the unwitting cause of Paul's arrest and imprisonment (Acts 21.27-34). He is sometimes identified with the unnamed brother who was famous among all the Churches for his preaching and whom Paul mentions in 2 Corinthians 8.18-22. Even if this identification is incorrect, there is no doubt that Trophimus was a close associate of

Paul, and it is therefore all the more surprising that he left him behind at Miletus sick, as he says in 2 Timothy 4.20 in explanation of why he was not with him as he wrote. His sickness was presumably an acute one but no clue is given about its nature. Again the problem arises about why no one exercised the gift of healing and restored Trophimus to health, so that Paul did not need to leave him behind because of illness.

The subject of health and healing in the epistles poses more problems than it solves, and yet what is written there allows us to draw a number of conclusions. Health concerns the whole man, body, soul and spirit, but is not fully realisable in this present life. In fact, the Christian concept of health provides a powerful argument for the life that is to come, for health is only possible for the whole man after the resurrection from the dead. One result of this is that healing is not always the answer to illness in the epistles. Disease may be allowed to take its natural course as in the case of Epaphroditus, or to become chronic and recurrent as in the case of Paul. Some members of the Church were given a gift of healing, but this does not appear to have been universally used for the healing of the sick. Finally, it is clear from the epistles that Christian faith and experience provide no immunity against disease. What it does provide is most fully illustrated by the experience of Paul with his thorn in the flesh.

REFERENCES

1. 1 Timothy 1.10; 6.3; 2 Timothy 1.13; 4.3; Titus 1.9, 13 and 2.1, 2. See the note on 1 Timothy 1.10 in J. N. D. Kelly, *A Commentary on the Pastoral Epistles* (A. & C. Black, London, 1963), p. 50.
2. J. A. T. Robinson, *The Body: A Study in Pauline Theology* (SCM Press, London, 1952), p. 9.
3. W. D. Stacey, *The Pauline view of man* (Macmillan, London, 1956), p. 182.
4. Cyril of Alexandria, *Commentary on St. John's Gospel*, book 12, 1 on John 20.28. Cyril quotes and then comments on the passage Luke 24.36-43. His life is usually dated A.D. 376-444.
5. A. Bittlinger, *Gifts and Ministries* (Hodder and Stoughton, London, 1974), pp. 17-29. The definition will be found on page 20.
6. A. Robertson and A. Plummer, *International Critical Commentary on the First Epistle to the Corinthians* (T. & T. Clark, Edinburgh, 1914), p. 266.
7. J. Calvin, *The First Epistle of Paul the Apostle to the Corinthians* (Oliver and Boyd, Edinburgh, 1960), ET by J. W. Fraser, p. 262.

Chapter Eleven

PAUL'S THORN IN THE FLESH

Throughout the Christian centuries the whole Church has had cause to be grateful to the young Christian community in Corinth whose lively relationships with the apostle Paul provoked his Corinthian correspondence, some of which still survives in our New Testament. This correspondence is concerned with the practical problems of a young enthusiastic Church living in a pagan cosmopolitan city whose very name was a synonym for immorality. The Greek verb *korinthiazomai* means to practise immorality and this sense still persists in the English verb *to corinthianise* which is derived from it.

One of the many problems which the young Corinthian Church raised for Paul was the question of his own authority as an apostle of Jesus Christ. The result was that throughout these letters he constantly asserts his apostolic authority which he claimed was ultimately based on the call to be an apostle he had received from God (1 Corinthians 1.1 *et passim*). On several occasions, however, he appeals also to his own experience in the service of God and of his Son Jesus Christ as displaying his credentials as an apostle and his fitness to exert pastoral authority over the Corinthian Church.

It is in the course of one of these autobiographical passages that Paul speaks of an experience of a heavenly vision and an ineffable revelation which had come to him, and which had been followed by the appearance of what he calls according to the common translation, 'a thorn in the flesh' (2 Corinthians 12.7). It is with some reluctance that he speaks of these experiences to demonstrate the basis of his authority. He calls it 'boasting' and uses the word *kauchomai* which is a characteristic word of the Corinthian letters in which it occurs twenty-six times. Boasting in this context does not mean the self-glorification which springs from pride, for to Paul that is of the essence of sin. Paul's boasting is not the glorification of himself but of God. Twice he quotes Jeremiah 9.24, 'If a man must boast, let him boast of the Lord' (1 Corinthians 1.31 and 2 Corinthians 10.17). Paul therefore speaks of his experience not to glorify himself, but to glorify God who gave him these experiences which served to verify his call to be an apostle.

It is in the eleventh chapter of the second letter to the Corinthian Church that Paul speaks of the wonderful mystical experience which he had fourteen years previously. It was an experience of surpassing wonder which would amply justify boasting of the baser sort had he wished to indulge in it. However, in order to forestall such pride and boasting God gave Paul 'a thorn in the flesh' which continued with him like a messenger of Satan to recur at intervals throughout his life.

The passage in which Paul describes this thorn in the flesh and which forms the basis of the present consideration of it is translated as follows in the RSV:

'And to keep me from being too elated by the abundance of revelations, a thorn was given me in the flesh, a messenger of Satan, to harass me, to keep me from being too elated. Three times I besought the Lord about this, that it should leave me; but he said to me, "My grace is sufficient for you, for my power is made perfect in weakness." I will all the more gladly boast of my weaknesses, that the power of Christ may rest upon me.'

2 Corinthians 12.7-9.

I. THE MEANING OF THE PHRASE

The phrase 'a thorn in the flesh' is a metaphor and not an exact literal description. Plummer suggested that the phrase may be derived from the LXX rendering of Numbers 33.55 which describes the discomfort which the inhabitants of the land of Canaan would cause to Israel if they were not entirely driven out when Israel occupied the land.[1] However, this suggestion does not seem very likely and has not been widely accepted.

In Greek the phrase is *skolops tē sarki* and we look first at the word *skolops*. This is an uncommon word and occurs only here in the New Testament. It means something which is pointed, and in Classical Greek denoted a pointed stake on which the heads were impaled after the decapitation of one's enemies (*Iliad* 18.177) or which was used for the construction of defensive palisades (*Odyssey* 7.45). It could also be used for the instrument used in execution by impalement. In Hellenistic Greek it came to mean a thorn or splinter stuck in the body and one of earliest usages in this sense is in the LXX where it occurs in Numbers 33.55; Ezekiel 28.24; Hosea 12.6 and Ecclesiasticus 43.19. In translation, therefore, the choice lies between a large pointed stake or a small thorn for the rendering of *skolops* in this passage. Both meanings can muster impressive lists of New Testament scholars in their defence, but it must be realised that the opinion of many of those who proposed 'stake' as the meaning of the word here dates from before the time when it was recognised that the New Testament was not written in bad Classical Greek, but in the Hellenistic or *koinē* Greek of the Graeco-Roman world. Had this fact been recognised earlier it is probable that many more scholars would have favoured the translation 'thorn' rather than 'stake'. This is suggested by an examination of the English versions of the New Testament for, when thirty-six of these were consulted, most of which were translated after the year 1900, twenty-eight of them were found to give 'thorn' as the preferred rendering, whilst only two gave the translation 'stake'. There seems to be no doubt therefore that we should prefer the meaning 'thorn' in translating the word *skolops* in the present passage.

By contrast to *skolops*, the second noun in the phrase is a common word, for *sarx* occurs almost one hundred and fifty times in the New Testament. It has various meanings and it is obvious that our choice of meaning will be determined by our view of the character of the thorn. Consequently we find that *sarx* or flesh has been interpreted of the physical body, of human nature either in contrast to the divine or in its lower aspect in man, and of the relationship of a man to his fellows by birth. Undoubtedly the commonest interpretation of the word here is that it refers to the physical body, but the relevance of the other interpretations will appear when we discuss the identity of the thorn.

The relationship between the thorn and the flesh depends on the significance of the dative case in which the word *sarx* is expressed. The translation 'for the flesh' has been suggested as on the whole more probable than 'in the flesh' because of the absence of the preposition *en*, in. There is little difference in meaning between these two phrases except that 'in the flesh' suggests a more permanent attachment of the thorn, whilst 'for the flesh' suggests that it might only be attached to the flesh on occasions. However, the eventual result is the same whether the thorn be 'in the flesh' or 'for the flesh', and the latter phrase is only infrequently used in modern European versions where the favoured translation is a 'thorn in the flesh'.

We end where we began, with the phrase 'a thorn in the flesh' firmly established as the most probable translation of the Greek *skolops tē sarki*. We cannot improve on the common translation although it is patently a metaphorical description of the condition from which Paul suffered. The significance of this phrase will occupy us for a large part of this chapter.

II. THE FEATURES OF THE THORN

Paul had been reluctant to mention the matter of visions and revelations of the Lord at all, and only did so because it illustrated the basis of his apostolic authority in his relationship with the God and Father of the Lord Jesus. The result is that he gives but scanty details of his experience, and this is true also when he comes to speak of his thorn in the flesh. There are, however, a number of the features of the thorn which we may discover by a closer examination of his description. These are details of its onset, its occurrence, its character and its effects. Consideration of these features will help us to come closer to an identification of the nature of the thorn, and it is to this that we now turn.

1. *Its onset.* The onset of the experience which Paul calls a thorn in the flesh was sudden and acute. It was given to him at a specific point in his life. This is suggested by the verb form which is *edothē*, the first aorist passive form of *didōmi*, give. It began when he was 'a man in Christ' (v. 2), that is to say when he was in adult life and had already become a Christian. It followed the experience in which Paul received visions and revelations from the Lord in such a way and at such an interval that he realised that it had been given to him to prevent his becoming too elated by them (v. 7). It does not however appear to have been part of that experience, but was distinct from it.

2. *Its occurrence.* The only clue to the first occurrence of an attack of the thorn in the flesh is the mention that the preceding experience of visions and

revelations of the Lord took place fourteen years before he wrote the twelfth chapter of Second Corinthians which is commonly dated about A.D. 56. This gives the year A.D. 42 as the approximate time when these events occurred in Paul's life, and since his conversion may have happened some nine years or so previously it is clear that they cannot be identified with his experience on the road to Damascus. Such an identification has already been excluded by Paul's statement that his experience of the visions and revelations dated from the time when he was already a Christian. We have no details of the time or place of the first attack of the thorn in the flesh, but it is clear that it was recurrent and liable to attack him at any time. He calls it the messenger (*angelos*) of Satan and says that it was sent to beat and bruise him. The word he uses is *kolaphizō* which means to beat with the fist (*kolaphos*), and it is used in the present tense to indicate that he was still suffering its attacks. It is clear that he was not affected by it all the time or he could never have done all the work he did do in the service of the gospel. The condition must therefore have been recurrent in nature. The present tense also suggests that it was a permanent affliction or 'a very steady companion' as Denney describes it.[2] This is also suggested by the tense in which Paul gives the Lord's reply to his request for the removal of the thorn, for when he mentioned what the Lord had said, he put it in the perfect tense which meant that it was to be his permanent answer for the whole of Paul's life. It is in keeping with this that his promise to Paul that his grace would be sufficient for him is expressed in the present tense since it would always be true when he was attacked by the thorn in the flesh.

3. *Its character.* The thorn in the flesh was personal to Paul. Although he began in the third person by describing himself as a man in Christ (v. 2), he soon changes to the first person and says that the thorn was given to him personally to keep him from being too elated (v. 7). It was therefore something which was personal to him and not shared with anyone else. According to the common interpretation it had to do with the physical part of him, his flesh in the sense of his body, and so its character was physical. We have already seen, however, that this view is not universally held, particularly by earlier commentators. Most authors describe the character of the condition as painful, and some prefer the translation of *skolops* as stake because it suggests greater pain than thorn. But there is no explicit mention of pain in the passage and the painful character of the condition is assumed by interpreters of the passage rather than explicitly described by Paul. The description of a thorn sticking into the flesh suggests a painful experience, and the use of a word which likens the experience to being beaten with a fist supports this suggestion. The fact remains, however, that Paul did not particularly emphasise the painful character of the thorn in the flesh.

4. *Its effect.* It was in terms of its effect that Paul described his thorn and not in terms of its painful character, and its effect was to produce weakness and humiliation. It was debilitating (v. 9) and produced a weakness in which Paul was supported by God's strength. It was also humiliating, for not only did it show his weakness (11.30), but it also prevented him from being too elated at the experiences which God had given to him and which he describes as an abundance of revelations (v. 7).

We may now summarise the features of the thorn in the flesh in so far as we can discover them from the passage in which Paul describes them:

1. Its onset was acute at a time when Paul was a mature adult and had become a Christian.
2. It persisted as a permanent state throughout his life, and manifested itself in recurrent attacks between which he enjoyed normal health and strength.
3. Its character was personal, physical and painful.
4. Its effect on him was debilitating and humiliating.

III. OTHER POSSIBLE EVIDENCE OF THE THORN

If this condition was part of the experience of Paul and affected him as much as he suggests it did, then it is reasonable to suppose that there may be further references to it either in the Acts or in his letters. A number of references have been regarded as providing other possible evidence about the thorn in the flesh, and these fall naturally into four groups.

1. *References which are expressed in general terms*

'I was with you in weakness and in much fear and trembling' (1 Corinthians 2.3).

'We are weak, but you are strong' (1 Corinthians 4.10).

'We do not want you to be ignorant, brethren, of the affliction we experienced in Asia; for we were so utterly, unbearably crushed that we despaired of life itself. Why, we felt that we had received the sentence of death' (2 Corinthians 1.8-9).

'For they say, "His letters are weighty and strong, but his bodily presence is weak"' (2 Corinthians 10.10).

'For we are glad when we are weak and you are strong' (2 Corinthians 13.9).

'You know that it was because of a bodily ailment that I preached the gospel to you at first; and though my condition was a trial to you, you did not scorn or despise me' (Galatians 4.13).

'I bear on my body the marks of Jesus' (Galatians 6.17).

'I rejoice in my sufferings for your sake, and in my flesh I complete what remains of Christ's afflictions for the sake of his body, that is, the church' (Colossians 1.24).

It is improbable that most of these references cast any further light on Paul's thorn in the flesh. It is tempting to regard the near fatal experience in Asia which he mentions in 1 Corinthians 1.8 as an example of an attack of the thorn in the flesh, but 'the most extraordinary thing about this passage is that we have no information at all about this terrible experience which Paul went through at Ephesus',[3] and so we must resist the temptation. The marks (*stigmata*) of Jesus to which Paul refers in Galatians 6.17 are neither signs of disease nor what we mean by the stigmata today, namely, the appearance of the wounds of Jesus which resulted from his crucifixion. They are the scars on his body which were the visible result of the personal violence he experienced in the service of the gospel and which he describes in 2 Corinthians 11.24-25. The only reference amongst those given above which might refer to the thorn in the flesh is Galatians 4.13. Here Paul reminds his readers in Galatia that the reason he was able to preach the gospel to them on the first occasion he did so was because he developed an acute illness which incapacitated him for travel and caused him to visit and to stay in Galatia for some time. We shall have to take account of this reference when we come to consider the identity of the thorn in the flesh.

2. *References which may indicate that Paul suffered from an eye affliction*

'For three days he was without sight' (Acts 9.9).

'Paul, looking intently at the council, said . . .' (Acts 23.1).

'Paul said, "I did not know, brethren, that he was the high priest"' (Acts 23.5).

'Though my condition was a trial to you, you did not scorn or despise me, but received me as an angel of God, as Jesus Christ. What has become of the satisfaction you felt? For I bear you witness that, if possible, you would have plucked out your eyes, and given them to me' (Galatians 4.14-15).

'See with what large letters I am writing to you with my own hand' (Galatians 6.11).

It is doubtful whether any of these verses taken individually would suggest that Paul had an affliction or infection of the eyes, and even their cumulative information and force is no more suggestive. Each verse is explicable on some basis other than that of a disease of the eyes. Paul's loss of sight on the Damascus road lasted only three days and did not recur (Acts 9.9). The verb *atenizō* which describes Paul's concentration of his attention on the members of the Sanhedrin is used on twelve occasions by Luke and twice by Paul. It never indicates any difficulty in seeing which might be due to a disease of the eyes, but refers to a special intensity of looking at a person as shown by its use in Luke 4.20; Acts 1.10; 3.4 and 14.9. Although the failure of Paul to recognise the high priest according to Acts 23.5 is surprising, there are several possible explanations other than that which suggests he suffered from poor eyesight due to eye disease. The high priest may not have been wearing his official robes because the council had been hurriedly called together by the tribune Claudius Lysias. Paul may not have known the high priest, having been only a few days in Jerusalem. Ramsay's suggestion that the tribune was in the chair and the high priest at the side with the other members of the council and so not readily distinguished is possible but unlikely.[4] Finally, Paul could have been speaking ironically, expressing surprise that anyone who ordered a defendant to be struck on the mouth whilst giving evidence in his own defence, could be a high priest.

As in the previous section the Galatian references appear to be the most relevant and promising. Paul in Galatians 4.13 speaks of 'a bodily ailment', as the RSV translates his phrase *astheneia tēs sarkos*, which he had suffered from and which appears to have been the reason why he paid his visit to Galatia. This had been a condition which produced a repulsive physical appearance in him as a result of which the Galatians would have been justified in regarding him with loathing and disgust (v. 14). In verse fifteen he makes a more specific reference to the possible nature of his disease when he says that the Galatians would if it had been possible have plucked out their own eyes and given them to him. Does this mean that Paul's bodily ailment was one which affected his eyes, and that in their concern for his recovery the Galatians would have been willing even to pluck out their own normal eyes in order to give them to Paul to replace his diseased ones? It certainly could mean this and we shall have to examine this possibility when we come to discuss the identity of the thorn in the flesh in more detail. The reference to 'large letters' in Galatians 6.11, however, need not imply poor eyesight. Paul did not usually write his own letters as we know from Romans 16.22, and it may be that at this point in the letter to the Galatians he took up the pen and wrote the concluding paragraph in larger script than his amanuensis had used. In this paragraph he sums up the essential issue of the letter and the large script would emphasise its importance.

3. *References which may suggest that Paul suffered from a fatal disease*

    (a) 'I die every day' (1 Corinthians 15.31).
    (b) 'We are . . . always carrying in the body the death of Jesus' (2 Corinthians 4.10).
    (c) 'We are always being given up to death for Jesus' sake' (v. 11).
    (d) 'Death is at work in us, but life in you' (v. 12).
    (e) 'We are treated as . . . dying, and behold we live' (2 Corinthians 6.9).
    (f) 'I am . . . often near to death' (2 Corinthians 11.23).
    (g) 'That I may . . . share his sufferings, becoming like him in his death' (Philippians 3.10).

These verses do not refer to a fatal disease, and neither do they lend any support to the notion that Paul regarded himself as suffering from one. They clearly refer to the constant exposure to violence which Paul faced in the course of his travels and preaching. This frequent possibility of injury is reflected in Romans 8.35, and is given in more detail in the Corinthian letters (1 Corinthians 4.9-13; 2 Corinthians 4.7-12; 6.4-10 and 11.23-28). It is significant for our present purpose that none of these lists includes a mention of sickness. Indeed his survival of such violence argues for his extreme physical fitness which allowed him to withstand such violent treatment. The fact was that Paul constantly faced death in the service of his Lord, and was in danger of dying by violence in the same way that Jesus died. This is the force of the unusual word *necrōsis* used by Paul in 2 Corinthians 4.10, unless we accept Denney's suggestion that Paul is saying that his apostolic work and sufferings were killing him.[5]

4. *References which mention hindrance by Satan*

    'We wanted to come to you – I, Paul, again and again – but Satan hindered us' (1 Thessalonians 2.18).

Paul regarded his thorn in the flesh as a messenger of Satan sent to harass him. This verse in First Thessalonians has sometimes been interpreted as referring to this thorn since it suggests a recurrent obstruction to his visiting the Thessalonian Church. But the reference is too indefinite to provide any real clue to the nature of the hindrance which Satan continually placed in the way of Paul and his companions to prevent their going to Thessalonica.

It is evident from this review of the other references which might have some bearing on the identity of the thorn in the flesh that few of them provide much further help, with the possible exception of the references in the letter to the Galatian Church. We shall have occasion to return to these in the course of the next section where we consider the possible identity of the thorn in the flesh.

IV. THE IDENTITY OF THE THORN

At the outset of our consideration of Paul's thorn in the flesh we do well to remind ourselves that we cannot at present know its precise identity. The very multiplicity of theories about its nature only serves to underline this fact. As Deissmann in his book on Paul points out, a small library could be collected of all the books and articles which have been written on Paul's illness.[6]

Merrins has suggested that if one day a contemporary statue of Paul were to be unearthed by the spade of the archaeologist somewhere in the eastern Mediterranean area, we might then be able to recognise some particular appearance which would allow us to identify the thorn in the flesh.[7] This is extremely unlikely, however, since almost all of the suggested identifications of the thorn are of such a character that they would not be obvious in the gross delineation of the facial features in a statue. Also, since the thorn affected him only from time to time it is most improbable that a statue would be made of him during an attack when his appearance would be abnormal if we accept the reference in Galatians 4.14 as relevant. The point remains theoretical, for we do not have any evidence of the existence of any contemporary picture or sculpture of Paul.

The best-known early description of Paul is in the late second century apocryphal Acts of Paul and Thekla. A man named Onesiphorus went with his family to meet Paul on the road from Lystra to Iconium in Asia Minor. He had not met him before and when he came he found that he was

'A man small of stature, with a bald head and crooked legs, in a good state of body, with eyebrows meeting and nose somewhat hooked, full of friendliness; for now he appeared like a man, and now he had the face of an angel.'[8]

There are similar descriptions of his appearance from later centuries but none of them gives us any clue to what his thorn in the flesh might have been.

It is not even clear that the Corinthian Christians themselves knew its precise identity. Stanley suggested that the obscurity of nature of the thorn for us was occasioned by the fact that it was plain to his contemporaries.[9] This, however, need not be so. Paul is boasting, albeit reluctantly, of things which support his claim to be an apostle and to have apostolic authority. He is appealing to evidence with which the Corinthians would not be familiar. They did not know about his experience of visions and revelations, and need not have known about the experience of the thorn in the flesh which followed them.

In the absence of any contemporary evidence about the nature of the thorn in the flesh we are left in the realm of conjecture, and it must be said at the outset of our review that we do not lack theories. They range from the bizarre and improbable to the reasonable and possible. They include suggestions which have no contact with the text and bear no relation to the metaphors which Paul uses to describe his experience. It is obvious that some of the suggestions have simply been snatched from the air and are without any foundation at all. In the case of others, Lightfoot has suggested that they have arisen from the circumstances of their originators who saw in Paul's experience of the thorn a more or less perfect reflection of the trials which beset their own lives.[10] A list of all the conditions which have been suggested for the diagnosis of the thorn reads like the index of a textbook of medicine.

For the purpose of discussion, however, the theories conveniently divide themselves into two main groups. On the one hand there are those theories which identify the character of the thorn as non-physical, and on the other those who regard it as physical in character.

Theories which identify the thorn as non-physical in character

    1. Religious opposition.
        a. By an individual, e.g. Alexander the coppersmith (2 Timothy, 4.14).
        b. By a group: Jews or pagans.
    2. Mental oppression.
        a. Exaggeration of a normal state such as grief or remorse.
        b. Neurosis, e.g. anxiety state, hysteria or 'neurasthenia'.
        c. Psychosis, e.g. depression or paranoia.
    3. Spiritual temptation.
        a. Pride   c. Sensuality
        b. Doubt   d. Ill-temper

Theories which regard the thorn as physical in character

    1. Physical defect.
        a. Stammering.
        b. Deafness.
    2. Bodily injury.
    3. Organic disease.
        a. A painful disorder.
        b. A nervous disease.
        c. An affection of the eyes.
        d. An infective disease.

Theories which identify the thorn as non-physical in character

The theories which belong to this group dominated the exegesis of the passage on the thorn in the flesh from the fourth to the eighteenth centuries, and any group of theories which endures for fifteen centuries without much opposition demands respect and discussion. However, they are not much favoured today, for most commentators prefer to regard the thorn as physical in character. One of the main reasons for this loss of favour is that most of these theories are not based on a careful examination of what Paul actually said, or upon a natural understanding of the words which he used. Many of the theories are examples of *eisegesis* rather than *exegesis*, of reading a meaning into the text rather than drawing one out of it. This is the significance of the remark made by Lightfoot about the influence of the circumstances of the originators of many of these theories which we have already quoted. The group as a whole can be divided into three sections according to whether the precise nature of the thorn was regarded as religious opposition, mental oppression or spiritual temptation.

1. *Religious opposition*. This was the view held by Chrysostom and the Greek Fathers in general. Chrysostom begins his exposition of the passage by denying that the thorn could be a headache inflicted by the Devil as some had said, because 'the body of Paul could never have been given over to the hands of the Devil, seeing that the Devil himself submitted to Paul at his mere bidding'. He went on to draw attention to the Hebrew name Satan in the phrase 'the messenger of Satan' which Paul used, and because this name meant an adversary, Chrysostom believed that his use of this name indicated that his thorn in the flesh was the opposition of adversaries such as Alexander the coppersmith (2 Timothy 4.14), and Hymenaeus and Philetus (2 Timothy 2.17).[11] Amongst modern commentators Knox, who regarded Chrysostom as 'St Paul's best interpreter', prefers this theory that the thorn was the opposition of adversaries, but admits that it 'does not impose itself on the mind'. He thought that the opposition came from the Jews, Paul's own flesh and blood.[12] Tasker also favours this theory after reviewing and dismissing the other ones. He points out that there is nothing so calculated to deflate spiritual pride as opposition encountered during the preaching of the gospel, and because of this 'it is not unlikely that Chrysostom's interpretation is nearer the truth than any other'.[13]

We know, however, from Acts 9.23-30 that Paul encountered religious opposition immediately after his conversion and this was therefore his experience some time before he was given the thorn in the flesh. Also, opposition was an experience common to all Christian believers and was not an experience peculiar to Paul. He would not have prayed to be delivered from an experience which was the common and expected lot of all who shared his faith. It appears unlikely therefore that we should identify the thorn in the flesh with the religious opposition which Paul encountered in his preaching, and so it is not necessary to decide whether its source was from an individual or a group.

2. *Mental oppression*. Numerous mental states have been proposed for the diagnosis of the thorn in the flesh, but it is unnecessary to enter into a detailed discussion of their nature or relevance. Some of the terms used are too imprecise to define what their proposers intended in terms of modern medical knowledge, e.g. the terms neurasthenia and depression. In most cases the suggestions are so widely at variance with what we know of the character and mind of Paul that they are not worth discussing. Whoever, for instance, would entertain the thought of the diagnosis of hysteria for the thorn in the flesh lacks insight alike into the character of Paul and the nature of hysteria. Modern authors who have thought that the thorn was some form of mental affliction include

Weatherhead who regarded it as 'some form of psychosomatic disorder'.[14] Amongst those who regard the thorn as the persistence of a normal state of grief or remorse, the most recent is Menoud who suggests that it was Paul's great sorrow at the unbelief of his own people, the Jews. Paul's prayer for the removal of the thorn was therefore a prayer that he might evangelise and convert them.[15] However, it is difficult to see how this view of Menoud and others explains the precise dating of the onset of the thorn some years after his own conversion, and its connection with his experience of visions and revelations.

3. *Spiritual temptation.* The final category of theories which identify the character of the thorn in the flesh as non-physical consists of those which derive it from spiritual temptation. This identification is given some plausibility by the description of his bodily ailment as 'my temptation' in Galatians 4.14 according to the AV rendering which was based on the Textus Receptus. However, the better textual tradition reads 'your temptation', and so removes any basis for this type of theory which has been found in this text assuming that it refers to the thorn in the flesh.

Calvin preferred to interpret the thorn in the general sense of including every temptation by which Paul was assailed. He paraphrases Paul's meaning as, 'To me there has been given a goad to jab at my flesh, for I am not yet so spiritual as to be exempt from temptations according to the flesh'.[16] In his view the flesh does not mean the body, but the part of the soul which is not yet regenerate. The only temptation he mentions specifically is pride, but it is clear that he is not very interested in exploring the possible identity of the thorn further than his general statement we have just quoted. He is more concerned with the significance of the thorn in the apostle's spiritual experience, and its lessons for us. Pride is an unlikely identification for the thorn if only because it was given to Paul specifically to save him from taking pride in the special visions and revelations which God had given him. It is of interest that in his notes on Galatians 4.13, Calvin does not link together the infirmity of the flesh spoken of there with the thorn in the flesh. There he interprets the flesh as meaning Paul's outward appearance, and explains the infirmity of the flesh as 'whatever might make him mean and despised'.[17]

Doubt also seems to be an improbable diagnosis for the thorn in the flesh. Paul had just been given greater visions and revelations than most men, and these would reinforce his faith rather than produce doubt.

Sensuality or concupiscence would also appear to be an unlikely identification for the thorn in the flesh in view of the fact that Paul has already explained how he came to terms with this problem in the seventh chapter of First Corinthians. This had been a popular identification in the Roman Catholic Church, and was set out in an authoritative fashion in the seventeenth century in the celebrated commentaries on the epistles of Paul by Estius (Willem Hessels van Est)[18] and Cornelius à Lapide (Van den Steel).[19] As Lightfoot points out, the latter author 'almost exalts this interpretation into an article of faith'.[20] Luther attributed the popularity of this view to the Vulgate rendering of *skolops tē sarki* by *stimulus carnis* which meant a goad for the flesh, with the flesh understood as the carnal or sensual nature of man. It is usually mentioned by modern Roman Catholic commentators, but is not commonly adopted. It has not been commonly accepted by Protestant writers, but its existence in Scotland is illustrated by its occurrence in Burns' cynical poem *Holy Willie's Prayer* (1785).[21] In this poem, after two verses describing incidents of fornication, Burns goes on,

> 'May be thou lets this fleshly thorn
> Beset thy servant e'en and morn
> Lest he owre high and proud should turn,
>   That he's sae gifted;
> If sae, thy hand maun e'en be borne,
>   Until thou lift it.'

Finally, the suggestion that the thorn in the flesh consisted of an infirmity of temper or fits of anger has been made by Lias in his commentary on Second Corinthians in the *Cambridge Bible for Schools and Colleges*,[22] and more recently by Holmes Gore.[23] These authors point to Paul's disagreements with Peter at Antioch (Galatians 2.11), and with Barnabas at the outset of his second missionary journey (Acts 15.37-40) as evidence of Paul's outbursts of anger. However, it cannot be said that this identification of the thorn in the flesh as fits of anger is at all convincing. It is difficult to explain why they began so late in Paul's life, and why they should follow an intense spiritual experience as the appearance of the thorn did.

The main objection to all these theories which regard the thorn as some form of spiritual trial or temptation is that God would hardly have told Paul to stop praying for their removal. Temptation of various kinds is the lot of all Christian believers and Paul would not have expected to be exempt from it. Equally, it is unlikely that Paul would regard spiritual temptations as something he was glad to boast about and content to suffer as he does in 2 Corinthians 12.9-10. In so far as these suggested identifications of the thorn are defects of character or of Paul's psychological make-up, they make strange bed-fellows with the insults, hardships, persecutions and calamities of verse ten of this passage, and this would imply that the thorn was not of the nature of spiritual temptation in any form. Finally, if Galatians 4.13 refers to the same conditions as the thorn in the flesh then it is difficult to see how a spiritual temptation could be the cause of Paul's preaching the gospel to the Galatians on the first occasion that they heard it from his lips.

So far we have not mentioned Luther's views on the nature of the thorn in the flesh although they also fall into the category of those which maintain the non-physical character of the thorn. This is because they underwent a change during his lifetime. His earliest view is contained in his earlier commentary on Galatians published in 1519, where in his comment on Galatians 4.13 he identifies the infirmity of the flesh and the thorn as religious opposition and persecution. In his later and fuller commentary published in 1535 he still believes that the two phrases refer to Paul's trials and temptations, but he now makes a distinction between outward trials and inward temptations. By the infirmity of the flesh he now understands Paul to refer to the religious opposition and persecution of his enemies, which may issue in physical violence and bodily injury. The thorn in the flesh on the other hand he now believes refers to inward and spiritual temptations such as Jesus experienced in the garden of Gethsemane before his arrest and which consisted of depression, anguish and terror.[24] His

final view is given in the Table-talk where he speaks only of spiritual temptations as the nature of the thorn in the flesh and speaks no more of outward
opposition and persecution.[25]

The conclusion of our review of the theories which propose a non-physical
character for the thorn in the flesh which afflicted Paul must be that such a
character is unlikely. This has emerged as we have considered the different
types of theory individually, and is reinforced by a consideration of the theories
as a group. In spite of recent attempts to revive them in one form or another,
no new evidence has been produced and it is no surprise that they have mostly
fallen out of favour today.

Theories which regard the thorn as physical in character

As a prelude to a more detailed discussion of the theories which regard the
character of Paul's thorn in the flesh as physical, we take up certain general
considerations. These consist of a number of observations on the two passages
relevant to our discussion which when taken together do at least create a pre-
sumption in favour of the general thesis that the thorn in the flesh was physical
in character.

1. *Observations on 2 Corinthians 12.7-10.* (a) The metaphor embodied in the
phrase 'a thorn in the flesh' (v. 7) is one which is derived from the physical
world and may be presumed to be intended to describe an experience which
was physical in nature.

(b) The primary and literal meaning of *sarx* or flesh is physical and denotes
the material which covers the bones of a human or animal body.[26] It is true that
sarx may also be used in an ethical sense to mean the carnal nature, but as
Hughes points out in his commentary on this epistle, Paul ordinarily reserves
the ethical usage for a doctrinal-ethical context in which the flesh is opposed to
the spirit, and in a narrative context such as our passage it is more likely to be
used in a physical sense.[27]

(c) The situations of weakness which include the thorn in the flesh and
which are listed in verse ten are all predominantly physical. Most commentators
speak of only four kinds of weaknesses in verse ten, but there are five words
and it is more natural to take them as specifying five kinds of weakness under
the general heading of 'the weaknesses' in verse nine. In verse nine *astheneiai*,
weaknesses, is used with the definite article to denote the class of things which
make Paul weak and in which God's power makes him strong. In verse ten,
five of these things are listed and the first one is *astheneiai*, weaknesses, but this
time without the definite article. It is possible that we should translate this
second use of *astheneiai* as sicknesses, for it forms part of a list of those things
which make Paul weak. The others are insolent maltreatment (*hubris*, here in
the passive sense), violent constraints (*anankai*), persecutions (*diōgmoi*), and difficulties (*stenochōriai*, literally refers to narrowness of space). All these make Paul
weak and unable to cope but God's power makes him strong even in these
situations and that is why he glories in their occurrence.

2. *Observations on Galatians 4.13-15.* It is customary to associate Paul's thorn
in the flesh with this passage in Galatians, but this association is not absolutely
certain as Tasker reminds us when he writes that in Galatians 4.13, 'Paul speaks

of "*an* infirmity of the flesh". There is no definite article, and there is no personal pronoun; he is not, in other words, referring to "that constantly recurring trouble of mine which elsewhere I call my thorn in the flesh". It may well have been a rather exceptional illness which had caused him to journey into Galatia at that particular time.'[28] It is only fair that we should remind ourselves of this possibility that the Galatian passage might be explained on another basis, because once we associate it with the passage from Second Corinthians which we have just considered, then the case for the physical character of the thorn in the flesh becomes much stronger. We can see this from the following observations.

(a) The meaning of the phrase *astheneia tēs sarkos*, a weakness of the flesh (v. 13), in this context is most naturally taken as physical and translated 'a bodily illness' as in the NEB. The same phrase occurs in Romans 6.19 where Paul uses it to denote the defective spiritual insight of the Roman Christians. It is clear that these two meanings of the phrase are not interchangeable in their contexts. The meaning in Romans would not fit the Galatian context, for this context demands a physical meaning.

(b) The condition which Paul calls a weakness of the flesh made him unable to travel and obliged him to stay and rest in Galatia for some time until he recovered. This would be more naturally understood of a physical illness.

(c) The condition which caused Paul to visit Galatia was visible to the Galatians in his appearance ('in my flesh') which was repulsive to behold (v. 14).

(d) The reaction of the Galatians to his appearance was to wish to do something physical to help him such as plucking out their eyes to give them to him (v. 15). This suggests that his condition was physical in nature.

These preliminary observations have served to set forth the general case in favour of regarding the character of the thorn in the flesh as physical. We now proceed to a consideration of the various theories which have been advanced about its specific identity.

1. *Theories of physical defect.* (a) *Stammering.* It would appear unlikely that an effective evangelist like Paul suffered from a defect of his speech such as stammering, but this has been suggested as the character of his thorn in the flesh. A convenient statement of this view is by Lowther Clarke in his book on *New Testament Problems* where he suggests that Paul was 'a victim to nerves' and suffered from a stammer.[29] Although in his concluding paragraph he indicates that he realises that this view may be thought fanciful, he claims support for it from two verses in Second Corinthians. The first is in 10.10 where Paul quotes his opponents as saying that his bodily presence was unimpressive and his speech of no account (*exouthenēmenos*). The second is in 11.6 where Paul admits, perhaps ironically, that he may be unskilled in speaking and uses the word *idiōtēs* meaning that he is a layman rather than an expert in rhetoric. It must be admitted that no one reading these verses in their context would think that they suggested that Paul had a speech defect, and it is very improbable that his thorn in the flesh was of this nature.

(b) *Deafness.* A defect of hearing was suggested by Knapp as the diagnosis for Paul's thorn in the flesh,[30] but it is difficult to find any evidence of this in the New Testament. Deafness is a permanent state and Paul clearly indicates that the thorn in the flesh affects him only intermittently. It does not explain any of the features of the attack described in the Galatian passage, and must be discarded as a possible diagnosis for Paul's condition.

2. *Theories of bodily injury.* There is no doubt that the opposition which Paul encountered often expressed itself in physical violence which led to bodily injury. Incidents involving Paul in bodily injury are mentioned in Acts 13.50; 14.19 and 16.23, and he gives details of others in 2 Corinthians 11.23-27. It is unlikely, however, that bodily injury constituted his thorn in the flesh, for violence against his person began soon after his conversion and some time before he had the ecstatic experience which preceded the appearance of the thorn.

An endeavour was made by Marcus Dods to identify the thorn in the flesh, or as least the weakness of the flesh Paul describes in Galatians, with what happened to him at Lystra immediately prior to his going to Galatia. At Lystra we are told that Paul was stoned and left for dead (Acts 14.19). This stoning would result in bodily weakness and produce a repulsive appearance such as he suggests the Galatians saw in him (Galatians 4.13-14), and so if this was an example of his thorn in the flesh, it could very well have been the result of personal violence resulting in serious bodily injury.[31] An even more dramatic suggestion is that at Perga in Pamphylia Paul was actually crucified by Jews who resented his charges that the Jewish people had crucified their Messiah. This occurred just before Paul went inland to visit the Galatians, and Turner finds support for this suggestion in the following references in the Epistle to the Galatians:

(a) 'I have been crucified with Christ' (Galatians 2.20).
(b) 'The cross of our Lord Jesus Christ, by which the world has been crucified to me, and I to the world' (6.14).
(c) 'I bear on my body the marks (*stigmata*) of Jesus' (6.17).

Turner expects the suggestion of crucifixion to be regarded as fantastic and it is difficult to take it seriously.[32] There is no mention of any violence at Perga, and if the Jews had crucified Paul there it would have been so unusual and significant that Luke would have mentioned it in the Acts. Paul's language in his references to crucifixion is clearly metaphorical and refers back to the crucifixion of Jesus and its significance in the spiritual experience of Paul and the Christian believer.

If we take the Galatian passage by itself the suggestion that Paul is describing the result of a violent assault upon his person is possible, although it must be said that to describe the result of an assault as 'a weakness of the flesh' reads strangely. If, however, we take it along with the passage in Second Corinthians, then the suggestion of bodily injury as the character of the thorn in the flesh becomes very improbable.

3. *Theories of organic disease.* The prevailing view today is that Paul's thorn in the flesh was physical in character and probably due to some identifiable syndrome or specific disease. Whether this change of view from that held in earlier times that it was not physical in nature can be attributed to any particular cause is difficult to decide. There has been an increasing understanding of

the nature of both mental and physical disease in modern times, and it may be that this has had some influence on the change of opinion. Also, the more recent views do attempt to do justice to the meaning of the passages in which the thorn in the flesh is described, and this may be attributed to the development of critical Biblical study and scholarship in the nineteenth century and after. Whatever the cause may be, the fact remains that many modern commentators accept the physical character of the thorn in the flesh, although they are not agreed on any specific identity for it. Numerous suggestions for this have been put forwards with varying degrees of plausibility.

a. *A painful disorder.* The earliest recorded tradition about the nature of the thorn in the flesh is quoted by Tertullian in his Montanist work *de Pudicitia* (On modesty) written about A.D. 220. In chapter thirteen of this work he writes that Paul's elation of spirit was restrained by buffeting by what 'they say' was earache or headache (*dolor auriculae vel capitis*). Jerome also mentions in his commentary on Galatians which he wrote about A.D. 386 the tradition that the physical weakness of Galatians 4.13 was a very severe headache (*gravissimus capitis dolor*). How authentic this tradition was is now impossible to say, but it does not of itself bring us much nearer a solution of the problem since headache is only a symptom and not a disease. Other more specific suggestions have included toothache due to dental caries, pain from some disease of the loco-motor system such as gout, sciatica and 'rheumatism', and finally we have the tradition which was preserved by Aquinas that it was a recurrent renal colic caused by the presence of a urinary stone in the kidney or ureter (*morbus iliacus*). These suggestions are either too imprecise or improbable to justify their further investigation. There is no doubt that the thorn in the flesh was painful, but it is doubtful if we can reach any definite conclusion about its identity by a con-sideration of pain alone.

b. *A nervous disease.* The two principal nervous diseases which have been proposed for the diagnosis of the nature of the thorn in the flesh are migraine and epilepsy.

The characteristic feature of *migraine* is a recurrent headache which occurs on only one side of the head. The name is a corruption of the term *hemicrania* used by the ancient Greek physician Galen because of the one-sided distribution of the pain.[33] Support for the theory of migraine as the thorn in the flesh has come from Johnson who appeared to describe an attack from her own personal experience and saw in it an explanation of what happened to Paul on the road to Damascus. She did not however relate her explanation very closely to Paul's descriptions in his two letters, but assumed that his conversion experience was the same as his thorn in the flesh, a name which she thinks he gave the affliction because he did not know the technical name for it.[34] But migraine as we know it today does not readily agree with Paul's experience. It usually begins at puberty, and in middle age becomes less frequent and less severe in its attacks. Paul is quite clear that his thorn was given him when he was about forty years of age and that he had never had it before. Also, since an attack of migraine lasts only a few hours, or at the most severe only a few days, it is unlikely that this would interfere with his travelling plans as much as the thorn or weakness of the flesh did. It is significant that medical commentators have rarely been

satisfied with the classical diagnosis of migraine in Paul's case, but have regarded it as a special type. Seeligmüller was a German neurologist who in 1910
wrote a booklet entitled *War Paulus Epileptiker?* (Was Paul an epileptic?) in
which he agreed that Paul might have suffered from migraine. When he went
into detail he defined the type of migraine as *Augen-migräne* or ophthalmic
migraine, and he described the features of this disease as including loss of consciousness and fits. This made it clear that he was in fact describing epilepsy and
not migraine. It is therefore possible that other authors who put forward the
diagnosis of migraine and did not describe its features in detail were in fact
thinking of epilepsy rather than migraine. When we compare the features of
migraine with the experience of Paul it is clear that his thorn in the flesh was
not migraine as we know it in medical practice today.

The most popular identification of the thorn in the flesh in the nineteenth
century was that of *epilepsy*. This identification appears to have been first made
in 1804 by K. L. Ziegler of Göttingen in the book *Theologische Abhandlungen*. It
was accepted and popularised in Britain by Lightfoot in his commentary on
the Epistle to the Galatians which was published in its first edition in 1865,
and in Germany by Krenkel in an article published in 1873, followed by a
book in 1890. After its introduction to Biblical scholarship by these authors
it was widely reproduced and accepted. The evidence that Paul was an epileptic is based on the description of his conversion experience in Acts 9.3-9;
22.6-11 and 26.12-18, and on his account of the experience of visions and
revelations in 2 Corinthians 12.1-4. We must therefore look at this evidence
first of all, before we consider whether the thorn in the flesh could have been
epilepsy.

The essential features of Paul's experience on the Damascus road can be
summarised by saying that he saw a bright light, he fell to the ground, he heard
a voice speaking to him, and he was blind for three days after the experience.
There is little positive evidence in these features for the diagnosis of epilepsy,
and a great deal of negative evidence against it.

(1) The bright light was also seen by his companions according to Acts
22.9 and therefore it could not have been the premonitory aura of an epileptic
fit.

(2) His companions fell to the ground along with him according to Acts
26.14.

(3) The sound of the voice was also heard by his companions but they
could not distinguish the words as we are told in Acts 9.7 and 22.9.

(4) At no point did he experience a loss of consciousness which is the
essential feature of an epileptic fit.

(5) There was no loss of memory for the events which happened during
the experience such as occurs after an epileptic fit.

(6) Blindness does not usually follow an epileptic fit, and if it did it would
not be expected to be complete, or to last as long as three days as it did in Paul's
case (Acts 9.9).

(7) The experiences of an epileptic during an attack, in so far as they may
be remembered which is very rarely the case, do not fit into a rational pattern
or have objective significance as they had in Paul's case.

(8) A profound change of personal belief and character such as occurred to Paul does not occur during or after an epileptic fit.

When we look at the second experience which Paul had and which he describes in 2 Corinthians 12.1-4, we find that the evidence for its being an epileptic fit is even less than it was for his conversion experience. This evidence against epilepsy in this second case is as follows:

(1) There was no loss of consciousness during this experience.

(2) There was no loss of memory for what happened during it.

(3) Epileptic attacks could never add to a man's knowledge of God as it
    is implied that the visions and revelations added to Paul's
    knowledge, and consequently to his apostolic authority.

In the light of all the evidence which we have considered, it is clear that neither Paul's conversion experience nor his ecstatic experience of visions and revelations were epileptic in nature.

What are we to say then of the thorn in the flesh? Was it epileptic in nature? The first thing to notice is how Paul carefully distinguishes the thorn from the ecstatic experience in his description in 2 Corinthians 12.1-10. It was given to him after that experience in order to counteract its possible elative effect on him (v. 7). Consequently it was not of the same nature, and if we had concluded that the ecstatic experience was epileptic in nature, this would mean that the thorn in the flesh was not. However, there are several considerations which make even its epileptic nature unlikely.

(1) The thorn in the flesh and the weakness of the flesh are not described in terms which would suggest a diagnosis of epilepsy.

(2) The thorn is usually regarded as a painful experience, but the features of epilepsy do not include pain.

(3) The majority of persons who develop idiopathic epilepsy do so before the age of thirty, and Paul was over forty years of age when the thorn appeared.

(4) An epileptic fit normally lasts only a few minutes and would not lead to an alteration in plans such as Paul suggests his illness did in Galatians 4.13.

The only exception to the first of these considerations which could be made is found in the use of the word *exeptusate* in Galatians 4.14. This is the only use of the verb *ekptuō* in the New Testament. Its literal meaning is 'to spit out' and it was suggested by Krenkel in his *Beiträge* published in 1890 that it referred to the custom of spitting at the sight of sick people in order to ward off the sickness from oneself. Paul is commending the Galatians for not observing this custom and so not rejecting him because of his disease. The disease in which this custom was observed more than for any other was epilepsy. Plautus, for instance, calls epilepsy *morbus qui insputatur*, the disease which people spit upon, in his comedy *Captivi* 3, 4, 18. But Plautus wrote in the late third century B.C., and by New Testament times the designation was applied to many more diseases than epilepsy as we see from Pliny, *Natural History*, 28, 7 where even the sight of a man with a lame right foot was said to provoke spitting. It was not therefore diagnostic of epilepsy. Schlier defends the literal meaning of the word in Galatians 4.14,[35] but it seems preferable to take it metaphorically and to believe that as its literal application widened, so it came to be used in a metaphorical sense of rejection without any necessary accompaniment of the physical act of spitting. In its literal usage it was a pagan word describing a pagan custom, and it is unlikely that Paul would use it in this sense to the Christians of Galatia. It is more likely that he used it simply to mean that they did not disdain or reject him because of his altered physical appearance produced by his illness. However, even if the literal meaning is insisted upon the word does not require the diagnosis of epilepsy, for, as we have seen, it may be applied to other diseases as well. In the absence, therefore, of any unequivocal supporting evidence we conclude that the use of the word here does not imply a diagnosis of epilepsy.

The final argument we must notice in favour of the epileptic nature of the thorn in the flesh is also as old as Krenkel, and has appeared frequently in the literature since his day. The argument is that since great men of history like Alexander the Great, Julius Caesar, Mohammed and Napoleon were epileptic, there is a strong probability that Paul was. The fallacy of this argument becomes obvious if we present it in the form of a syllogism:

> Some great men had epilepsy,
> Paul was a great man;
> ∴ Paul had epilepsy.

The evidence for the diagnosis of epilepsy in the case of almost all the great men of whom it is alleged is very scanty. In the case of Napoleon, for example, Allo mentions that the diagnosis is based on one page in the *Mémoires* of Talleyrand where the author describes how one day in Strasbourg in 1805 the Emperor fainted from fatigue and indigestion.[36] This argument has no firm foundation in fact and is not worth preserving amongst those used to support the case for the epileptic nature of Paul's thorn in the flesh.

By this time it should be clear that there is no real evidence either that Paul was an epileptic, or that his thorn in the flesh was epilepsy.

Before we leave our consideration of nervous disease as a possible cause of the thorn in the flesh, we should refer to a modern medical attempt to explain both Paul's conversion experience and his thorn in terms of one condition in much the same way as epilepsy has been used. Hisey and Beck of Alabama have suggested that Paul's conversion experience was due to a small acute brain haemorrhage which occurred in the area of the brain cortex which is concerned with sight and hearing. The permanent sequel to this haemorrhage was a unilateral loss of vision (hemianopsia) and perhaps minor epileptiform attacks, either of which or both of them together constituted his thorn in the flesh.[37] This theory is open to most of the objections we have already urged against the view that the thorn in the flesh was epilepsy. The fact that at his conversion Paul's sensory impressions of light and sound were shared by his companions excludes any cause which was intrinsic to himself. Cerebral haemorrhages like epileptic visions do not produce profound religious changes in a man, and do not inspire him to turn the world upside down as Paul was accused of doing at Thessalonica in Acts 17.6. The description of Paul's thorn in the flesh is not given in terms which would suggest the effects of brain haemorrhage, and so we must conclude that this theory can be safely discounted as an explanation both of Paul's conversion and his thorn in the flesh.

c. *An affection of the eyes.* The view that an affection of the eyes constituted Paul's thorn in the flesh was originally advanced by Lewin in 1851 when he published the first edition of his two-volume work *The Life and Epistles of St Paul*.[38] This view was adopted by Farrar in his work *The Life and Work of St Paul* published in 1879, although he appears to accept the possibility that the thorn was epilepsy and that Paul suffered from eye disease and epilepsy concomitantly.[39] The basis for this view is found in certain references in Paul's Epistle to the Galatians, and it assumes that the illness he mentions there was identical with the thorn in the flesh described in Second Corinthians. The references are Galatians 4.13 which is interpreted as meaning a physical illness; 4.14 which means that the condition was visible to the Galatians; and 4.15 which suggests that it had something to do with the eyes. Both Lewin and Farrar refer to verses in the Acts and Galatians which might mean that Paul suffered from defective vision and to which we have already referred. In a later edition of his book Lewin added a further point when he derived the word *skolops*, thorn from the words *skellō*, dry up and *ops*, the eye, and suggested that *skolops* therefore meant something which withered the sight, but this derivation did not prove acceptable to later authors.

Lewin's original suggestion, which was accepted by Farrar, was that the disease of the eyes was ophthalmia, which we would call today conjunctivitis. He suggested that Paul's eyes had been inflamed and weakened by the bright light on the Damascus road, and in Damascus itself he had contracted an infection of the eyes which never left him, and whose acute exacerbations incapacitated him from time to time. A more specific description of the nature of the disease which is sometimes given is that of trachoma which was known in the nineteenth century as Egyptian ophthalmia because it was brought to Britain by soldiers returning from the campaign against Napoleon in Egypt in 1801.

This theory sounds plausible until it is examined closely. To place its origin in Damascus as both Lewin and Farrar do, is to forget that the first appearance of the thorn was some years after Paul's Damascus experience. To find support for the theory by adducing apparent examples of poor vision is to place an interpretation on certain incidents which might not otherwise have occurred to commentators. Finally, to interpret Galatians 4.15 of an affection of the eyes is to misconstrue the emphasis of the verse.

This theory that the thorn was a disease of the eyes depends solely on the mention of eyes in Galatians 4.15. Here Paul says to the Galatian Christians in the words of the AV translation, 'I bear you record, that, if it had been possible, ye would have plucked out your own eyes, and have given them to me'. The question then arises whether the reference to eyes in this verse requires us to understand that Paul's disease was one of the eyes, or can be explained in some other way. Lightfoot's comment on this view is that 'the stress of the argument rests on what I cannot but think a mistaken interpretation of Galatians 4.15'.[40] He goes on to point out that the emphasis is not on *your* eyes but on your *eyes*, i.e. not on your healthy eyes as opposed to my diseased ones, but on your eyes as your most precious possession which you would have been willing to give up to make me well again. The NEB adopts this interpretation when it renders this verse by 'I can say this for you: you would have torn out your very eyes, and given them to me, had that been possible'. If this interpretation of the verse is correct, and it appears to be very reasonable and satisfactory, then there is no real basis here for the theory that Paul's thorn in the flesh was an affection of the eyes. This finds confirmation too in the fact that the other evidence quoted from the Acts and elsewhere in the Epistle to the Galatians to suggest that Paul suffered from defective eyesight, can be explained just as adequately on other grounds. We conclude, therefore, that there is no real basis for the view that the thorn in the flesh was an affection of the eyes.

d. *An infective disease.* The final category of physical disease which has been proposed to explain the nature of the thorn in the flesh is that of infective or communicable disease. A number of the conditions suggested can be safely set aside as unworthy of discussion. These include lice infestation, smallpox and leprosy.[41] However, an infective recurrent febrile disease is a strong possibility and appears to have been considered as early as the time of Chrysostom (A.D. 347-407) who was himself a sufferer from 'ague-fever'. In his twenty-sixth homily on Second Corinthians, he comments on 12.10 and gives his opinion that in speaking of the kind of infirmity he had Paul did not speak of fevers, or of any intermittent fever (*periodos*), or of any bodily ailment.[42] Since Chrysostom believed that the thorn in the flesh consisted of persecution we may assume that he is here denying those theories which held it to be a febrile disease, and therefore witnessing to their existence in his own time. Whether this deduction is valid or not, there is no doubt that a febrile disease has been put forward as Paul's thorn in the flesh by modern authors. The two main diseases which have been suggested are brucellosis and malaria.

Brucellosis is the modern name for undulant or Malta fever. This disease is due to the brucella group of bacteria which infect man through the milk of affected goats or cows. It occurs around the shores of the Mediterranean and in other parts of the world, and is characterised by a chronic variable fever which persists for about a year and then clears up, and is accompanied by weakness and sweating with pains in various parts of the body. In 1904 Alexander, who was a medically qualified theologian and held the chair of divinity in the Glasgow College of the Free Church of Scotland, wrote an article in the *Expository Times* identifying Paul's thorn in the flesh as brucellosis.[43] He began by rejecting eye disease, epilepsy and malaria as possible identifications, and went on to describe what he regarded as Paul's three attacks of illness on each occasion of which he asked the Lord to deliver him according to 2 Corinthians 12.8. The first attack was in Cilicia and is described in 2 Corinthians 12.2-8; the second one was at Pisidian Antioch (Acts 13.13-14), and the third at Troas is described in 2 Corinthians 1.8-9. Alexander claimed that these attacks were those of brucellosis and constituted the three occasions on which Paul prayed to be rid of his illness which he mentions in 2 Corinthians 12.8. His article concluded with a table in which he compared the effects of Malta fever, as he called brucellosis, with the features of Paul's infirmity. Neither the details in the table nor the comments in the article suggest that the diagnosis of brucellosis can explain any of the features of Paul's illness any better than malaria can, whilst malaria can explain other details which brucellosis cannot explain. We conclude, therefore, that brucellosis is a less probable diagnosis than malaria.

Malaria was first suggested by Sir William Ramsay as the disease which best explained the nature of Paul's thorn in the flesh in his book *The Church in the*

Roman Empire before A.D. *170* which was first published in 1893.[44] The suggestion arose out of Ramsay's own experience as a traveller and archaeologist in
Asia Minor. In his experience, malarial fever was endemic in the coastal plain
of Pamphylia where he believed Paul contracted this disease. His comments on
the behaviour of the disease are all the more interesting because they were
written before Ross finally demonstrated the transmission of the disease to man
by the bite of the spotted-winged anopheline mosquito in 1897.

We believe that of all the diseases which we have so far considered, malaria
best satisfies the requirements of the two passages where Paul's sickness is described. This can be seen by setting these requirements down one by one and
comparing them with the effects of malaria. We begin with the requirements
of the passage in Second Corinthians, chapter twelve.

(1) The disease should be a physical one, for the thorn was *in the flesh*
(v. 7). No special comment is necessary here, for malaria is a physical disease
caused by the various species of the malarial parasite.

(2) It should produce pain as a thorn does, and also aches like those which
follow a beating about the head and the body with fists (*kolaphizō*, v. 7).
Headache and aches in muscles, bones and joints are typical of malaria.

(3) It should produce depression as opposed to elation (v. 7). Untreated
malaria with its intermittent fever, chills and sweating soon produces a profound state of miserable depression in its victim.

(4) It should not be connected with his conversion experience for it occurred some years after it as we know from the date mentioned in verse two.
Malaria would not be connected with such an experience if its onset was some
years after it had occurred.

(5) It should not be of the same nature as the ecstatic experience described
in the first four verses of the chapter. Although malaria may produce dreams
and even hallucinations, it never produces an ecstatic experience such as Paul
describes out of which comes the apprehension of new truth about God which
he calls revelations (*apokalupseis*, vv. 1 and 7).

(6) It should have a definite point of onset in time which could be described by the aorist tense as in verse seven where Paul says that there was given
(*edothē*) to him a thorn in the flesh. About ten or more days after the bite of an
infected mosquito the first attack of malaria begins with a sudden rise of temperature and shivering.

(7) It should be recurrent and should return to affect him from time to
time. This is the implication of the present tenses in which the two verbs *hupe-
rairō*, be elated, and *kolaphizō*, beat with the fists, are given in verse seven.
Untreated malaria of the type which Paul probably contracted is notorious for
producing relapses at intervals of weeks or months, and even for some years
after the initial infection.

(8) It should be a chronic disease lasting at least fourteen years and even for
the life of the sufferer. Untreated malaria is a chronic disease and has been
known to last for many years. In Paul's case there would also be the possibility
of constant re-infection as he journeyed in lands in which malaria was endemic.

(9) It should be a disease which may be prone to relapse after the kind of
ecstatic experience which Paul describes earlier in the chapter. As the thorn in

the flesh was associated with this experience, so a relapse of malaria is believed often to be provoked by exposure to stress of different kinds, and there seems no reason to deny the possibility that a malarial relapse could follow the stress of an intense ecstatic experience.

We now turn from an examination of the requirements of the passage in Second Corinthians to consider those of the account of Paul's infirmity of the flesh in the fourth chapter of Galatians.

(1) The disease is again required to be a physical one, for it is described as disease (*astheneia*) 'of the flesh' (v. 13), and its effects were visible in the flesh (v. 14). As we have noted already, no special comment is necessary here, for malaria is clearly a physical disease.

(2) It should be a disease which could be contracted in Pamphylia because immediately prior to his visit to Galatia he had been on the low-lying plain which lies between the Taurus mountains and the sea on the south coast of Asia Minor. This plain constituted the region of Pamphylia and particularly in summer was hot, humid and fever-ridden. The fever was malaria carried by the mosquitoes which bred in the swamps and marshes of the well-watered plain. Paul had come from Paphos in Cyprus and had sailed up the river Cestris to land at the port of Perga (Acts 13.13). It was here according to Ramsay that he contracted malaria.

(3) It should be a disease which arises suddenly and lasts long enough to result in a change of plan for an enterprise such as Paul and his companions were engaged upon. It was, therefore, not of short duration as an epileptic fit would be, but a condition which could be expected to last some days if not weeks, and one which would call for a period of convalescence. This requirement fits in with the picture of malaria.

(4) It should be a disease in which the removal of the patient from a hot humid climate to a cooler mountain atmosphere would normally be advised if this were possible. It was well recognised that patients suffering from malaria were more comfortable in a cool mountain climate and ran less risk of further infection when removed from beside the swamps of a fever-ridden plain. This would explain Paul's change of plan which caused him to cross the high Taurus mountains to reach Antioch in Pisidia which stood at an altitude of 3,600 feet above sea-level (Acts 13.14). If he had not contracted malaria he would not have sought a cooler climate and higher ground, and so he was able to say to the Galatians that his first visit to them was the result of illness (v. 13). This illness had caused him to change his plans which did not originally include a visit to Galatia, but because of his illness such a visit became a medical necessity.

(5) It should be a disease which could so alter the appearance of the patient that those who saw him might find his appearance unpleasant and even repulsive, and a reason for spurning him (v. 14). An untreated attack of malaria particularly if it were a severe infection could quickly produce a drawn, haggard, hollow-eyed appearance of the face which would be unpleasant and even repulsive to those unaccustomed to the sight of people severely affected by malaria.

(6) It should be a disease whose cure at that time was unknown, and whose course was unaffected by even the greatest expression of sympathy by the

patient's friends. In the case of the Galatians that sympathy was expressed by their willingness to tear out their very eyes in order to help Paul (v. 15). Although malaria was described by Hippocrates and the Greek physicians, its cure was unknown for many centuries after their time. Sympathy might have influenced the course of a mental illness, but could have no effect on the course of malaria.

(7) It should be a disease from which the patient would recover and be able to travel and to preach between attacks and relapses. Malaria is such a disease.

In the circumstances no conclusion can be final, but it seems reasonable to conclude that a diagnosis of malaria is in keeping with the features required of the thorn in the flesh in the two passages we have just considered, more than that of any other disease which has been suggested. It also has the advantage of harmonising with the earliest tradition which described headache as the nature of the thorn, for headache is a characteristic feature of malaria.

V. THE SIGNIFICANCE OF THE THORN TO PAUL

Whatever the identity of his thorn in the flesh may have been, Paul leaves us in no doubt about its significance for him and his spiritual experience. This appears from the description of the thorn and its effects which he gives in 2 Corinthians 12.7-10, where he has the following things to say about it.

1. *It was a given thing* (v. 7). The appearance of the thorn in the flesh was not an accident due to chance, for chance had no place in Paul's thinking. It was given to him at a definite point in time with a specific relationship to another event, namely the ecstatic experience which he had just described. He tells us that to prevent him from being too elated after that experience 'there was given' (*edothē*) to him a thorn in the flesh. Paul uses an impersonal passive form of the verb as though he were reluctant to say it, but it is clear that he means us to understand that the thorn was given to him by God, for its purpose was to keep him from spiritual pride. It was this realisation of who gave it to him which helped him to accept it and to understand its purpose.

2. *It was a messenger of Satan* (v. 7). Although it was given by God, it was provided by Satan. What God willed for a good purpose was supplied by Satan for an evil one. The word for messenger is *angelos* but it need not have its technical meaning of an angel here, but simply mean an ordinary messenger, and indeed may mean no more than that the thorn was Satanic in origin. The thorn is personified, but that is not to say as Barth understands Paul to say, that 'like a thorn in the flesh, an angel of Satan stands at his side to buffet him'.[45] The thorn in the flesh was sent by Satan to remind Paul of his weakness, and was allowed by God in order to preserve him from spiritual pride. Physical disease is clearly associated with Satanic activity in Scripture. The supreme example in the Old Testament is the affliction of Job (Job 2.1-7), and the outstanding New Testament example is found here in Paul's thorn in the flesh.

3. *It proved a recurrent source of harassment* (v. 7). The thorn came like an enemy to fight with Paul and to belabour him as an opponent might do with

his fists. This is the sense of the verb *kolaphizō* which he uses to describe its effect. It harassed him repeatedly as the present tense of the verb suggests, whenever he was over-elated by the abundance of revelations. It was a source of weakness to him, for its attacks sapped the strength of both his body and his mind. As we learn from his Galatian experience it affected his plans, for it was an attack of the thorn which resulted in the evangelisation of Galatia, an area which had not been in Paul's original plan (Galatians 4.13). Indeed we may go so far as to attribute the letter to the Galatians to his thorn in the flesh, for had he not turned aside into Galatia to recover from his sickness he would not have preached to the Galatians, and there would have been no reason for him to write a letter to them afterwards. This is another example of how God controls the evil intention of Satan in order to produce good.

4. *It was an antidote to spiritual pride* (v. 8). Paul gives this as the primary purpose of the thorn in the flesh, and he repeats it twice as though for special emphasis. The word he uses to describe his temptation to spiritual pride is *huperairomai* which means 'exalt oneself exceedingly'. It was this state to which the thorn in the flesh was to form the antidote. The tense of the verb is again in the present implying that the temptation to excessive elation still recurred although it first came to him fourteen years previously (v. 2). Paul does not say that he had more than one experience of visions and revelations, although there is no reason why he should not have had, and in our discussion of the possible malarial identity of the thorn we indicated how the stress of an ecstatic experience might precipitate an attack of malaria. However, the thorn was given as an antidote to spiritual pride and not to the ecstatic experience which was its cause. Excessive elation or spiritual pride could result simply from the recollection of the experience of ecstasy, and so occur more frequently than the ecstatic experience itself. The antidote was the thorn in the flesh which produced in Paul a feeling of weakness and depression which counteracted his feeling of over-elation and pride. The fact that the thorn was to prevent excessive elation indicates that even if Satan provided it, God still controlled it. Left to himself, Satan would have wished to cripple Paul completely and made him incapable of continuing his work of preaching the gospel, but God prevented this, and did not allow Satan to do more than check Paul's spiritual pride.

5. *It provided a subject for prayer* (v. 8). Paul prayed on three occasions that the thorn might leave him, and there is no reason why we should not take this literally. However, commentators from Chrysostom[46] to Barrett[47] have understood this verse to mean that Paul prayed earnestly and repeatedly about his thorn. We have no note of the three occasions on which he prayed but we may presume that they were related to recurrent attacks of his disease. The prayers were directed to the Lord by whom Paul clearly means Jesus Christ, and as Denney comments,[48] we may be sure that the Lord had full sympathy with those prayers, for he had himself prayed three times that his cup of suffering might pass from him (Matthew 26.39-44). Paul had to persevere in prayer, for he did not receive an answer to his first two prayers, or if he did, he failed to recognise it or to accept it. After the third request he was in no doubt about the Lord's reply, and recognised that reply as final. He describes the reply in the perfect tense *eirēken*, he has said, or as Moule suggests we translate it, his

answer to me has been.[49] It was his answer to Paul when he prayed, it remains his answer, and will remain his answer to the end of Paul's life. Paul accepted this and knew he need not pray about the matter again even though it had not been settled in the way he had expected.

6. *It produced an accession of strength* (vv. 9-10). The answer to Paul's prayer was the unexpected one that the Lord would not remove the thorn in the flesh which was causing weakness, but would supply strength to counteract the weakness. The Lord told Paul in words which the apostle quoted to his readers that his grace (*charis*) was all-sufficient for Paul and would provide for all his needs. In the case of the thorn, his need was for strength (*dunamis*) and the Lord would supply this to show that in human weakness, divine strength finds its full scope, as Knox translates the verb *teleioō*. Grace is not to be identified with strength, for this would be to impoverish the concept of grace. On this occasion grace provided strength for Paul, but it had much more to provide when other occasions with other needs arose. Both the verbs in this statement which Paul quotes are in the present tense to indicate that the all-sufficiency of grace and the perfect provision of strength applied not only to Paul's immediate situation but for the rest of his life. The statement applies equally to us today, for it is an expression of a permanent principle of the Christian life. Paul accepted the assurance of God's help and the implication that the experiences he describes as weaknesses will continue secure in the knowledge that in his time of weakness he will be clothed with God's strength. The verb he uses to describe this is *episkēnoō* which means to pitch a tent (*skēnē*) upon. There may be a reminiscence here of the glory and power of the Lord descending on to the tabernacle in the wilderness in Exodus 40.34-38. In the same way as the glory of God filled the tabernacle of old, so the strength of God would fill the frail tent of Paul's earthly body and strengthen him in the hour of his weakness.

7. *It was a reason for boasting* (v. 9). In this section of the epistle Paul is boasting of certain things which demonstrate the basis of his authority as an apostle. He has in mind those whom he calls false apostles in 11.13 and who are at work in the Church at Corinth and who are boasting of their credentials to be apostles. He answers their boasting by boasting himself, but he finds it distasteful and does it only reluctantly and because the Corinthians have forced him into it (v. 11). His boasting, however, ends in irony. He began by mentioning visions and revelations of the Lord probably because the false apostles at Corinth had claimed to have them, but he refuses to boast about them, preferring to boast about his weaknesses instead (v. 5). He then describes the appearance of the thorn in the flesh and its antidote in the grace and power of the Lord, and concludes that he would now rather boast of the things which caused his weakness than ask the Lord to remove them (v. 9). The reason for this unexpected attitude is to be found in the Lord's reply to Paul's prayer in which he was assured of the strength he needed whenever weakness came upon him, so that he could say that when he was really weak was the time when he was truly strong. So he boasted of the thorn in the flesh not because of the weakness it produced, but because of the accompanying experience of divine strength. It was this experience which really demonstrated how closely he lived to the Lord who was the source of his calling and apostleship.

8. *It caused a change of attitude* (v. 10). As the ground of his boasting had changed from that of having special ecstatic experiences to that of experiencing weakness so that he might know the power of Christ (v. 9), so his attitude to those things which caused his weakness had changed. No one could be ex-pected to welcome sickness, ill-treatment, hardship, persecution and distress even when they are experienced for the sake of Christ, but this is now Paul's attitude to all these things. The word he uses is *eudokeō* which means be well pleased with. Paul had asked for the thorn to be removed, but the Lord had not agreed and had shown him how the weakness it produced could be overcome by the strength provided by divine grace. This changed his attitude to those things which he called his weaknesses, so that he did not now ask for them to be removed nor did he resign himself passively to endure them, but he wel-comed them and took delight in them, for they revealed more to him of the grace of God and the power of Christ than otherwise he would have known. His change of attitude is seen in the final statement of the passage where he declares that he now welcomes those things which cause weakness because he realises that God's power comes to its full strength in weakness as the NEB translates it.

There can be no doubt that the experience of the thorn in the flesh had great significance for Paul. In his brief account of it we are taken into his con-fidence and told of something which was at once a cause of weakness and a source of strength. This paradox of spiritual experience found expression in the words which as we have already noted Paul quotes as the very words of the Lord to him, 'My grace is sufficient for you, for my strength is made perfect in weakness'. The general principle of grace being all-sufficient Paul was already familiar with, but he was now to see the application of the general principle to his state of weakness in which grace was to provide strength. The result was that when he was writing to the Philippian Christians from prison he could tell them that he had learned to be self-sufficient (*autarkēs*) in all circumstances because his sufficiency was of Christ who continually infused strength into him (Philippians 4.11-13). It was experiences like that of the thorn in the flesh which lay behind Paul's confidence in his Lord and contentment in his service what-ever that service may involve.

VI. THE SIGNIFICANCE OF THE THORN FOR US TODAY

Our discussion so far in this chapter could be dismissed as merely antiquarian in nature and in interest, but this would be to misunderstand the real significance of the thorn in the flesh for those who suffer. It not only had meaning for Paul; it also has meaning for us today. Its meaning is all the greater because we do not know the identity of the thorn in the flesh with any certainty. If it were certain that the disease which Paul contracted was malaria, then it might be argued that his experience was significant only for those who suffered from malaria, and not for those who suffered from other diseases. The fact that Paul did not describe the nature of his illness in any detail, but dwelt mainly on the fact that he became ill, makes his experience relevant and meaningful for us today in any situation of sickness in which we may find ourselves.

Paul's refusal to go into details about his thorn in the flesh illustrates a basic difference between the Biblical attitude to events and that which characterises man today, which we need to keep in mind as we come to consider the significance of the thorn in the flesh today. The Bible is concerned with the primary causes of events and usually ignores the secondary ones, whilst modern man is more satisfied with information about secondary causes and does not commonly enquire about the primary ones. In other words, the Bible is more interested in the *why* than in the *how* of events, whilst modern man is more concerned with the *how* and does not ask about the *why*. If Paul suffered from malaria, then modern man would be satisfied to know that he had been exposed to the bite of an infected mosquito on the malaria-infested Pamphylian plain. The Bible, however, is interested in knowing why he fell ill at all. This difference in approach explains why the Bible is not specially interested in identifying the disease or answering those questions whose answers we today would regard as of interest and significance.

1. *An explanation of sickness.* The first thing we can learn from Paul's experience of the thorn in the flesh is that sickness has a meaning which is deeper than the merely physical and pathological. Sickness is a universal human experience and our natural instinct is to deny that it belongs to the ideal scheme of things. We could dismiss Paul's experience with a comment such as this as one which is common to all men, and fail to realise that in this experience of Paul's the veil is temporarily lifted for us and we are allowed to glimpse something of the context and purpose of human sickness.

The first point to notice is that Paul fell ill at all. He was subject to disease and sickness like any other man and had he not been executed would eventually have died of some disease or injury. It is important to note this because the view still prevails in some quarters that when a man becomes a Christian he need never again suffer from any illness, and if he should do so this is a sign that he lacks real faith. One of the main exponents of this view in North America at the end of last century was the Rev A. B. Simpson, a Presbyterian minister in New York City. In 1884 he wrote an influential book on *The Gospel of Healing* in which he maintained that Christ came into the world to save men not only from sin, but also from its physical effects which included disease. Paul's thorn in the flesh gives the lie to this view, and it should be added that Simpson himself died of cerebrovascular disease in 1919 aged 75 years.

The second matter which arises from Paul's experience is that there is always a reason for sickness and the time at which it occurs. Its onset is not an accident. Even if Paul's disease was malaria and was due to the bite of an infected mosquito, it was not an accidental occurrence, the result of his not observing anti-malarial precautions as we might say today. It was given to him as an antidote to spiritual pride. In Paul's case the reason for his sickness was revealed to him, but it is not often revealed to us. This is not to say, however, that a reason does not exist.

The third thing to note has to do with the origin of sickness. We have already mentioned our natural human instinct which refuses to accept disease and sickness as part of the ideal scheme of things, and there is no doubt that such an instinct is right. The Bible associates disease with evil and suggests that disease in the physical realm corresponds to evil in the moral and spiritual, and that disease spoils physical health as evil mars spiritual holiness. This is what Paul means when he regards his disease as a messenger of Satan. It was supplied and sent by the great Adversary of God and goodness. If there were no evil in the world there would be no disease. There were those in Judaism who believed that sickness was the result of the sin of the one who was sick. Rowley has shown that this was not the orthodox Israelite view and that it was not characteristic of the Old Testament as a whole.[50] It receives no support either from the experience of Paul, for his thorn in the flesh did not arise from his personal sin. It was not the result of pride, but was given to him in order to prevent him succumbing to the temptation to be proud because of his special relationship to the Lord because of which he was given visions and revelations. This was the explanation of Paul's sickness. It formed part of his spiritual experience and development.

2. *An illustration of providence.* The thorn in the flesh also provides a good illustration of the working of divine providence. The word providence does not occur in Scripture, but the fact of providence is reflected on its every page, as we see how God provides for his creation and his creature man. In the case of Paul's thorn we may distinguish a number of different aspects of providence.

a. *The control of evil.* The thorn in the flesh was given to Paul by God for a beneficient purpose, but was supplied by Satan for a malicious one. That malicious one was overruled and kept in check by God. Instead of the thorn crippling Paul permanently, it was allowed to operate only periodically as it was required to control Paul's temptation to spiritual pride. It never got out of God's control.

b. *The prevention of sin.* Paul makes it very clear that the thorn was given to keep him from falling into the sin of spiritual pride from becoming too elated at his visions and revelations. It was not given to him as a punishment for sin as in the case of Miriam in Numbers 12.9-15 or Gehazi in 2 Kings 5.27, nor as a test of faithfulness as in the case of Job in Job 2.3-8. It was given to him as a preventive against sin, and he emphasises this point by repeating it in the same verse (2 Corinthians 12. 7).

c. *The provision of strength.* God in his providence actively supplies man with what he needs in his different situations, and this is illustrated by his reply to Paul's prayer. Grace is sufficient to cope with any situation, and provided the strength which Paul needed to overcome his weakness and to counteract the effect of his thorn in the flesh.

3. *A source of reassurance.* The third way in which Paul's experience of his thorn in the flesh has significance for us today is as a source of reassurance and encouragement. It is not usually given to us today to have the curtain drawn back to reveal the purpose and background of our experience of illness as it was for Paul. It is noteworthy that even in his case it was not drawn back at his first request for help. However, he has recorded his experience for our encouragement so that when illness comes to us we can be reassured that it has a providential background, and that in our experience of weakness we, like him, can

expect to know the strength which God's grace in Jesus Christ can provide. This grace working through the various methods of healing which God has provided and revealed to man may produce healing. If it does not produce removal of the disease with which we are afflicted, as it did not in Paul's case, then it will still be true that God's power will increase in us as our strength declines. For us, as for Paul, it is still true that God's power comes to its full strength in weakness.

In a world where men still suffer from sickness and disease, this record of Paul's experience of what he called his thorn in the flesh cannot be dismissed as either simply antiquarian or irrelevant. In the hour of pain and suffering the Christian can know that his experience is not an accident outside the purpose of God resulting from a suspension of his providence, but a situation in which God is active for the Christian's good with everything under control. From this he can draw encouragement and reassurance as he faces his own experience and follows the example of Paul in seeking healing from the Lord.

REFERENCES

1. A. Plummer, *International Critical Commentary on the Second Epistle of St Paul to the Corinthians* (T. & T. Clark, Edinburgh, 1915), p. 349.
2. James Denney, *Expositor's Bible on The Second Epistle to the Corinthians* (Hodder and Stoughton, London, 1903), p. 353.
3. W. Barclay, *The Daily Study Bible on The Letters to the Corinthians* (The Saint Andrew Press, Edinburgh, 1956), p. 192.
4. W. M. Ramsay, *The Bearing of Recent Discovery on the Trustworthiness of the New Testament* (Hodder and Stoughton, London, 1914), pp. 90-95.
5. J. Denney, *Expositor's Bible on The Second Epistle to the Corinthians* (Hodder and Stoughton, London, 1903), p. 168.
6. A. Deissmann, *Paul, A Study in Social and Religious History* (Hodder and Stoughton, 1926), ET, second edition, p. 60, n. 5.
7. E. M. Merrins, 'St Paul's Thorn in the Flesh', *Bibliotheca Sacra*, vol. 64 (1907), p. 661.
8. E. Hennecke, *New Testament Apocrypha* (Lutterworth Press, London, 1965), ET, vol. 2, p. 354.
9. A. P. Stanley, *The Epistles of St Paul to the Corinthians* (John Murray, London, 1876), fourth edition, p. 547.
10. J. B. Lightfoot, *Saint Paul's Epistle to the Galatians* (Macmillan, London, 1902), tenth edition, p. 186.
11. *The Homilies of St John Chrysostom on Second Corinthians* (Parker, Oxford, 1848), ET by J. Ashworth, p. 293.
12. R. A. Knox, *A New Testament Commentary for English Readers* (Burns Oates and Washbourne, London, 1956), vol. 2, p. 204.
13. R. V. G. Tasker, *The Second Epistle of Paul to the Corinthians* (The Tyndale Press, London, 1958), p. 176.
14. L. D. Weatherhead, *Psychology, Religion and Healing* (Hodder and Stoughton, London, 1952), second edition, p. 143.
15. P. H. Menoud in *Studia Paulina* (Bohn, Haarlem, 1953), p. 170.
16. J. Calvin, *The Second Epistle of Paul the Apostle to the Corinthians* (Oliver and Boyd, Edinburgh, 1964), ET by T. A. Small, p. 159.
17. J. Calvin, *The Epistles of Paul the Apostle to the Galatians, Ephesians, Philippians and Colossians* (Oliver and Boyd, Edinburgh, 1965), ET by T. H. L. Parker, p. 79.

18. Estius, *In omnes Pauli Epistolas Commentarii* (Douay, 1614).

19. Cornelius à Lapide, *Commentaria in omnes divi Pauli Epistolas* (Antwerp, 1614).

20. J. B. Lightfoot, *Saint Paul's Epistle to the Galatians* (Macmillan, London, 1902), tenth edition, p. 188, n. 3.

21. Robert Burns, *The Poetical Works* (Oxford University Press, 1904), edited by J. L. Robertson, p. 88, lines 55-60.

22. J. J. Lias, *The Second Epistle to the Corinthians* (Cambridge University Press, 1882), pp. 17-18.

23. V. A. Holmes Gore, 'The Thorn in the Flesh', *Theology*, vol. 32 (1936), pp. 111-112.

24. M. Luther, *Commentary on Saint Paul's Epistle to the Galatians* (William Tegg, London, 1854), ET by E. Middleton, pp. 332-334.

25. J. B. Lightfoot, *Saint Paul's Epistle to the Galatians* (Macmillan, London, 1902), tenth edition, p. 189n.

26. Arndt and Gingrich, p. 750, s.v. *sarx*.

27. P. E. Hughes, *Paul's Second Epistle to the Corinthians* (Marshall, Morgan and Scott, London, 1962), p. 448.

28. R. V. G. Tasker, *The Second Epistle of Paul to the Corinthians* (The Tyndale Press, London, 1958), p. 175.

29. K. Lowther Clarke, *New Testament Problems* (S.P.C.K., London, 1929), chap. 16, 'Was St Paul a Stammerer?' pp. 136-140.

30. M. L. Knapp, 'Paul the Deaf', *The Biblical World*, vol. 47 (1916), pp. 311-317.

31. Marcus Dods in *Hastings' Dictionary of the Bible* (T. & T. Clark, Edinburgh, 1899), vol. 2, p. 94, art, 'Epistle to the Galatians'.

32. Nigel Turner, *Grammatical Insights into the New Testament* (T. & T. Clark, Edinburgh, 1965), p. 94.

33. Galen, *Opera omnia* (ed. C. G. Kühn, Leipzig, 1821-33), vol. 12, p. 592.

34. Eleanor A. Johnson, 'St Paul's "Infirmity"', *Expository Times*, vol. 39, pp. 428-429 (1927-1928).

35. H. Schlier in *Theological Dictionary of the New Testament*, ed. G. Kittel (Eerdmans, Grand Rapids, 1964), vol. 2, p. 448, s.v. *ekptuō*.

36. E. B. Allo, *Saint Paul, Seconde Épître aux Corinthiens* (Librairie Lecoffre, Paris, 1956), p. 317, n. 1.

37. A. Hisey and J. S. P. Beck, 'St Paul's "Thorn in the Flesh": A Paragnosis', *Journal of the Bible and Religion*, vol. 29 (1961), pp. 125-129.

38. T. Lewin, *The Life and Epistles of St Paul* (Bell, London, 1851), vol. 1, pp. 213-219.

39. F. W. Farrar, *The Life and Work of St Paul* (Cassell, London, 1879), Excursus x, pp. 710-715.

40. J. B. Lightfoot, *Saint Paul's Epistle to the Galatians* (Macmillan, London, 1902), tenth edition, p. 191, n. 1.

41. Although Schoeps appears to regard leprosy as a possible diagnosis. See H. J. Schoeps, *Paul* (Lutterworth Press, London, 1961), ET, p. 81, n. 1.

42. *The Homilies of St John Chrysostom on Second Corinthians* (Parker, Oxford, 1848), ET by J. Ashworth, p. 295.

43. W. M. Alexander, 'St Paul's Infirmity', *Expository Times*, vol. 15 (1903-1904), pp. 469-473, 545-548.

44. W. M. Ramsay, *The Church in the Roman Empire before* A.D. *170* (Hodder and Stoughton, London, 1893), p. 63.

45. K. Barth, *Church Dogmatics* (T. & T. Clark, Edinburgh, 1956), ET, vol. 1, part 2, p. 332.

46. *The Homilies of St John Chrysostom on Second Corinthians* (Parker, Oxford, 1848), ET by J. Ashworth, p. 294.

47. C. K. Barrett, *The Second Epistle to the Corinthians* (Black, London, 1973), p. 316.

48. J. Denney, *Expositor's Bible on The Second Epistle to the Corinthians* (Hodder and Stoughton, London, 1903), p. 354.

49. C. F. D. Moule, *An Idiom Book of New Testament Greek* (Cambridge University Press, 1953), p. 15.

50. H. H. Rowley, *The Faith of Israel* (SCM Press, London, 1956), pp. 114-116.

Chapter Twelve

HEALING IN THE EPISTLE OF JAMES

The Epistle of James is one of the most Jewish of the New Testament letters, and yet it is written in excellent Greek. By some authors its language is ranked along with that of the Epistle to the Hebrews as most nearly approaching classical purity of all the books of the New Testament,[1] whilst other authors are not so enthusiastic in their opinion.[2] The epistle is traditionally ascribed to James the brother of Jesus, and there is no adequate reason for rejecting that view. The letter must, therefore, have been written before James died a martyr's death in A.D. 62,[3] and it will reflect the thought and practice of the apostolic Church.

Its character is described by Hunter as pithy, prophetic and practical.[4] It is written in a simple, vivacious and direct style with its meaning often expressed in aphorisms and epigrams, and illustrated by apt similes from nature and from human life. It breathes a prophetic passion and his attitude to the rich in 1.9–11; 2.1-7 and 5.1-4 has earned James the name of the Amos of the New Testament. The practical character of the epistle is shown by the fact that its one hundred and eight verses contain no less than fifty-four imperatives, giving an average of one imperative in every second verse. It is, therefore, an epistle of exhortation and of practice.

The epistle has lain long under the undiscerning condemnation of it by Luther as 'an epistle full of straw' containing little to feed the Christian soul because it contained nothing about the gospel.[5] In fairness to Luther, however, it must be said that he agreed that it contained many good sayings and he thought highly of its emphasis on the law of God. Although we can understand the reason underlying his attitude to the epistle, we can also be glad that it has been preserved in the canon of the New Testament to remind us that the Christian life may begin and continue in faith, but unless the daily life of the believer exemplifies his faith in Christ, then that faith is not a living reality.

Every commentator on this epistle remarks on the difficulty of reducing its contents to a logical plan. Hunter describes it as 'the despair of the analyst'.[6] It appears to consist of a series of sayings and admonitions which follow one another without any apparent order or connection, although the repetition of themes and catchwords has been recognised as giving a measure of unity to the epistle.[7] This feature has led to the suggestion that basically the epistle is a sermon in the Jewish tradition and one which shows many parallels with the Sermon on the Mount for, as Knox remarks, 'James has always kept the Sermon on the Mount well in view'.[8] Another theory regards the epistle as essentially an exposition of the contents and implications of the *Sh^ema* of the sixth chapter of Deuteronomy. Recent study has recognised a substantial literary coherence of the epistle combined with a carefully styled opening thematic statement (1.2-27) and an equally carefully constructed closing section (5.7-20).[9]

Our present concern is with one short paragraph of the closing section of the epistle, namely, James 5.13-18. This paragraph provides one of the few glimpses into the healing practice of the apostolic Church that we have in the epistles of the New Testament. As we have already seen from our study of Paul's mention of the gift of healing in his Corinthian correspondence, it is not easy to construct a coherent picture of the healing activity of the apostolic Church. The few references which we have to it only raise more questions than they answer.

I. WHAT JAMES SAID

When we turn to the paragraph in question, we note first of all that its main subject is prayer. The key verse of the paragraph is verse 16b, 'The prayer of a righteous man has great power in its effects' (RSV). Thus the topic of healing is dealt with in the context of prayer. It is worth emphasising this fact because many commentators have obscured it. Even so sane and learned a commentator as Alfred Plummer introduced his remarks on this paragraph by saying, 'Two subjects stand out prominently in this interesting passage—the elders of the Church and the anointing of the sick.'[10] These two subjects became very prominent in the use made of the passage in the later history of the Church, but we cannot feel that they were as prominent in the mind of the author or of his readers as Plummer suggests. Other commentators characterise the contents of this paragraph as simply a list of miscellaneous Church activities, and they fail to notice the occurrence of the word *prayer* in each verse of the paragraph which ends with the great example of Elijah as a man of prayer whose prayer was effective. Prayer is the basis of all the activities of the Church, and healing is no exception.

The passage before us readily divides into the following three sections:
1. Three groups of people are characterised and advised what to do (verses 13 to 14a).
2. The advice for the third group (the sick) is described in more detail (verses 14b-16).
3. The effectiveness of the recommended procedure is illustrated from the experience of Elijah (verses 17-18).

The three groups of people consist of those who are suffering, those who are cheerful, and those who are sick. James begins by asking, *Is any one among you suffering?* The verb is *kakopatheō* which means 'to be in trouble, to suffer misfortune'. The cognate noun has already been used in verse ten to describe the example of the prophets in suffering affliction. Here in verse thirteen, the emphasis seems to be neither on the misfortune, nor on the suffering, but on the feeling of unhappiness or depression which these produce. The Vulgate was therefore correct in translating this question as '*Tristatur aliquis uestrum?*', which

Knox translated in his English version as 'Is one of you unhappy?' This feeling of unhappiness is in contrast to that of happiness in the latter part of the verse. The first group of people consists of those who are unhappy or depressed because they are in trouble of some kind. This need not be because of their faith as it was in the case of the prophets in the previous paragraph, but because of the misfortune which is the common lot of man in this world.

Is any cheerful? The AV has *merry* which is not a good translation as it refers to outward hilarity rather than inward cheerfulness. The verb is *euthumeo* and like *kakopatheo* is used only three times in the New Testament. The other two occasions are in Acts 27.22 and 25 where Paul exhorts his companions to take heart as they face the wreck of the ship on which they are sailing with all the danger which that entailed. The verb can therefore refer to being in good heart in spite of facing misfortune and being in trouble, and thus indicates an attitude of mind rather than a specific situation in life. James has no particular situation in mind, but has in view all those whose present lot is happiness as opposed to the unhappiness of which he has just spoken.

All men fall into one or other of these two groups. They are either happy or unhappy, in trouble or out of it, facing good fortune or misfortune. It might seem that James had included all men in his two groups, but he goes on to include a third category of people when he asks, *Is any among you sick?* This third category can be regarded as a special section of the first. Here the misfortune or the suffering is due to sickness, and so the unhappiness has a physical cause and this justifies the recognition by James of a third category, those who are sick.

Each of these three groups is recommended to do something. Those who are unhappy as they face misfortune or are in trouble are advised to pray. There is no promise that prayer will remove the cause of the unhappiness, but it will remove the unhappiness itself. Those who are happy and cheerful are recommended to sing hymns of praise to God. In both cases the tense of the verb is the present imperative which implies that the action of praying or praising should go on constantly and repeatedly. The first verb is the common one for praying in the New Testament, *proseuchomai* which always means praying to God. The second verb is one of the three verbs used for singing in the New Testament. There is not as much about singing in the New Testament as we might expect. The three verbs are only used thirteen times between them, and the corresponding nouns only nine times. The verb used here is *psallo* which originally meant to play a stringed instrument with the fingers, and ultimately to sing praise to God without necessarily specifying any instrument or type of hymn.

The procedure recommended for the third group is significantly different from that which was advised for the first two groups. In their case, the procedure did not necessarily involve anyone but the person concerned. Those in the third group, however, are to call in the elders of the Church. This may well be the reason why James separated the sick into a third group rather than leaving them in the first group, since the Church had a special responsibility for the sick. Harnack regarded this verse as 'a clear proof that all aid in cases of sickness was looked upon as a concern of the Church'.[11] As if to underline this difference in procedure where the sick are concerned, James changes the tense from the present imperative to the aorist imperative which implies that the action of the verb is to be done immediately and on one occasion only. The third significant difference in the procedure for the third group is that it is described in more detail than in the case of the other two groups. This leads us on to the second section of the paragraph.

The sick man is to call for the elders of the Church and when they come they are to do two things. They are to pray over the sick man, and they are to anoint him with oil in the name of the Lord (v. 14b). It is difficult to dogmatise on the time relationship of these two procedures. The instruction to anoint with oil is expressed by an aorist participle which usually means that the action it describes precedes that of the main verb which in this case concerns prayer.[12] This is why the RVm translates the clause, 'Let them pray over him, having anointed him with oil in the name of the Lord'. However, since there are numerous examples where the aorist participle appears to denote simultaneous action it is impossible to exclude it here,[13] and so the anointing with oil may have preceded the prayer or may have accompanied it. It should be noted that James gives no guidance on where or how extensively the sick man was to be anointed.

The elders are to pray over (*epi*) the sick man, presumably as he lay in bed, and perhaps as they stretched their hands over him. The type of prayer which would be effective is defined in verse fifteen as 'the prayer of faith'. In response to this believing prayer the sick man will be saved, will be raised up by the Lord, and will be forgiven any sins he has committed. James does not instruct the sick man to confess his sins to the elders and there is no justification here for the practice of auricular confession to a priest. The fact that the prayer of faith will result in healing for the sick man shows that it is not offered in anticipation of his death but of his recovery.

In verse sixteen James appears to ignore the elders, and he goes on to say that all members of the congregation can take part in healing. They should confess their sins to one another, and pray for (*huper*) one another and they will be healed (*iaomai*). These imperatives are again in the present tense implying that both confession and prayer should be the usual activities in the circumstances of sickness. This encouragement to mutual confession and prayer for each other is an indication of the close sympathy and fellowship which existed between members of the early Christian community. It is noteworthy that there is no mention of anointing of the sick with oil in this verse. That appears to be reserved for the elders to do.

The final sentence of this second section (v. 16b) is the key to the whole paragraph. Here James defines the kind of prayer which is the most effective. It is the earnest prayer of a righteous man, of a man who walks daily with God. There has been much debate about James' comment on prayer here, and in particular on the meaning of the present participle *energoumenē*, which the RSV translates 'in its effects'. James uses a less common word for prayer in this sentence. This paragraph is the only one in which he mentions prayer in his epistle and with one exception he always uses the verb *proseuchomai* or its derived noun *proseuchē*. The exception is in our sentence where he uses the noun *deēsis* which denotes prayer which arises out of a definite need, a specific petition for help in a particular situation. He goes on to say that this type of prayer is powerfully effective. This is the plain meaning of James here, but the debate has centred around the participle *energoumenē*, whether it should be construed actively or passively. Mayor, who wrote the classic commentary on this epistle, argues strongly for the passive meaning that the prayer of a righteous man is powerful when it is set in operation by the Holy Spirit.[14] The active meaning on the other hand is that the prayer of a righteous man is powerful in its working, and it is this meaning which is preferred by most modern translations.[15]

James goes on to give an example of one who was a righteous man and whose prayer was effective. He chooses Elijah, an example which is not obviously related to the subject of healing and which is a reminder that the subject of this paragraph is prayer and not healing. Elijah had come to hold a special place in Jewish thought. This is shown by the twenty-eight references to him in the gospels, or nineteen if we exclude the nine parallel references, as well as such passages as Ecclesiasticus 48.1-9. James reminds his readers that Elijah was a man of like nature with themselves, and then goes on to give them an example of his effective prayer.

If we turn to the Old Testament record of the incident to which James alludes in this passage, we find that he has deduced from it certain matters which are not explicitly stated in the text.[16] We are not told in the text, for example, that Elijah prayed for drought. We are told in 1 Kings 17.1 that he was able to declare on the authority of the God of Israel that there would be a drought, and we may deduce his prayer from the phrase 'before whom I stand'. The reference to the length of the drought as three and a half years which is also mentioned in Luke 4.25 is a deduction from 1 Kings 18.1 which speaks of the third year. Finally, there is no reference to Elijah's prayer for the end of the drought in the Old Testament narrative, although it may be assumed that it was offered.

II. WHAT JAMES MEANT

In the previous section we have seen what James said in his short paragraph. We now turn to ask what he meant by what he said. His injunctions to the first two groups of people, those who were unhappy and in trouble and those who were cheerful even though they might be in trouble, are clear. Prayer and praise cover all life's situations and sanctify both sorrow and joy for God's people.

In the case of the third group, those who are sick, James' meaning is not at once clear. There are several words and phrases which he uses which need closer examination in order to discover what they mean.

1. *Sickness.* First of all we must ask what James understood about the nature and cause of sickness. He uses two different words for sickness in this paragraph and both of them describe the physical effect of illness rather than sickness itself. This is typical of the words used of sickness in most languages, for such words are descriptive of the effect of sickness rather than indicative of its

nature. This derives from the obvious fact that men experience the symptoms which sickness produces before they reflect on its nature, and explains why the traditional names for many diseases are descriptions of their symptoms rather than indications of their nature or cause.

The first word he uses is the verb *astheneō* which occurs in verse fourteen. Its basic meaning is 'to be weak', and presumably it came to be applied to sickness because of the bodily weakness it caused. This verb and its derivatives form the commonest words used for sickness in the New Testament. The second word used by James occurs only three times in the New Testament. It is the verb *kamnō* whose present participle is employed in verse fifteen to describe the sick man on his bed. The verb originally meant 'to work', then it meant 'to be weary as the result of work' (as in Hebrews 12.3 and Revelation 2.3), then 'to be weary from sickness', and finally 'to be sick'. Although these two words have different etymologies there is no valid reason for distinguishing between them in usage. They both mean 'to be sick'. Outside the New Testament, however, a further extension of meaning of *kamnō* occurs and the verb comes to mean 'to die' as in Wisdom 4.16 and 15.9, and this has been used to justify basing the practice of extreme unction on verse fifteen. The sick referred to in this verse are thus taken to be those who are about to die. It is true that the verb in its past tenses was used as a description of the dead, 'but as there is no instance of the present participle conveying the meaning of "the dying", it is most improbable that this is the sense here, and that the writer means to suggest that the sufferer is *in extremis*'.[17] Even apart from the question of tense usage, the context would appear to exclude any extension of meaning of *kamnō* here. If we accept the extended meaning of this verb in verse fifteen as Arndt and Gingrich (p. 403) suggest we may, then the meaning of the passage would be that although Christians should call in the elders of the Church for all sickness (v. 14), only those who were actually dying would be healed. This is unlikely to be what James meant, and so we see no real reason for distinguishing between the meaning of these two verbs in this context.

What kind of sickness did James have in mind? This question is of importance because some authors maintain that what James describes here is exorcism and not the healing of physical disease. The main clue lies in the usage of the verb *astheneō* and its derivatives, as we may ignore the rare verb *kamnō* in this case. A close examination of the usage of the verb *astheneō* and its derived forms in the New Testament will show that these words are always applied to physical disease when they are used in a pathological sense and do not simply mean weakness. In at least three cases the condition they describe is carefully distinguished from demon possession. These are in the verses Luke 4.40; 8.2 and Acts 5.16. In view of this clear indication of usage, we feel that we are justified in concluding that James meant physical sickness when he spoke of anyone being sick in the community to which he wrote. The nearest we can come to the type of sickness which James had in mind is to say that it appears to have been sickness of acute onset, and which confined the sick one to bed or at least to the house so that he could not go to the elders but had to call them to come to him (v. 14).

The important question here, however, is the relationship between sickness and sin. It is frequently maintained that the Old Testament view is that sickness is due to personal sin, and that this is the view which James sets forth in this paragraph. Neither of these suggestions can be sustained. As Rowley points out the rigid equation of desert and fortune or of sin and suffering 'is nowhere characteristic of the Old Testament as a whole'.[18] Likewise whoever insists that James teaches such a rigid doctrine has missed the significance of the particle 'if' in verse fifteen. James says that if the sickness is the result of some personal sin, then this sin will be forgiven the sick man in response to the prayer of faith of the elders. The clear implication of this is that there are some illnesses which are due to personal sin, and there are some which are not. It is certainly true that there is an organic connexion between sickness and sin, for there would be no sickness in the world if there were no sin, but we cannot go on to say that a man's sickness is always due to his own personal sin. This is contrary to human experience and is certainly not what James says here.

2. *Healing*. James speaks of healing only twice in this paragraph and uses a different word each time. In verse fifteen he uses *sōzō* and in verse sixteen he uses the verb *iaomai*. We have already discussed the meaning and usage of these two words in chapter four,[19] and we do not need to do so again. We should note, however, that in verse fifteen we are given the elements of a definition of healing. Here we are told that in response to the prayer of faith three things will happen:

(1) The sick man will be saved,
(2) he will be raised up by the Lord, and
(3) he will be forgiven any sins he may have committed.

Here we have the three basic components of the Christian definition of healing. First, we are told that the sick man will be saved. The verb is *sōzō* which may mean physical healing or spiritual salvation which together compose the complete healing of the whole man. In this case the physical meaning predominates because the forgiveness of sins which forms an essential part of spiritual salvation is specified separately. Also, we are never told in the New Testament that a man will be saved in a spiritual sense by prayer, whilst we are often told of physical healing in response to prayer. Furthermore, physical healing would naturally precede the raising up which forms the second part of the definition. The first part of the definition means, therefore, the healing of physical disease.

The second clause of the definition says that in response to the prayer of faith, the Lord will raise up the sick man. The word *egeirō* is the usual one used for the physical resurrection of our Lord from the dead, but it is plainly not used of raising from the dead in our paragraph. In Mark 1.31 it is used of the healing of Simon Peter's mother-in-law, and in Matthew 9.6 of the cure of the paralytic. We therefore take it in a physical sense here. The Lord not only heals the sick of his disease, he also raises him up from his bed and puts him on his feet again with new strength and vitality.

The final part of the definition is clearly spiritual and so completes the definition of healing by extending it to the whole of man's being. If the sick man has committed sins he will be forgiven by God. There is no suggestion that the sick man may never have sinned, but only that his present sickness may or may not be connected with his sins. The tense of the verb is the perfect which suggests that he may be in a state of having committed some sin and the present sickness may be a consequence of this. If this is so, then his cure will include forgiveness.

Healing in the Christian meaning of the term may be summed up in the three following propositions:

(1) Deliverance from physical disease,

(2) Restoration of bodily strength, and

(3) Forgiveness of sins.

James is quite clear that healing is always more than physical, and that it includes the whole man.

3. *The elders of the Church.* The sick man was to call for the elders of the Church. Who and what were these *presbuteroi*? We may be quite certain that they are not priests in the sacerdotal sense, for the New Testament word for this office is *hiereus* which is never applied to a separate class of people in Christian usage, but only to the saints or Christian believers in general. In this sense all Christians are priests (1 Peter 2.5, Revelation 1.6; 5.10 and 20.6). Having said this, however, we must add that we know very little about the elders of the New Testament Church in spite of all the intensive study of the origins of the ministry of the Church in recent years. In contrast to his account of the appointment of the first deacons in the sixth chapter of Acts, Luke says nothing about how elders came to be appointed. This suggests that they were not a novelty in the apostolic Church, and when we put this together with the fact it is at Jerusalem that we first hear of elders (Acts 11.30), it seems probable that the Church organised itself along the same lines as the synagogue, at least in its early years. We may conclude, therefore, that the synagogue custom of choosing a body of senior men or elders to have oversight of its worship and well-being was also followed by the early Church. It is a body such as this to which James refers in this passage. The *ekklēsia* or Church of which they were elders was the local Christian community or congregation which was the local embodiment and expression of the Church universal.

Why were the elders called in? Were they called in as representatives of the community they led, or did this healing function belong to their office as elders? This is an important question for the healing ministry of the Church today. In so far as the office of elder is defined in the New Testament there is no suggestion that healing the sick was a specific function of this office. There is no reference to healing as a function of elders or bishops in the Pastoral Epistles although these terms describe the same office. In the Corinthian Church healing gifts were not associated with the elders, but were given to those to whom the Holy Spirit willed to give them (1 Corinthians 12.9, 28 and 30). Even in our present passage James says that healing is possible for all members of the Church to practise in verse sixteen, whilst in verses fourteen and fifteen he associates healing with the elders alone. The most probable view is that the elders were called in as the representatives of the congregation and not because of any healing function which was inherent in their office. Intercession for others was part of their pastoral care and duty certainly, but it was a duty which was shared by every member of the congregation.

This view is the one most in line with the evidence of the New Testament and need not be disturbed by the exhortation of Polycarp to the elders of the Church at Philippi to care for the *astheneis* which may mean either the weak or the sick (Polycarp to the Philippians, 6.1), nor by the eighth canon of the *Canons of Hippolytus.*[20] This canon suggests that anyone who manifestly possessed a God-given gift of healing might request ordination as a presbyter on this ground. Even if Hippolytus Romanus was the author of these *Canons*, they are not earlier than the end of the second century A.D. Whatever their date may be, it is difficult to know the relationship of the practice they recommend to the advice given by James in our passage. In the absence of evidence that a healing gift was recognised as a qualification for the office before the time that James wrote his letter, it seems more reasonable to conclude that the *Canon* was based on James than that both were based on a practice for which there is no evidence. This *Canon* need not therefore disturb our conclusion that the elders of the Church were to be called to the bedside of the sick as the representatives of the Church, rather than those with special gifts of healing.

The elders were to be summoned as a body, and it is of interest to note that Luke always refers to the elders in the Acts as a body and never as individuals. James does not envisage an individual elder acting as a healer in private, but only of healing as a corporate function of the body of elders of a congregation. Bengel in his comments on this passage speaks of the elders as the highest Medical Faculty (*Facultas Medica*) of the Church and deplores its loss because of lack of faith.[21]

4. *Prayer.* Prayer is the main topic of this paragraph, and in verses fifteen and sixteen it is specifically stated that prayer will heal the sick. It is important therefore that we should understand what type of prayer James means here. He sets this out in three phrases:

(1) 'The prayer (*euchē*) of faith'(v. 15).
(2) 'The prayer (*deēsis*) of a righteous man' (v. 16).
(3) 'He prayed fervently (*proseuchē proseuxato*)' (v. 17).

We may deduce the type of prayer which James regards as effective for healing from an examination of these phrases. It is to be prayer based on faith and proceeding from faith, without doubting (cp. James 1.6). It is to be the prayer of a righteous man, a man who is in a right relationship with God and stands before him as Elijah did. It is to be specifically related to the need out of which it arises. This is the significance of the word *deēsis* used in the second phrase. It is to be a prayer for the healing of the sick man to whom the elders have been called, and not vague intercession for the sick in general. Finally, if the prayer is to be effective it is to be made fervently. This phrase in verse seventeen is one of the Hebraisms in James, reflecting the infinitive absolute in Hebrew. *Proseuchē proseuxato* means literally that 'he prayed with prayer', and is a means of expressing the intensity of his prayer. We may summarise the type of prayer which James regards as effective in healing as that which is earnest and believing, which is specifically directed to its object, and which springs from the offerer's close relationship to God. It should be noted too that the prayer arises out of the faith of the elders. There is no mention of faith on the part of the sick man although faith of some kind is implied in his initial act of calling in the elders.

The unqualified nature of the two statements in verses fifteen and sixteen that prayer will result in healing is worth noting. However, we may not draw from this unqualified relationship of the prayer of faith and healing, the apparent corollary that if healing does not occur then either the prayer has not been earnest enough or the faith has not been strong enough. This apparently sound logic is not the logic of faith, for there may be other reasons why healing has not occurred. This is why most commentators tone down these statements by saying that we must understand the unexpressed qualification that healing will only occur if it is the will of God. This is a legitimate qualification and is in accord with the teaching of the rest of the New Testament. For instance, we have already seen how Paul prayed three times to be healed of his thorn in the flesh according to 2 Corinthians 12.8, but healing was not granted. God had another reason why his affliction should continue, and so healing in his case did not include the removal of the disease, but a new use for it in Paul's relationship to God and to his fellow-men.

5. *Anointing with oil.* We come now to one of the most interesting questions associated with our passage, although it cannot be regarded as the most important. When the elders were called in by the sick man they were to anoint him with oil. James gives the impression that this was not a new procedure he was suggesting, but simply what he would expect to be the normal custom with which his readers would be familiar. Had it been something new, we would have expected him to give more details about it and to explain its significance.

The oil specified was olive oil (*elaion*) which was freely available in the Mediterranean world of the first century A.D. as it is today. It would be readily available in every household, for it was used for toilet, dietetic and medicinal purposes, as well as in domestic lamps and religious rites. Two different words are used in the New Testament for the application of oil to the body. *Aleiphō* is the humbler one and usually means to apply oil for toilet purposes (Matthew 6.17 and Luke 7.46). The other word is *chriō* which is the ritual and official word for anointing with oil and is used only in the figurative sense of anointing by God to denote his commissioning such as he gave to his Son Jesus Christ. Here in James the humbler word is used, and the same word occurs also in Mark 6.13 which is the only other reference in the New Testament to anointing the sick with oil.

Two views have been taken of the significance of anointing the sick with oil in this passage. The first view is that it was a medical procedure, and the oil was being used medicinally. James was saying that normal medical methods should be used in the name of the Lord along with believing prayer. On this view we should translate the clause in verse fourteen in modern terms such as those suggested by Sugden, 'Let them pray over him, giving him his medicine in the name of the Lord'.[22] If it be objected that this instruction of James could not now apply to all cases of sickness, for olive oil was specific in only a few, then the evidence is that in the first century A.D. anointing with oil was a common supportive procedure in many forms of systemic illness. Our most complete information on medical practice at this time, albeit from a Roman source and giving an account of Greek medical practice, is the treatise *De Medicina* by Celsus. In the first four books of this work there are numerous references to the use of anointing with oil (*unctio*) in the treatment of different systemic diseases, and a general statement that 'it is desirable that even in acute and recent diseases the body should be anointed' (Book II, 14, 4). It is this type of disease which James appears to be referring to in our paragraph.

The second view regards the anointing with oil as a religious act with no medical significance. Those who hold this view usually regard the act of anointing as partly or wholly sacramental in character, and so this view finds its ultimate development in the sacrament of extreme unction. This name may refer either to the anointing as the last of the three sacramental unctions of the Roman Catholic Church with the others given at baptism and confirmation, or to the anointing as given to one who is *in extremis* and about to die. In neither case has the name any warrant in this passage which speaks of anointing the sick in anticipation of healing, not of the dying in anticipation of death. In recognition of this fact, the second Vatican Council suggested the name 'anointing of the sick' might replace that of 'extreme unction'. [23]

There is probably not enough evidence in this passage to allow us to decide which of these two views is correct. However, an analysis of the usage of the verb *aleiphō* in the New Testament appears to support the medical view rather than the religious one. This verb is used nine times, once here and eight times in the gospels. It is never used in the gospels of anointing for a religious purpose, but only for toilet or medical purposes. In seven instances it is used for smearing or rubbing the body with oil for toilet purposes. The remaining instance of its use is in Mark 6.13 where it refers to anointing for healing. This verse describes the practice of the Twelve after they had been commissioned and sent out by Jesus to preach and heal. Mark says that 'they cast out many demons, and anointed with oil many that were sick and healed them' (RSV). There is a distinction here which should be noted. In spite of several contrary opinions, including that of Schlier,[24] anointing with oil is never used as part of the practice of exorcism in the New Testament, and Mark here carefully distinguishes the anointing with oil of the sick from the casting out of demons. This means that anointing with oil was used only for the healing of physical disease in the New Testament. This fact would be difficult to explain on the view that such anointing was religious in nature for, if this were so, there is no reason why its use should be confined to one type of disease or one kind of situation. Further, if anointing with oil had only religious significance and not medical, it is difficult to explain why it was so often omitted, and in particular why it was never practised by Jesus himself, but only by his disciples.

In the history of the Church there were several changes in the practice of anointing the sick with oil which are more readily understood if the oil is regarded as a medicine rather than the symbolical material of a religious rite. One very significant change came in the ninth century when in A.D. 852 anointing of the sick with oil was finally restricted to the members of the priesthood. This was done first by Hincmar, the archbishop of Rheims, in that year, but the restriction soon became universal throughout the Church.[25] Prior to this, anointing of the sick had been performed freely by laymen and laywomen who were either the sick themselves or the friends of the sick. The late origin of this restriction of the practice to presbyters in the history of the Church is difficult to understand, if from the beginning it had been regarded as a religious rite. It means that for almost eight centuries the practice of the Church was in conflict with the clear instruction of James that presbyters or elders should anoint the sick and the ordinary members of the Church need not. Prayer and confession were all that was required of Church members for healing (v. 16). For the Church therefore to leave anointing to be carried out by the sick or their friends was contrary to what the instructions of James required. This would suggest that anointing of the sick with oil was not regarded by the Church as a religious rite whose exact observance was binding on it from the beginning and for all time.

There were also two further changes in the practice and usage of anointing which indicate an acceptance of the fact that the oil frequently failed to heal, and such an acceptance is more readily understood if the oil was regarded as a medicine which would often fail to heal rather than a ritual symbol which was not expected to fail. The first of these changes was the introduction of measures which were designed to supplement or boost the efficacy of the oil. The oil came to require special consecration for the purpose of anointing. At first this was carried out by a layman, but eventually required to be done by a bishop. The oil might be taken from the lamps used in churches, or might be stored in martyrs' tombs or mixed with the relics of saints, all in order to increase its efficacy. The second of these changes was the association of anointing with oil, not with healing, but with dying. This occurred about the twelfth century and marked the final loss of faith in the oil as a medicinal agent. This loss of faith reflected a change in medical opinion about the oil, which would have had no influence on the practice if it had been only a religious rite with no medical significance.

We cannot escape the feeling that a reference by James to contemporary medical practice to illustrate a principle has been mistaken for a binding instruction on the Church. James held that healing should be by a combination of medical and non-medical methods, and in illustration referred to the contemporary medical method of anointing sick people with oil which he said the elders should now do in the name of the Lord Jesus Christ and with prayer. This illustration has been taken to mean that the contemporary method described by James should be permanently used in the healing ministry of the Church even though it would eventually fall out of use in medical healing, as more effective medicines and procedures were discovered and used. But Jesus never used this method of anointing and James attributed healing to the prayer of faith which accompanied it rather than to the application of the oil. The fact is not without significance that the Church did not appear to understand the practice of anointing, and eventually came to change its meaning from that of a prelude to healing to that of a preparation for death. This would explain why the modern Church commonly neglects the practice altogether, and commonly shows some embarrassment when the subject is raised.

III. WHAT JAMES DID NOT SAY

In any study of healing in this letter, significance must also be given to what
James did not include in his description of what to do in cases of sickness.
When we consider his omissions it is clear that he did not intend to give a
complete account of the healing practice of the apostolic Church, and this was
for the very good reason that he was writing to those who were already familiar with its methods. It is unfortunate for us that we are not in a similar
position. There are three topics in particular with which James does not concern himself.

1. *The laying on of hands.* James makes no mention of the common method
of touching or the laying on of hands for the healing of sickness which was
used by Jesus and the apostles. According to the New Testament records this
method was used far more often than anointing with oil. James must have seen
hands laid on the sick to heal them, but he does not include this procedure in
his advice to the sick and those who sought to heal them. It is true, of course,
that anointing involves touching the sick and so it may be argued that James
did recognise touching as a means of healing. However, the method he described was not the simple laying on of hands that Jesus had used, but one
which involved in addition the application of oil to the body.

2. *Demon possession.* There is no mention of demon possession or of exorcism in this passage. The sick are described by the verb *astheneō* which is never
used to describe those who are demon-possessed in the New Testament. Exorcism in the New Testament never includes touching the possessed person and
since anointing with oil would involve touching the person it would not be
used as a means of exorcism.

3. *Gifts of healing.* In 1 Corinthians 12.9 Paul spoke of 'gifts of healing', and
how these were bestowed by the Holy Spirit on whom he will, and how they
were to be used for the benefit of all members of the body of Christ. James does
not mention such gifts, but assumes that all elders and even all members of the
Church can heal. His emphasis is on the place of prayer in healing rather than
on special gifts. There need be no real contradiction here. The presence of some
with a special gift of healing does not mean that healing is necessarily confined
to them, nor that all cannot share in healing. In any case we do not know how
extensively these gifts were present in the apostolic Church, for they are only
mentioned in connection with the Church at Corinth. The fact is that James
does not mention them here.

IV. WHAT JAMES TEACHES

There are several principles concerning the Church and the healing of the sick
which are embedded in this paragraph we have been considering.

1. *The Church has a concern for the sick.* This is the clear implication of James'
instruction to the sick man to send for the elders of the Church. They are to be
summoned because they are concerned. This is the first obvious deduction from

this passage. It is true that the primary application of the instruction is to the sick of the Christian community, just as the original commission of Jesus was to heal the sick of the lost sheep of the house of Israel in Matthew 10.5-8. In practice, however, the Church has never been able to confine its healing ministry to its own sick. This appears in the Acts and has increasingly appeared in the history of the Church, especially in missionary situations.

In the minds of many people today the concern of the Church is one that is essentially peripheral to the main task of healing. The minister stands aside whilst the doctor does the real work of healing. Finally, when the doctor has done all he can, the minister is allowed to come in with the assumption that no more healing is possible and that all the minister can do is to prepare the sick man for death. This is not the view which James takes here. The clear implication of this passage is that the concern of the Church is not peripheral but central.

2. *Healing is part of the normal work of the Church.* There is no suggestion in this passage that the healing work of the Church was something abnormal or extraordinary. It was part of the normal routine of Church life. If a man fell sick he sent for the elders of the Church, and they came without any apparent reluctance or embarrassment to carry out a recognised procedure which was normally expected to result in the healing of the sick man who had called them.

3. *Healing is based within the Christian community.* Healing is here based within the Christian community. It was to be practised by the elders and by the ordinary members of the Church. This continued to be the case for many centuries of the history of the Church. It was only with the rise and organisation of the medical and nursing professions that the basis of healing moved out of the Church into the community at large. It is this change which has resulted in so much uncertainty in the Church's attitude to healing and produced the tendency for the Church to withdraw from its healing ministry or to identify it with the practice of certain procedures which are usually included under the category of 'faith-healing'.

4. *The healing ministry of the Church includes all methods of healing.* If our interpretation of the reference to anointing with oil in this passage is correct, then James is here recommending the employment of both physical and non-physical methods of healing. Even if this interpretation is not correct the point still remains in view of all the benefits of modern medical healing. These benefits are the gift of God to suffering humanity and are to be used in the healing of the sick. They are applied by Christian doctors in the course of their daily work, and therefore are included in the healing ministry of the Church. The Church uses all methods in its ministry of healing, whether they be medical or non-medical. The method used in any particular case will depend on the training of the person concerned. Methods which need medical knowledge or skill can only be applied by persons who are medically trained. Every method of healing is represented amongst the members of the Church, and when those members are practising the method of healing in which they are trained they are sharing in the healing ministry of the Church. All methods of healing are thus available for the healing ministry of the Church and should be included within it.

5. *Sickness and healing always have more than a physical dimension.* James reminds us that there are more dimensions to sickness and healing than the purely physical. This is implied in the need for prayer and the involvement of the Christian community in cases of sickness. The other dimensions have been obscured by the Cartesian separation of body and soul which still dominates much of popular thought today. Sickness has always more than a physical dimension even if it be so minor as the common cold. It always has mental, social and spiritual dimensions, and this paragraph of James reminds us of all of these. Similarly healing cannot be confined to the physical or medical dimension, but must include the other dimensions too.

The paragraph which has formed the basis of our study is short, but the history of its exegesis reveals that much has been based on it and much read into it. It has been the main proof text for auricular confession to a priest, unction, extreme unction and so-called faith-healing. It would be tragic if the Church continued to treat this passage as it has treated it in the past and missed what we believe to be its clear teaching. We may summarise that teaching in the following terms. The Church has a healing function to perform in all cases of sickness. This function includes the use of all forms of healing through those who are professionally qualified and those who are not. All methods are to be applied in the name of Jesus Christ and supported by prayer. In this way and in other practical ways all members of the Christian community can share in the healing of the sick. This healing of the sick is not confined to the repair of the body or the saving of the soul but includes both in the redemption of the whole man.

REFERENCES

1. J. B. Mayor, *The Epistle of St James* (Macmillan, London, 1892), p. clxxxix.
2. C. L. Mitton, *The Epistle of James* (Marshall, Morgan and Scott, London, 1966), p. 234.
3. Flavius Josephus, *Antiquities of the Jews*, 20:9.1.
4. A. M. Hunter, *Introducing the New Testament* (SCM Press, London, 1957), second edition, p. 167.
5. M. Luther, *Preface to the New Testament*, concluding paragraph.
6. A. M. Hunter, op. cit., p. 165.
7. W. E. Oesterley, *The General Epistle of James* in *The Expositor's Greek Testament* (Hodder and Stoughton, London, 1910), vol. 4, p. 407.
8. R. A. Knox, *A New Testament Commentary for English Readers* (Burns Oates and Washbourne, London, 1956), vol. 3, p. 111.
9. F. O. Francis, 'The Form and Function of the Opening and Closing Paragraphs of James and 1 John', *Zeitschr. f. die Ntl. Wissenschaft*, vol. 61 (1970), pp. 110-126. Cp. also P. B. R. Forbes, 'The Structure of the Epistle of James', *Evangelical Quarterly*, vol. 44 (1972), pp. 147-153.
10. Alfred Plummer, *Expositor's Bible on St James and St Jude* (Hodder and Stoughton, London, 1891), p. 323.
11. A. Harnack, *The Mission and Expansion of Christianity* (Williams and Norgate, London, 1908), ET vol. 1, p. 121.
12. See J. H. Moulton, *A Grammar of New Testament Greek* (T. & T. Clark, Edinburgh, 1963), vol. 3 (by Nigel Turner), p. 79.

13. It is accepted as 'a contemporaneous aorist' by J. R. Ropes in *The International Critical Commentary on the Epistle of St James* (T. & T. Clark, Edinburgh, 1916), p. 305, and by J. Adamson in *The New International Commentary on the Epistle of James* (Eerdmans, Grand Rapids, 1976), p. 197.

14. J. B. Mayor, *The Epistle of St James* (Macmillan, London, 1892), pp. 177-179.

15. See the excursus on the translation of *energoumenē* in J. Adamson, op. cit., pp. 205-210. C. L. Mitton in his commentary thinks it is unimportant to decide between the two possible renderings (op. cit. p. 206).

16. See C. L. Mitton, *The Epistle of James*, pp. 207-208.

17. R. V. G. Tasker, *The General Epistle of James* (Tyndale Press, London, 1957), p. 133.

18. H. H. Rowley, *The Faith of Israel* (SCM Press, London, 1956), p. 114.

19. See above, pp. 31-32.

20. R.-G. Coquin, 'Les Canons d'Hippolyte', *Patrologia Orientalis* (Firmin-Didot, Paris, 1966), vol. 31, fasc. 2, p. 360.

21. J. A. Bengel, *Gnomon Novi Testamenti* (1742), in loc.

22. E. H. Sugden, *Abingdon Bible Commentary* (Epworth Press, London, 1929), p. 1337.

23. W. M. Abbott (editor), *The Documents of Vatican II* (Geoffrey Chapman, London, 1967), p. 161.

24. H. Schlier in *Theological Dictionary of the New Testament*, ed. G. Kittel (Eerdmans, Grand Rapids, 1964), vol. 1, p. 231, s.v. *aleiphō*.

25. W. E. Scudamore in *A Dictionary of Christian Antiquities*, ed. by W. Smith and S. Cheetham (John Murray, London, 1880), vol. 2, p. 2004, art. 'Unction'.

Part Four

HEALING IN THE CHURCH TODAY

OUR STUDY of the teaching and practice of the apostolic Church in Part Three has shown that the apostles and others associated with them healed men and women of disease, and also on occasion raised them from the dead. It follows, therefore, that they had the authority and the ability to heal which they must have derived from Jesus Christ, their Risen Lord.

Nevertheless, we have seen that the use of this power of healing was not a prominent feature of the life of the apostolic Church, and was not always manifest even when a clear indication for it was present. Miracles of healing were not so marked a feature of the book of Acts as they were of the gospels, even though the period of activity of the apostolic Church recorded in that book is about ten times longer than that of the earthly ministry of Jesus. We did not read there of any failures such as occurred in the case of the epileptic boy in the gospels where it was said in Matthew 17.16 of the disciples that 'they could not heal him'. However, in the epistles it is recorded that Paul and three of his colleagues remained unhealed even though the Church had the power to heal them.

The question now arises whether the modern Church still possesses the authority and the ability to heal men and women of disease. All down the centuries of the history of the Church there have been claims that men and women have been healed just as they were in the gospels and in the apostolic age. The early Christian apologists pointed to the miracles of healing by the Church as proof of the divine origin of Christianity, and the Roman Church recognised and accepted them as the required proof of sanctity prior to the beatification and canonisation of some faithful member of that Church.

In dealing with the question of healing in the Church today we begin by discussing in some detail the healing commission which Jesus gave to the Twelve and the Seventy disciples as recorded in the gospels. We do so because of the frequency with which this commission to heal is referred to in the modern literature on the healing ministry of the Church. Having decided about the validity of this commission for the Church today, we then go on to discuss the healing ministry of the modern Church in the light of the principles and practice of such a ministry set forth in the New Testament.

Chapter Thirteen

THE HEALING COMMISSION TO THE DISCIPLES

Jesus commissioned his disciples to heal the sick on two separate occasions in the gospels. The first occasion was in the Mission Charge to the Twelve disciples, and the second in Mission Charge to the Seventy.

I. IN THE MISSION CHARGE TO THE TWELVE

The record of the Mission Charge to the Twelve is given in the synoptic gospels in Matthew 10.5-14; Mark 6.7-11 and Luke 9.1-5. The record varies in length and detail between the three gospels but there can be no doubt of its authenticity, for it was written and published within the lifetime of at least some of those to whom the charge was given. Of the mission itself, T. W. Manson writes that it 'is one of the best attested facts in the life of Jesus'.[1]

The version of the Charge which we shall consider is that given by Matthew since he gives it in the fullest form, and his version is the common one quoted in the literature on healing. He places the Mission Charge in the context of the compassion of Jesus. Jesus saw the crowds harassed and helpless because they were leaderless without a shepherd (Matthew 9.35-38). They were like a harvest without labourers to gather it in, and so Jesus proceeds to appoint labourers and give them their instructions. It is these instructions which constitute the Mission Charge.

The content of the Mission Charge consists of seven imperatives.

1. *Go . . . to the lost sheep of the house of Israel* (Matthew 10.5-6). The commission of the disciples was confined to the house of Israel as Jesus' own original commission was according to Matthew 15.24. They were not so much as to set foot on any road which led to a Gentile centre of population such as a city of the Decapolis. They might use a road which led to a Samaritan city, but they must pass by the city when they reached it and go only to the lost sheep of the house of Israel. As Jesus was most probably in Galilee when he spoke these words, the mission of the disciples was in effect confined to this region. There were Gentiles to the north in Phoenicia and Syria, to the east in the Decapolis, and there were Samaritans to the south. The roads of Samaria were open to them and so they could reach Judaea if they wished, but is is unlikely that they went there. It was in Galilee that they attracted the attention of Herod Antipas, its tetrarch, who attributed their doings to a resurrected John the Baptist (Mark

6.14-16). The unexpected exclusiveness of this command is a mark of its authenticity. No one would put a restriction on the mission of the disciples if Jesus had not actually done so in his Mission Charge. The reference to 'the lost sheep of the house of Israel' is not a further restriction by Jesus as though he meant only the criminal class of the population, but a reference to the whole house of Israel represented by the crowds he had just seen looking like sheep without a shepherd (Matthew 9.36).

2. *Preach as you go* (v. 7). The first purpose stated for their going was to preach. The theme of their preaching was to be 'The kingdom of heaven is at hand', combined with a call to repentance according to Mark 6.12. This message was the same as the Baptist had preached up and down the Jordan valley (Matthew 3.2), and the one which Jesus had preached in Galilee (Matthew 4.17). In view of this, it is difficult to derive from the Mission Charge a new sense of urgency as though Jesus had suddenly come to the realisation of an imminent crisis in his ministry and was preparing for it as Vincent Taylor suggests in agreement with Albert Schweitzer.[2] There was no new message, but new and more messengers as the natural development in the expansion of the Christian movement.

3. *Heal the sick* (v. 8). The second purpose of their going was to heal the sick. This command is the first of what we may call the four clinical imperatives in which their task of healing is more specifically defined. This fuller definition is given by Matthew alone, and not by Mark or Luke. Mark does not mention the command to heal the sick in his account, but he records that the disciples did heal when they went out (Mark 6.13). The verb in Matthew is *therapeuō* which Luke changes to *iaomai* (Luke 9.2) in line with his preference for the latter verb which we have already noted. The command is a simple one with no details of how the disciples were to heal. The only hint of the methods they used is given in Mark 6.13 where we are told that 'they anointed with oil many that were sick and healed them'.

4. *Raise the dead* (v. 8). Jesus raised the dead and here gave his disciples authority to do the same. The existence of no fewer than five variant readings involving this clause shows that the early Church had some difficulty with this command. In some manuscripts it is omitted, whilst in others its place in the commission varies.[3] Its omission suggests that those who omitted the command took the Mission Charge as valid in their own day, but doubted the authenticity of this part of it. The manuscript evidence leaves little doubt that the command is authentic. This command has caused difficulty in our own day too, and has been interpreted of raising the spiritually dead from sin to goodness.[4] However, there is no real need to avoid the plain meaning of the words if we accept that Jesus had the power to raise the dead which is so clearly illustrated by the gospel record. Also, it should be noted that Jesus does not speak of men being dead in sin and so any reference he made to raising them from the dead would be in a physical and not a spiritual sense.

5. *Cleanse the lepers* (v. 8). At first sight this command to cleanse lepers appears to be anomalous. Jesus is commanding his disciples to do what he did not do himself, and what in fact they could not do because they were not of the levitical priesthood. It is clearly laid down in the fourteenth chapter of Leviticus

that only a priest could perform the ceremony of cleansing a leper. Jesus himself observed this regulation and when he cured a leper of his leprosy, he was always very careful to send him on to a priest to fulfil the levitical law (Matthew 8.4; Mark 1.44; Luke 17.14). The explanation of this apparent anomaly lies in the fact that in both Old and New Testaments the word *cleanse* can refer to both the physical cure of the leprosy and to the ritual cleansing of the leper or to each separately. Our Lord's command to his disciples on this occasion was not therefore anomalous or contrary to the levitical law. He healed the physical disease but did not carry out the levitical ritual, and his command was that his disciples should do the same.

6. *Cast out demons* (v. 8). The disciples were given authority over demons and were commissioned to cast them out of those whom they had possessed. Demon possession is clearly distinguished from sickness and from leprosy, and its treatment is to be of a different character from theirs. Jesus does not call this exorcism, for this word by derivation means the casting out of demons by oaths, incantations and magic, and is not used in the New Testament of the casting out of evil spirits by Jesus or by the apostles. The disciples cast out demons in the name and by the power of Jesus Christ.

7. *Take no gold . . . no bag . . .* (vv. 9-10). Money, haversack, sandals, staff and a spare tunic were all items which a prudent traveller would provide for his journey, but the disciples were to go as they were and not put off time to collect these things before they left. It has often been pointed out that the Mishnah tractate *Berakoth* directs that a man 'may not enter into the Temple Mount with his staff or his sandals or his purse' (9.5), and that this part of the Mission Charge may therefore mean that the mission was to be undertaken as a sacred task comparable with setting out to worship in the Temple at Jerusalem. This parallel is interesting but it is doubtful if it is significant since the disciples are to lay aside more than the three articles mentioned in the Mishnah, and a sufficient reason for doing so is to be found in their need to travel light as well as the short period of time they are to be away.

From this brief survey of the contents of the Mission Charge to the Twelve, it is clear that four out of the seven imperatives which make up the Charge are concerned with healing. There is no doubt therefore that the Twelve were given a healing commission on this occasion as they set out on their first experimental mission without Jesus. As if to underline the importance of this first mission Matthew gives the disciples for the first and only time in his gospel the name of *apostles* (Matthew 10.2), as those sent out by Jesus.

II. IN THE MISSION CHARGE TO THE SEVENTY

Luke alone records the Mission of the Seventy, and this fact has led to the conjecture that he was himself one of their number. This is improbable as he indicated in the prologue to his gospel (1.1-4) that he was not an eye-witness of the events he recorded, but only a compiler of the experiences of others. It has also led to a denial of the authenticity of the Mission since the instructions contained in the Mission Charge to the Seventy are very similar to those which were given to the Twelve. As a result of this some scholars have taken the view that Luke's account of the charge to the Seventy is but a doublet of the charge to the Twelve.[5]

The Mission Charge given by Jesus to the Seventy is recorded in Luke 10.1-11, and whilst it is not as systematically set out as that to the Twelve in Matthew, nevertheless the main items of the charge are clear enough.

1. *Go your way* (v. 3). Here there is no restriction to the house of Israel and no mention of the Gentiles. Luke's editorial comment states that the reason for sending out the Seventy was that they might prepare the way for Jesus' own visit to the places which he was about to include in his own itinerary (v. 1.).

2. *Say to them* (v. 9). The message they were to declare to those they met on their journey was, 'The kingdom of God has come near to you'. This was the same message as that given to the Twelve in Matthew 10.7. The nearness of the kingdom 'is the local nearness of a present reality not the chronological nearness of a future reality'.[6] The implication of the message is that its hearers can accept or reject the kingdom; it does not come upon them automatically or forcibly. When they hear it, that is their day of opportunity and decision.

3. *Heal the sick* (v. 9). The verb is *therapeuō* as in the Mission Charge to the Twelve in Matthew 10.8, although on that occasion Luke changed the verb to his favourite *iaomai* as we see in Luke 9.2. No details are given beyond the bare command and there is no mention of casting out demons, but we know from the report which the disciples gave on their return that they did cast out demons in his name (v. 17). It is significant that on this occasion the commission to heal was extended to others than the Twelve.

4. *Carry no purse, no bag, no sandals* (v. 4). This instruction is similar to that given to the Twelve in their commission, and like it it suggests that the Seventy were being sent on a short preaching and healing mission to prepare for the coming of Jesus on a later occasion.

III. THE MODERN VALIDITY OF THE HEALING COMMISSION

The question which now arises is whether the healing commission in both or either of its forms is still valid today. Is the healing commission which Jesus gave to his disciples, both the Twelve and the Seventy, still binding on the Church? This is an important question because the commission to heal the sick is commonly regarded as the justification of the medical missionary movement which arose within the Protestant Church in the late eighteenth and early nineteenth centuries and still continues to this day. Also, it is often used as a proof text in our own day by those who practise 'divine healing'.[7] The only way to answer this question is by a closer examination of the details of the two healing commissions.

The Healing Commission to the Twelve

The first significant point about the Mission Charge to the Twelve which includes their healing commission is its restriction to the lost sheep of the house of Israel according to Matthew 10.6. This point alone raises and may even be held to settle the question of its modern application and validity. Today the mission of the Church is to all men, and not only to the house of Israel.

The next thing to notice is that the message which the disciples were to preach was defined in pre-crucifixion and pre-resurrection terms. These terms were 'the kingdom of God' and 'repentance'. They were not the terms used in the final commission to the disciples or in the *kērugma* of the apostolic Church. The preaching of the apostolic Church was in terms of the death and resurrection of Jesus Christ and the salvation which flowed from these two events. Obviously the terms of the message of the Mission Charge could not be other than they were, for they came before the great events of the gospel. The character of the message which the disciples were to preach is therefore another indication that the Mission Charge was for the circumstances in which it was given, and not for the post-resurrection Church.

Furthermore, two of the clinical imperatives of the Mission Charge are not the common practice of the Church today. The first one is the command to raise the dead. So far as we know, the disciples did not raise any dead person to life again before the Ascension of Jesus although they were given authority to do so on this occasion. In the Acts of the Apostles both Peter and Paul are recorded as raising the dead, but since that time this command has rarely if ever been fulfilled. It was the realisation of this non-fulfilment which presumably led to the attempts to remove the command from the text which we have already noted. We can say with certainty that this command is not observed by the modern Church, which suggests that it does not recognise itself as having the necessary power and authority to raise the dead.

The second clinical imperative not commonly practised today is the command to cast out demons. On this there is less certainty, however. On the one hand there is the denial of the existence of demons and demonic phenomena which would make the command meaningless. On the other hand there is an increasing modern acceptance of the reality of demons and their activity. The fact is, however, that the casting out of demons has been but little practised in the normal activity of the Church in modern times which suggests that the Church has not felt this command of Jesus binding on it.

The modern relevance of the command to cleanse lepers has been questioned on the ground that the leprosy of the New Testament was not the disease we know by that name today.[8] Most of the evidence on this subject comes from the detailed descriptions of the book of Leviticus,[9] and the identity of the disease in the New Testament is uncertain for no descriptions are given. Harrison goes so far as to say that in the New Testament the word *lepra* 'appears to be restricted to specific dermatological conditions exclusive of true leprosy'.[10] If it is true that the leprosy of the New Testament is not the disease caused by the leprosy bacillus which we know today, then this provides a further reason for doubting the modern validity of the healing commission of which the command to cleans lepers forms a part.

The final aspect of the Mission Charge to the Twelve which bears on its modern validity is the minimum provision which the disciples were required to make for their preaching and healing tour. This provision envisaged only short-term activity on their part and does not suggest that Jesus was laying down the terms of their permanent activity.

In a section which is peculiar to Luke's gospel, Jesus refers to an occasion on which he sent out the Twelve 'with no purse or bag or sandals' (Luke 22.35). It is after the Lord's Supper, and Jesus asks them if they had lacked anything when he sent them out at that time, and they replied that they had not. The actual occasion which Jesus had in mind is not specified. On the basis of the words used by Jesus some commentators have identified the occasion with the sending out of the Seventy, for only on that occasion was the wording used by him in his instructions to the disciples the same as that used by Jesus in this later reference. The Seventy were told to 'carry no purse, no bag, no sandals' (Luke 10.4).[11] However, Jesus was now speaking to the Twelve, and it would appear more natural for him to refer to the Mission Charge he had given to them rather than that to the Seventy who are carefully distinguished from the Twelve by the word *others* in Luke 10.1. In Matthew, the Twelve were instructed to take no money (and therefore they needed no purse), no bag, and no sandals (Matthew 10.9-10). If Luke 22.35 is a reference to the Mission of the Twelve, as we think it must be, then it clearly envisages that Mission as a distinct event with its own separate instructions with which Jesus now contrasts those he is about to give for a new situation (Luke 22.36). In other words, the instructions given to the Twelve prior to their previous Mission were for that Mission alone.

The conclusion seems to be inescapable that the Mission Charge and therefore the healing commission given to the Twelve applied only to the situation and circumstances in which it was originally given. It was not a permanent commission applicable to the Church in all ages.

The Healing Commission to the Seventy

The Mission Charge to the Seventy and the healing commission which it contained can also be seen to be local and temporary. Luke in his editorial comment says that Jesus appointed the Seventy and sent them out by twos to prepare for his visit in every town and place where he was to go (Luke 10.1). There is no restriction to the house of Israel but there is a geographical restriction to the land of Israel and its immediate neighbourhood which contained the places which Jesus would be likely to visit. The message they were to declare concerned the kingdom of God and was in pre-crucifixion terms. They were to carry no baggage, to engage in no time-consuming greetings on the road, and not to spend time eating in different houses each day. These features of the commission to the Seventy indicate that like the commission to the Twelve it was not permanent, but local and temporary. Its local and temporary nature is further suggested by the fact that Luke records the completion of the mission of the Seventy after a period of time which is not specified, but could have been several months according to Arndt. In Luke 10.17-24 it is suggested that their mission was now complete and had been strikingly successful although Jesus' comment on it is that 'the highest thing in life is not spectacular outward success but the assurance of possessing God's favour'.[12]

Our conclusion, therefore, must be that neither the commission given by

Jesus to the Twelve and recorded in Matthew 10.5-15 and Luke 9.1-5, nor that given by him to the Seventy and recorded in Luke 10.1-11 was intended to be permanently valid and binding on the Church. Nevertheless we know from history and from experience that the modern Church does have a healing ministry, and it is to a consideration of the basis and practice of this ministry that we now turn.

REFERENCES

1. T. W. Manson, *The Sayings of Jesus* (SCM Press, London, 1949), p. 73.
2. V. Taylor, *The Life and Ministry of Jesus* (Macmillan, London, 1961) p. 107.
3. B. M. Metzger, *A Textual Commentary on the Greek New Testament* (United Bible Societies, London, 1971), p. 27.
4. W. Barclay, *The Daily Study Bible: The Gospel of Matthew* (Saint Andrew Press, Edinburgh, 1958), vol. 1, p. 375.
5. See the discussion by I. H. Marshall in *The New International Greek Testament Commentary* on *The Gospel of Luke* (Paternoster Press, Exeter, 1978), pp. 412-414.
6. E. E. Ellis, *The New Century Bible: The Gospel of Luke* (Nelson, London, 1966), p. 155.
7. J. C. Peddie, *The Forgotten Talent, God's Ministry of Healing* (Collins, Fontana Books, London, 1966), pp. 13-14.
8. S. G. Browne, *Leprosy in the Bible* (Christian Medical Fellowship, London, 1974), second edition, pp. 21-22.
9. J. Wilkinson, 'Leprosy and Leviticus: The problem of description and identification', *Scottish Journal of Theology*, 30 (1977), 153-169.
10. R. K. Harrison, *Interpreter's Dictionary of the Bible* (Abingdon Press, Nashville, 1962), vol. 3, p. 112, art. 'Leprosy'.
11. See the note on this verse in I. H. Marshall, *The Gospel of Luke* in *The New International Greek Testament Commentary* (Paternoster Press, Exeter, 1978), p. 824.
12. W. F. Arndt, *The Gospel according to St Luke* (Concordia Publishing House, St Louis, Missouri, 1956), p. 284.

Chapter Fourteen

THE HEALING MINISTRY OF
THE CHURCH TODAY

The phrase *The Healing Ministry of the Church* is a modern one and does not occur in the New Testament or in the literature of the Church before the nineteenth century. The earliest usage of the phrase *The Ministry of Healing* we have been able to trace is for the title of a tract published in 1881 by the Rev A. J. Gordon, D.D., a Baptist minister of Boston, Massachusetts in the United States. In the following year he used it again as the title of a book of 283 crown octavo pages which was published first in the United States and then in Britain. This book was the first extended study of healing in the Church to appear, although Gordon confined his attention to miraculous or non-medical healing as indicated by the alternative title which he gave to his book of *Miracles of Cure in all Ages*. We cannot say whether he first coined the phrase which he used as the main title of his book, but it is a phrase which has come into common use in recent years and is preferred by many because it begs fewer questions than other terms which are used such as faith-healing, divine healing and spiritual healing.

I. THE MODERN INTEREST IN HEALING

The tract and book published by Gordon are an illustration of the great interest in healing which was present in church life in the United States of America in the late nineteenth century. This interest was associated particularly with the names of Dr Gordon, Dr Charles Cullis and the Rev A. B. Simpson, but it does not appear to have had much influence within the major denominational traditions at this time. It was largely confined to the more enthusiastic branches of the Church, and healing of the sick became a major article of belief and practice in the Pentecostal Churches which arose in the United States in the early years of the twentieth century. Amongst the leaders of these Pentecostal Churches, the man mainly responsible for bringing the healing of the sick into the foreground of their work was John A. Dowie whose antipathy towards doctors and medical healing is said to date from his experience as an honorary chaplain to the Royal Infirmary of Edinburgh.[1]

An interest in the healing of the sick also arose in Church circles on the continent of Europe in the nineteenth century, and somewhat earlier than in the United States. The best known example is that of the work of the Blumhardts in South Germany. In 1838 Johann Christoph Blumhardt became the Lutheran pastor of the village of Möttlingen in the Black Forest. In 1841 he was confronted by the two sisters Gottliebin and Katharina Dittus who exhibited signs of demon possession. After two years of constant prayer Katharina was cured, but Gottliebin became much worse. One night in 1843 matters reached a climax in her violent behaviour and convulsions, and after Blumhardt prayed all night with her the demon came out shouting, '*Jesus ist Sieger*, Jesus is Victor', and she too was cured. This was the beginning of Blumhardt's healing ministry which after 1852 was centred in the sanatorium at Bad Boll. Blumhardt did not use anointing with oil and only rarely used laying on of hands, but healed in the context of a service of divine worship which included the proclamation of the healing word of God. When he died in 1880 his work was continued by his son Christoph Friedrich who took charge of the Bad Boll sanatorium.

In Switzerland one of the well-known names connected with healing in the nineteenth century is that of Dorothea Trüdel of Männedorf on Lake Zurich. She ran a factory for the making of artificial flowers, and she began her work of healing when in 1847 four of her employees became ill with a sickness which medicine only made worse. She could find no elders willing to act as the Epistle of James required, and so she laid hands on the sick and prayed with the result that they were healed. After this experience she continued her work of healing using the Bible, prayer, laying on of hands and anointing with oil, and she was able to heal many whom the medical profession had given up as incurable. After she died in 1862 from typhus fever, her work was carried on by Samuel Zeller assisted by his sister and several of Miss Trüdel's former helpers.

In Britain there had been miraculous cures associated with the ministries of George Fox (1624-1691) and John Wesley (1703-1791), but nothing in the nineteenth century corresponded to the experiences we have just noted in Europe and North America. If we are to judge from the production of literature on the subject, it would appear that interest in miraculous healing in Britain lagged behind that of the other countries. It is only in the twentieth century that books on this subject written by British authors begin to be published in Britain.

The interest in healing, of whose modern expression in Church life we have been speaking, has so far concerned only non-medical healing. The fact that the Church was concerned only with this type of healing was the result of the divorce between the Church and medicine which occurred at the Renaissance and has continued to our own day. The philosophical grounds for the divorce are usually found in Descartes' rigid dualistic separation of the body and the soul which according to him met only in the *conarium* or the pineal gland at the base of the human brain. These two separate entities of body and soul came to have separate curators. The body was handed over to the care of the medical profession and the soul to the care of the Church, and this division of care and responsibility still persists particularly in popular thought to this day. Prior to the Renaissance the Church had practised all forms of healing, and had not confined its concern to matters of the soul alone. It is not surprising therefore to find that eventually the Church came to reassert its right to practise both medical and non-medical healing, and to reject the view which confined its activity to only one part of man's being. This did not occur by any

dramatic gesture or even at a single stroke, but through the gradual introduction of medical practice into the Church missionary activity. It is not without
significance that there were strong links between those who practised non-
medical methods of healing and the modern missionary movement in the
Protestant Churches. This is illustrated by the connection of the Blumhardt
family with the Basel Mission.

It is therefore through the modern medical missionary movement that the
Church has regained a place in the practice of medical healing, and has come
to include both medical and non-medical healing in its ministry of healing.
Medical missionaries have been trained in the methods of modern medicine and
have used those methods in the name of the Church and in the service of
humanity. It is of interest to note how this happened without its real significance being realised by the Church initially. This is shown by an examination
of the nature of the literature which arose out of the work of medical missionaries. The books and articles which were written by them or about their work
were almost all purely descriptive, and only rarely was any attempt made to
relate that work to any theological concept of health and healing, or to regard
it as part of the healing ministry of the Church. It is only in recent years that an
attempt has been made to consider the theological basis of healing whether
medical or non-medical. This attempt has to a large extent arisen out of the
difficulties with which the overseas medical work of the western Churches has
been confronted now that medical services have become so expensive to provide, and the younger Churches who have now assumed responsibility for these
services in their own countries have found it very difficult to finance even the
present standard of services. It was because of appeals for help from both East
and West Africa in 1962 to the Division of Inter-Church Aid of the World
Council of Churches that a consultation was called at Tübingen in 1964 to
consider the situation. This consultation produced the report entitled *The
Healing Church* which has been so influential in modern thinking about the involvement of the Church in healing.

II. THE AUTHORITY TO HEAL IN THE CHURCH TODAY

The modern interest in the ministry of healing of the Church and its practice
raises the question of its basis and authority. We have already seen that the
evidence does not suggest that the commissions given to the Twelve and the
Seventy in the gospels were any more than local and temporary. Has the
Church then any authority to heal? We believe that it has, and for the following reasons.

1. *The promise of Jesus.* Jesus promised that the disciples after his Ascension
would do the same works as he had done when he was with them. In John
14.12 he says to Philip, 'He who believes in me will also do the works that I do;
and greater works than these will he do, because I go to the Father'. These
works (*erga*) of which Jesus speaks include his works of healing for the word is
frequently used of his miracles of healing in this gospel.

2. *The practice of the apostles.* The apostles continued to heal the sick after his

Ascension as we know from the book of Acts. They would not do that which they had no authority to do, and if they had no authority to heal the sick, how were they able to do this? The fact that they did continue to heal the sick successfully must mean, not that the previous commissions to the Twelve and the Seventy were still valid, but that the final commission was regarded by them as including the authority to heal the sick, cast out demons and raise the dead.

3. *The scope of the gospel.* Healing the sick was part of the gospel which the apostles and the Church were commissioned to preach. This is the implication of the fact that the apostles did heal the sick after the Ascension. The gospel included the healing and salvation of the whole man in his body, mind and spirit. It is the same gospel that is still entrusted to the Church to proclaim today, and since it included healing of the sick in apostolic times, it still does so today.

4. *The power of prayer.* The main agent in the Church's ministry of healing is prayer, and that is still available to the Church today. After Jesus had promised that his disciples would do the same works as he did, he goes on immediately to say, 'Whatever you ask in my name, I will do it, that the Father may be glorified in the Son' (John 14.13). This suggests that when they came to do the same works as he had done they would request the power to do them through prayer. We have examples of this in the Acts where prayer preceded healing in the case of the raising of Tabitha by Peter (Acts 9.40), and in the healing of the father of Publius by Paul (Acts 28.8). When James writes of healing in the fifth chapter of his epistle he does so in the context of prayer, and he recommends the elders and the Church members to pray for the healing of the sick (James 5.14-18). Healing occurred in the apostolic Church in response to the prayer of faith, and there is no reason that what happened then should not still happen in the Church today.

III. THE CONTEXT OF HEALING TODAY

When we turn from the New Testament scene to that of the situation today we become aware of several features in the contemporary scene which are very different from those of the first-century Hellenistic world. It is important to remind ourselves of what these features are because they profoundly affect the modern attitude to healing and the concept of the involvement and role of the Church in healing.

1. *The status of modern medicine.* In the Hellenistic world medicine did not enjoy a very high status. Amongst the Greeks the influence of Hippocrates had already waned, and with a few outstanding exceptions medicine was practised on the basis of theories and *theriac*.[2] The Romans according to the elder Pliny had got on well without doctors for six hundred years.[3] However, with the fall and destruction of Corinth in 146 B.C. Roman power over Greece became supreme and Greek medicine began to migrate to Rome although it was not held in very high repute there. The practice of medicine was beneath the dignity of a Roman citizen and was left to slaves and foreigners. Its pharmacopoeia of effective drugs was small and its instruments few and crude, and the basis of its practice was all too often empiricism and superstition.

Today medicine enjoys a very high status in the community. Its practice is no longer based on empiricism and superstition but on an advanced knowledge of the structure and function of the human body, the origin and processes of disease and of the external and internal factors which influence the course of diseases. The great advances in surgical technology and the discovery of potent drugs have combined to give modern medicine a prestige and a status higher than it has ever known. The physician is now a prominent and trusted member of modern society and tends to be credited with an astonishing omnicompetence. The existence of this attitude to modern medicine is in marked contrast to that held in the world of the New Testament and is a factor which must be taken into account when considering the modern context of the healing ministry of the Church. It is true, of course, that such an attitude is being eroded today and it is being maintained that much healing occurs in the world for which orthodox medicine is not responsible. There is even a view which regards modern medicine as no more effective in the control and treatment of disease than primitive medicine was, and dismisses its claims as myth.[4] However, the majority still believe in its effectiveness and modern medicine continues to enjoy great prestige within the communities of the Western world.

2. *The organisation of the medical profession.* There exists today in most countries a well-organised medical profession which has established professional corporations designed to protect its rights and to control entry into its ranks and the practice of its art. This appears to be a new phenomenon in the history of the world, although from the provisions of the law code of Hammurabi, king of Babylon ca. 1792-1750 B.C., it has been assumed that there was an organised medical profession in Babylonia with its own rules of professional etiquette and a standard scale of fees.[5] However, we know very little about Babylonian medicine and even less about its practitioners.[6] We know a little more about Egyptian medicine which achieves a passing mention in the Old Testament in Genesis 50.2, but even in Egypt there was nothing approaching an organised medical profession such as we know today, although the calling of the physician was recognised.[7] The physician was known in Israel and is mentioned in the Old Testament in 2 Chronicles 16.12; Job 13.4 and Jeremiah 8.22. The Hebrew name for the physician is *rōphē'* which is commonly derived from a Semitic root meaning to stitch or repair.[8] This may imply that the earliest Hebrew physicians were surgeons concerned with the repair and treatment of wounds. It is significant that in Israel it is never recorded that the priest was also the physician as he commonly was in the countries surrounding Israel.

In New Testament times we have seen how the Romans left the practice of medicine to slaves and Greeks who were certainly not organised into a medical profession. We know that there were physicians in Palestine who treated the sick. Jesus confirmed this by his comment that those who were healthy did not need a physician but those who were sick (Mark 2.17). The Talmud advised scholars not to live in a town where there was no physician,[9] but no indications survive of how many towns did have a physician. There were complaints about the high fees charged by physicians,[10] but physicians in general were held in high regard as we can see from Ben Sirach's advice to patients in Ecclesiasticus 38.1-15. According to Munter some kind of medical guild existed in Rabbinic times which had for its insignia the *harut* which is the branch of a palm tree or a balsam bush,[11] but we know little about it and it certainly cannot be compared to the modern medical profession.

After New Testament times the care of the sick became the responsibility of the Church in the lands where it was established, and this responsibility was discharged in its name by the monastic orders whether itinerant or attached to the *hospitia* which were the guest houses of the monasteries where sick people found shelter, food and rest. When a papal edict of 1130 forbad monks to perform operations involving contact with blood, they employed the barbers who already combined shaving with phlebotomy or blood-letting as indicated by the traditional barber's pole. Guilds or Companies of Barber-Surgeons were formed in different centres such as Paris (1210), London (1461), Edinburgh (1505) and Dublin (1572). These guilds were the first of the professional organisations which were set up to supervise and control the practice of medicine and surgery. They and their modern successors in Britain, the Royal Colleges of the various branches or medical practice represent an organised medical profession such as was unknown in the world of the New Testament. This means that if the Church wishes to become involved in the practice of medical healing today it must do so in accordance with the rules and regulations governing the practice of medicine which have been drawn up by representatives of the medical profession and embodied in the laws of the State. No one may practise medical healing who is not qualified to do so, and anyone who is qualified to do so may not practise in conjunction with one who is not qualified.

Over a century ago in Switzerland, Dorothea Trüdel experienced the displeasure of the medical profession when she established a hospital at Männedorf to accommodate those who sought healing from her. The local medical profession disapproved of her work and a case was brought against her by the local state prosecutor at their instigation, and she was found guilty of malpractice in 1856 and fined. She continued her work of healing on those whom the medical profession had pronounced incurable, and in 1861 she was again convicted in court, but this second conviction was quashed on appeal by a higher court. After this she was left alone and the value of her work was recognised.[12] Her experience of the opposition of the medical profession is one from which the Church must learn if it is to include medical healing within a comprehensive involvement in its ministry of healing.

3. *The establishment of national health services.* The third feature of the modern situation which affects the practice of the healing ministry of the Church is the establishment in Western countries of national health services. These services have been established as part of the provision made by the Welfare State for its citizens.[13] The concept of the Welfare State arose out of the Christian doctrine of man and the Christian concern for one's neighbour. The Christian view of man gave human personality a status, worth and dignity independent of the State and superior to the State which it should be the function of the State to recognise and preserve. After the Reformation the State began to assume responsibility for the welfare of its citizens and to provide services which in former times had been provided by the Church. These services include those required for the care and cure of the sick. Today, therefore, there exists in Great

Britain a comprehensive national health service which provides facilities for the prevention, diagnosis and treatment of disease and disability. In other words, it is a service which seeks to promote health and practise healing. This means that any service provided by the Church as part of its ministry of healing must take account of those services which are already provided by the State in a national health service.

4. *The loss of the spiritual dimension of life.* One marked difference between New Testament and modern times so far as the Western world is concerned is the loss of the spiritual foundation of private and community life. In Western society today the emphasis tends to be on the physical and the material with the result that the health of the body takes precedence over the health of the soul. This is in marked contrast to the world in which the healing ministry of the Christian Church began, and in marked contrast to the life and thought of African and Asian communities today.

This is clearly a difference of which the practice of a healing ministry by the Church must take account. This ministry will be rendered more difficult in a situation where a defective view of human personality prevails, and the reality of spiritual forces is ignored or denied. In such a situation the health which it is the object of healing to restore is inadequately defined, and healing ceases to be complete and comprehensive in its scope and practice. The Church in its healing ministry must, however, insist on the wholeness of man in all aspects of his being, and not least in the spiritual, and seek to recover the spiritual dimension of human life of which former generations in the West were very much aware.

IV. THE PRACTICE OF HEALING BY THE MODERN CHURCH

If it is accepted that the modern Church has the authority to heal men in the name of Jesus Christ, and is called to do so in a situation which is very different from that of apostolic times, the next questions which arise concern the practice of healing by the Church today.

1. *Where is the healing ministry of the Church to be practised?*

In the gospels the healing ministry of Jesus was practised in the community at large, wherever the sick were brought to him, or wherever he found those whom he healed. In the Acts, healing was carried out equally in the community at large and within the newly established Christian community. In the epistles, however, the healing ministry of the Church is confined within the Christian community. Healing is no longer regarded as a Messianic manifestation to the Jew, or as a demonstration of power to the Greek, but is a practical consequence of belonging to the Christian community although, as we have seen, it did not always occur when it was sought. The gift of healing is to be used within the Christian community for the common good of that community (1 Corinthians 12.7). If a Christian believer falls ill he is to call for the elders of the Church to come to heal him (James 5.14). This means that healing does not play a primary role in evangelism although in the Acts it had resulted in believers being added to the Church (Acts 9.35 and 42). The healing ministry of the Church is therefore to be practised within the Christian congregation. This was one of the insights of the first Tübingen consultation on the ministry of healing of the Church,[14] and it is one which should not be lost sight of, for it is true to the teaching of the New Testament.

However, there is more to be said than this when we consider the Church's practice of its healing ministry in the modern situation. As well as the congregational practice of healing in which the Church acts corporately to practise what is essentially non-medical healing, there is also the individual practice of healing by Christians trained in the art and science of healing and of the various healing professions. As members of the Church they are practising a healing ministry in the community at large in their daily work. They are the Church scattered in the world and their healing work is part of the Church's healing ministry exercised in a secular society. They do not, however, practise in isolation, for in their daily work they are upheld and supported in other practical ways by the Church gathered as a community in worship and in witness.

The ministry of healing of the Church is therefore practised within the Christian community by the corporate concern and activity of the congregation, and in the secular world by the activity and witness of its members engaged in the practice of the healing professions.

2. *Who practises the healing ministry of the Church?*

In the epistles three groups of people are expected to practise healing.

a. Those who have been given the gift of healing by the Holy Spirit (1 Corinthians 12.9).

b. The elders of the Church who are called for by the sick (James 5.14).

c. The ordinary members of the Church who by confession to each other and by prayer for each other can produce healing (James 5.16).

The emphasis in all these references is not on the individual but on the Church as a community. Those who are given the gift of healing by the Holy Spirit are placed by God in the Church to manifest and use their gift for the common good (1 Corinthians 12.7 and 28). The elders and Church members are spoken of by James in the plural which suggests that the authority to heal is not vested in them as individuals but in the Church as a corporate body which they represent in their ministry of healing. There is no mention of any special training of any members of these three groups. It is implied that they are able to heal by virtue of their belonging to the Church and because of their function in it. Their healing is non-medical in character and does not depend on any medical training or skill.

In the Church today there is no difficulty about the recognition of the elders and the ordinary members of whom James speaks, but there is controversy about those who possess the gift of healing. When we discussed what the epistles had to say about healing we took the view that the gift of healing was neither wholly natural nor wholly supernatural, but shared the characteristics of both spheres. It was given by God to certain individuals as a natural endowment which was supernaturally enhanced by the Holy Spirit once they became

Christians. Healing is possible in some cases on the basis of this natural endowment, for only thus can we explain how healing results from the activity of the traditional healers of Africa, or exorcism results from the practice of the non-Christian exorcists such as those whom Jesus himself recognised in Matthew 7.22 and Luke 11.19. This natural endowment includes such characteristics as sympathy or the ability to enter into another person's difficulties, patience or the facility to listen to their story, wisdom to know how to advise them and what to do in their particular case, and confidence to encourage them to expect recovery and healing. To these natural characteristics the Holy Spirit adds a new dimension by intensifying them and including with them faith in God's promise to heal through the prayer of faith.

In the modern situation it is possible to combine these gifts whether they consist of a natural endowment alone, or a natural endowment supernaturally enhanced, with training and experience in the art and practice of modern medicine and surgery. Some members of the three groups in the Christian community already mentioned may therefore be medically qualified or trained in some branch of the healing professions. By virtue of their training and the professional recognition of their qualifications they are able to practise medical healing and in their practice to bring medical healing into the ministry of healing of the Church. They are able to do this most obviously in the medical missionary situation where they practise in a hospital or primary health care scheme provided by the Church as part of its healing ministry. It is less obviously so, although equally true, that where the State provides a comprehensive health service, the Christian staff who work within it are also practising the healing ministry of the Church. In the work of medical missionaries and in the work of Christian doctors fulfilling the Church's ministry of healing in a State health service, a new synthesis has occurred between medical healing and non-medical healing in the healing ministry of the Church.[15] By staffing the health services of the Welfare State and by bringing into those services a fuller concept of health and healing than can be provided on a secular basis, the Church is practising its ministry of healing and enriching the services provided by the State.

3. *How is the healing ministry of the Church to be practised?*

The same methods of healing are available to the Church today as Jesus and the apostles used in the New Testament. These methods are four in number:

> a. By prayer.
> b. By word.
> c. By touch.
> d. By means.

a. *Prayer*. The basic method by which the Church practises its healing ministry today is by prayer. Prayer is the foundation of all Christian healing. It may be all that is required in any particular situation, or it may be accompanied by the use of other methods. This paramount importance of prayer was pointed out by Jesus after his cure of the epileptic boy. Mark records how after the miracle the disciples asked Jesus why they had not been able to expel the demon, and he answered simply, 'This kind cannot be driven out by anything but prayer' (Mark 9.29). Prayer for healing may be made in the presence of the sick as in Acts 9.40 and 28.8, but also in the absence of the sick just as Jesus healed the Syrophoenician girl (Mark 7.24-30) and the centurion's servant (Luke 7.1-10) at a distance. Individual members of the Church join in its healing ministry as they pray for the sick privately, or corporately in meetings for intercession at which the sick are usually not present. Prayer also forms an essential part of services which may be held for the sick, often with the sick themselves present.

God's promises to answer the prayers of his people are recorded in the gospels in such passages as Matthew 7.7-11; 18.19; 21.22; John 14.13-14; 15.7 and 16.23. These promises are applied to healing by James in his epistle (5.15-16), and might be understood to make any special gift of healing unnecessary for earnest, believing prayer which avails for healing is available to all members of the Church. However, there is no doubt that there are those in the Church who appear to have a special gift of healing from God. This is true of such men as Cameron Peddie, whose experience must be included in any description of the healing ministry of the Church today.[16] Nevertheless, the teaching of the New Testament is that prayer is the essential element in that healing ministry.

b. *Word*. In their sanatorium at Bad Boll the Blumhardts practised healing in the context of worship and the proclamation of the Word of God.[17] The words of Jesus in the gospels and the accounts of his healing miracles can still bring healing to men and women today as they are read and expounded.

The word is still the means of casting out demons as it was with Jesus in the gospels. In the case of the epileptic boy, although Jesus said that the kind of demon which possessed him came out only by prayer, he expelled the demon by a word addressed to him which is recorded for us in Mark 9.25. Every form of service for the casting out of demons from a person possessed by them suggests a form of words to be addressed to the demon for it is by prayer and the authority of Jesus Christ that demons are still cast out today.[18]

c. *Touch*. The laying on of hands or the touching of a sick person was a method of healing used by Jesus and the apostles, and consequently we have their practice as an example to follow in the modern practice of healing by the Church. Touch is a means of conveying sympathy to a person, but it is more than this when it is done in the name of Jesus Christ. It was never used in the casting out of demons, and so has no place in Christian exorcism. It may be used alone with prayer, or be combined with other methods. In the New Testament it was often combined with a word as in the case of the bent woman in Luke 13.13.

It is not always stated where Jesus or the apostles applied their hands. Sometimes it was to the affected part of the body as when Jesus touched the eyes of the two blind men in Matthew 9.29 to restore their sight, or the wounded ear of Malchus in Luke 22.51. At other times we are simply told that Jesus laid his hands on the sick person without any indication of whereabouts he did so, as for example in the case of the patient with advanced leprosy in Matthew 8.3. In modern practice hands are commonly laid on the head or shoulders of the sick person, but they may also be laid on the part of the body that is diseased if this is known.

d. *Means*. There are several instances where medical means are used in the healing of sickness in the Bible. The most unequivocal example in the Old Testament is where the prophet Isaiah prescribes a fig poultice for King Hezekiah's boil in 2 Kings 20.7 and Isaiah 38.21. In the New Testament we find Jesus using saliva as part of the treatment in three of his healing miracles, once in the case of a deaf and dumb man in Mark 7.33, and twice in the case of blind persons in Mark 8.23 and John 9.6. Also in the gospels there is a mention of his disciples anointing the sick with oil and healing them in Mark 6.13. Anointing the sick with oil as part of the healing procedure is mentioned also in James 5.14, and we suggested in our discussion of this verse in chapter twelve that it is probable that we should understand the use of oil here as medicinal rather than ritual.[19] In the ancient world the use of olive oil was widespread as a method of treatment. It was applied to open wounds in the same way as we apply white or yellow petroleum jelly[20] today, to act as an emollient covering to protect the surface of the wound and to prevent dressings from becoming adherent to it. This use of olive oil is referred to in Isaiah 1.6 and Luke 10.34. This latter reference is in the parable of the good Samaritan and describes how the Samaritan treated the wounds of the victim of the robbers by applying olive oil to act as a protective emollient and fermented wine (*oinos*) as an antiseptic. In doing so he followed the same principles as those which are followed today in the treatment of wounds. As well as being used on wounds, olive oil was also rubbed on the unbroken skin and was commonly recognised as a useful supportive and even curative medicinal agent in the ancient world for many different diseases and injuries. The elder Pliny has much to say about the olive in the fifteenth book of his *Natural History*, and observes that 'olive oil has the property of imparting warmth to the body and protecting it against the cold, and that of cooling the head when heated' (Section V, 19).[21] The use of olive oil in sickness continued to be recommended even into the twentieth century. An illustration of this is provided by the last edition of Professor Kirk's *Papers on Health* which was published as one volume in 1904 and was reprinted in 1912. These papers were written in a popular style and in the words of the Introduction 'set forth a series of simple remedies and preventives of many common troubles'. They were widely used as a guide to household medicine in the latter part of the nineteenth century, and their significance for our present purpose is found in the frequency with which rubbing the patient with olive oil was recommended as a form of treatment for sicknesses of various kinds.[22]

The final undoubted reference to the use of means in the treatment of disease in the New Testament epistles is in 1 Timothy 5.23 where Paul describes a little wine for Timothy's frequent attacks of dyspepsia. The term used is *oinos* which means the fermented juice of the grape as opposed to the unfermented. The wine was presumably prescribed for its stimulant effect on the stomach and its production of gastric juice. It is often suggested that this verse was 'written with an ascetic kind of gnosticism in mind'[23] and that Timothy had abstained from wine and taken only water for religious reasons. Timothy's total abstinence may equally well be explained as a testimony against those who were addicted to too much wine (cp. 3.8). Whatever the reason for his abstinence, there is no doubt that he was advised to take wine as a remedy for frequent attacks of illness, rather than to demonstrate that he was not an ascetic.

A book to which we have not so far referred in our study of health and healing in the New Testament is the book of the Revelation to John. In Revelation 22.2 there is a reference to healing in which the use of means in healing is described. The leaves of the tree of life which is mentioned in that verse 'were for the healing (*therapeia*) of the nations'. The same idea occurs in Ezekiel 47.12 where the prophet speaks of trees whose fruit will be for food and whose leaves will be for healing. We do not need to enter deeply into the exegesis of these verses, for the principle they set forth is obvious. The leaves of these trees produce healing. No detail of the method of use is given, whether they are applied as leaves to the body as a dressing, or swallowed by mouth to have a healing effect, or whether extracts of the substance or juice of the leaves are to be made and used for healing. This does not matter for our present purpose, for it is plain that we have here a reference to a medicinal agent of botanical origin which may be used to produce healing. Both these verses may therefore be used to justify the use of means in the healing ministry and added to those which we have already considered. These references may not be numerous but they are sufficient to allow us to conclude that the application of means whether medical or non-medical is described and recognised as a legitimate method of healing in the New Testament. As means were used in New Testament times in the healing of the sick, so they may be used today in the treatment of illness and disease.

The Church today is therefore able to practise a healing ministry using the same methods as Jesus used during his earthly ministry. Prayer still forms the basis of the Church's ministry of healing, but a far greater variety of means is available now than was available then. More is known of the identity and activity of drugs and of the efficacy of medical and surgical procedures than was known in New Testament times, and this knowledge is at the disposal of those who practise healing and may be used along with the other recognised methods of healing as part of the healing ministry of the Church.

REFERENCES

1. W. J. Hollenweger, *The Pentecostals* (SCM Press, London, 1972), ET by R. A. Wilson, pp. 116-118.
2. D. Guthrie, *A History of Medicine* (Nelson, London, 1945), p. 70. *Theriac* was a universal antidote to the poison of venomous animals especially snakes. Its basis was treacle, a name which is derived from *theriac*.
3. Quoted by F. H. Garrison, *Introduction to the History of Medicine* (Saunders, Philadelphia, 1929), p. 105.
4. See for example Ivan Illich, *Medical Nemesis. The Expropriation of Health* (Calder and Boyars, London, 1975).
5. J. B. Pritchard (ed.), *Ancient Near Eastern Texts relating to the Old Testament* (Princeton University Press, 1969), third edition, pp. 175-176.
6. D. Guthrie, op. cit., p. 19.
7. J. H. Breasted, *A History of Egypt* (Methuen, London, 1912), p. 85.

8. BDB, p. 950, s.v. *rāphā'*.

9. Babylonian Talmud, *Sanhedrin*, 17b.

10. Mishnah, *Kiddushin*, 4.4.

11. S. Munter, *Encyclopaedia Judaica* (Keter, Jerusalem, 1971), vol. 11, p. 1182, art. 'Medicine'.

12. P. Dearmer, *Body and Soul* (Pitman, London, 1909), pp. 374-376.

13. The term *Welfare State* appears to have been first used in print by William Temple in his book *Citizen and Churchman* published in 1941 by Eyre and Spottiswoode in London (see p. 35 of this book). Its first appearance in a dictionary was in the addenda included in the *Shorter Oxford Dictionary* in 1956.

14. See *The Healing Church* (World Council of Churches, Geneva, 1965), pp. 36-37.

15. Phyllis Garlick, *Man's Search for Health* (Highway Press, London, 1952). See especially Part Six entitled 'Towards a New Synthesis'.

16. J. Cameron Peddie, *The Forgotten Talent, God's Ministry of Healing* (Collins, Fontana Books, London, 1966).

17. Dorothee Hoch, *Healing and Salvation* (SCM Press, London, 1958), p. 39.

18. R. Petitpierre (ed.), *Exorcism: The Report of a Commission convened by the Bishop of Exeter* (SPCK, London, 1972), pp. 37 and 45.

19. See above, pp. 152-154.

20. The modern proprietary name for petroleum jelly is *Vaseline* which is derived from the combination of the German *wasser*, water, and the Greek *elaion*, olive oil, with the addition of the ending *-ine* denoting a derived substance. See the *Concise Oxford Dictionary of Current English* (Oxford University Press, 1976), sixth edition, p. 1287, s.v. *vaseline*.

21. H. Schlier lists a number of other references to the therapeutic use of olive oil in ancient writers in his article on *elaion* in the *Theological Dictionary of the New Testament*, ed. G. Kittel (Eerdmans, Grand Rapids, 1964), vol. 2, pp. 472-473.

22. John Kirk, *Papers on Health* (Simpkin Marshall, Hamilton, Kent and Co., London, 1912), p. 9. These papers appeared originally as a weekly column in the *Christian News* of Glasgow, and were published in eleven volumes, the first one of which was issued in 1875. They were revised and edited by his son Edward Bruce Kirk, and published in one volume in 1904. Kirk was Professor of Pastoral Theology in the Congregational Theological Hall in Edinburgh (1859–1876). His wife Helen wrote his biography under the title *Memoirs of Rev. John Kirk, D.D.* (John B. Fairgrieve, Edinburgh, 1888).

23. C. K. Barrett, *The Pastoral Epistles* in the *New Clarendon Bible* series (Oxford University Press, 1963), p. 81.

SELECT BIBLIOGRAPHY

The modern literature on the subject of health and healing is voluminous, and this bibliography consists of only a selection of the books which are available. Those books which are listed are the ones which were used in the preparation of the studies which compose the present volume, or which appear to make a significant contribution to some aspect of the subject of health and healing in Biblical and Christian thought and practice. Books which have already been mentioned in the text in connection with specific points of information or interpretation have not usually been included in the bibliography.

I. GENERAL REVIEWS AND DISCUSSIONS

1. W. Barclay, *Prayers for Help and Healing* (Collins, Fontana Books, London, 1968).
2. R. V. Bingham, *The Bible and the Body: Healing in the Scriptures* (Marshall, Morgan and Scott, London, 1921).
3. W. H. Boggs, *Faith Healing and the Christian Faith* (Elek Books, London, 1957).
4. M. Botting, *Christian Healing in the Parish* (Grove Books, Bramcote, Notts., 1977).
5. E. H. Cobb, *Christ Healing* (Marshall, Morgan and Scott, London, 1933).
6. J. Crowlesmith (ed.) *Religion and Medicine. Essays by Members of the Methodist Society for Medical and Pastoral Psychology* (Epworth Press, London, 1962).
7. G. G. Dawson, *Healing: Pagan and Christian* (S.P.C.K., London, 1935).
8. P. Dearmer, *Body and Soul. An Enquiry into the effects of Religion upon Health, with a description of Christian works of Healing from the New Testament to the Present Day* (Pitman, London, 1909).
9. L. Dougal, *The Christian Doctrine of Health* (Macmillan, London, 1916).
10. V. Edmunds and C. G. Scorer, *Some Thoughts on Faith Healing* (Tyndale Press, London, 1979).
11. E. Frost, *Christian Healing. A consideration of the place of Spiritual Healing in the Church of Today in the light of the Doctrine and Practice of the Ante-Nicene Church* (Mowbrays, London, 1949).
12. H. W. Frost, *Miraculous Healing. A Personal Testimony and Biblical Study* (Marshall, Morgan and Scott, London, 1951).
13. P. L. Garlick, *The Wholeness of Man. A Study in the History of Healing* (The Highway Press, London, 1943).
14. ———, *Man's Search for Health. A Study in the inter-relation of Religion and Medicine* (The Highway Press, London, 1952).

15. A. J. Gordon, *The Ministry of Healing, or Miracles of Cure in all Ages* (Hodder and Stoughton, London, 1882).

16. H. Hutchison, *The Church and Spiritual Healing* (Rider, London, 1955).

17. A. G. Ikin, *New Concepts of Healing* (Hodder and Stoughton, London, 1955).

18. M. T. Kelsey, *Healing and Christianity in Ancient Thought and Modern Times* (SCM Press, London, 1973).

19. G. W. Kirby (ed.), *The Question of Healing. Some Thoughts on Healing and Suffering* (Victory Press, London, 1967).

20. G. S. Marr, *Christianity and the Cure of Disease* (Allenson, London, n.d.).

21. B. Martin, *The Healing Ministry in the Church* (Lutterworth Press, London, 1960).

22. F. MacNutt, *Healing* (Ave Maria Press, Notre Dame, Indiana, 1974).

23. ———, *The Power to Heal* (Ave Maria Press, Notre Dame, Indiana, 1977).

24. A. Schlemmer, *Faith and Medicine* (Tyndale Press, London, 1957).

25. A. R. Short, *The Bible and Modern Medicine* (Paternoster Press, London, 1953).

26. P. Tournier, *A Doctor's Casebook in the Light of the Bible* (SCM Press, London, 1954).

27. B. B. Warfield, *Counterfeit Miracles* (Scribners, New York, 1918).

28. L. D. Weatherhead, *Psychology, Religion and Healing* (Hodder and Stoughton, London, 1951).

29. M. Wilson, *The Church is Healing* (SCM Press, London, 1966).

30. ———, *Health is for People* (Darton, Longman and Todd, London, 1975).

31. B. E. Woods, *The Healing Ministry* (Rider, London, 1961).

The books by Boggs (3), Kelsey (18), Weatherhead (28) and Wilson (29) contain useful bibliographies.

II. REPORTS ON HEALTH AND HEALING

The decade which began with the year 1958 saw the publication of a number of reports on the healing ministry of the Church which were of two types. There were those which were the production of denominational committees specially appointed to consider the subject, and those which were the record of discussions in ecumenical consultations. These reports are listed in chronological order of publication.

A. Reports of Church Commissions

1. Church of Scotland, *Spiritual Healing. The Report of the Church of Scotland Commission* (Saint Andrew Press, 1958).

2. Church of England, *The Church's Ministry of Healing. Report of the Archbishop's Commission* (Church Information Office, London, 1958).

   The memorandum of evidence submitted to the Archbishops' Commission by the British Medical Association was published as *Divine Healing and Co-operation between Doctors and Clergy* (British Medical Association, London, 1956).

3. United Presbyterian Church in the United States of America, *The Relation of Christian Faith to Health* (Office of the General Assembly of the United Presbyterian Church, Philadelphia, Pa., 1960).

4. United Lutheran Church in America, *Anointing and Healing* (Board of Publication of the United Lutheran Church in America, New York, 1962).

5. Presbyterian Church of England, *The Ministry of Healing in the Church. A Handbook of Principles and Practice* (Independent Press, London, 1963).

6. United Church of Canada, *Sickness and Health* (Board of Evangelism and Social Service, United Church of Canada, Toronto, 1967).

B. *Reports of Ecumenical Consultations*

1. The First Tübingen Consultation, *The Healing Church* (World Council of Churches, Geneva, 1965).

2. The Makumira Consultation, *Health and Healing* (Evangelical Lutheran Church of Tanzania, Arusha, 1967).

3. The Legon Consultation, *Making Man Whole* (Reprinted from *The Ghana Bulletin of Theology*, vol. 3, nos. 2 and 3, 1967).

4. The Coonoor Consultation. *That Thy Saving Health May be Known. An Evaluation of the Coonoor Conference on the Healing Ministry of the Church. Coonoor, South India, March 1967* (Published as *Concordia Theological Monthly*, Occasional Paper No. 2, May 1968).

5. The Umpumulo Consultation, *The Healing Ministry of the Church* (Lutheran Theological College, Mapumulo, Natal, South Africa, 1967).

6. The Second Tübingen Consultation, *Health: Medical-Theological Perspectives. A Preliminary Report* (World Council of Churches, Geneva, 1967). Some of the papers prepared for this consultation were published in *The International Review of Missions*, vol. 57, no. 226 (April 1968).

7. The Limuru Consultation, *Health is Wholeness* (Protestant Churches Medical Association, Nairobi, Kenya, and the Lutheran Institute of Human Ecology, Park Ridge, Illinois, 1970).

8. The Dar-es-Salaam Consultation, *Like Lightning from Heaven* (Tanzania Christian Medical Association, Dar-es-Salaam, 1975).

In addition to the above consultations, other conferences have been held in various parts of the world, but their reports exist in only limited typescript editions and are not readily available.

III. HEALING IN THE GOSPELS

1. W. Barclay, *And He had Compassion on them. A Handbook on the Miracles of the Bible* (Saint Andrew Press, Edinburgh, 1955).

2. H. van der Loos, *The Miracles of Jesus* (E. J. Brill, Leiden, 1965). This book is the fullest modern treatment of the miracles of Jesus.

3. M. A. H. Melinsky, *Healing Miracles. An Examination from History and Experience of the Place of Miracle in Christian Thought and Medical Practice* (Mowbrays, London, 1968).

4. E. R. Micklem, *Miracles and the New Psychology* (Oxford University Press, 1922).

IV. DEMON POSSESSION AND EXORCISM

1. W. M. Alexander, *Demonic Possession in the New Testament. Its Relations Historical, Medical and Theological* (T. & T. Clark, Edinburgh, 1902).
2. E. Langton, *Essentials of Demonology. A Study of Jewish and Christian Doctrine: Its Origin and Development* (Epworth Press, London, 1949).
3. F. S. Leahy, *Satan Cast Out. A Study in Biblical Demonology* (Banner of Truth Trust, Edinburgh, 1975).
4. S. V. McCasland, *By the Finger of God. Demon Possession and Exorcism in the light of modern views of Mental Illness* (Macmillan, New York, 1951).
5. J. W. Montgomery (ed.), *Demon Possession. A Medical, Historical, Anthropological and Theological Symposium* (Bethany Fellowship, Minneapolis, Minnesota, 1976).
6. J. L. Nevius, *Demon Possession and Allied Themes: Being an Inductive Study of Phenomena of our own Times* (Fleming H. Revell, New York, 1897, and republished by Kregel Publications, Michigan, 1968).
7. T. K. Osterreich, *Possession, Demoniacal and Other, among Primitive Races in Antiquity, the Middle Ages and Modern Times* (Paul, Trench and Trübner, London, 1930).
8. R. Petitpierre (ed.), *Exorcism. The Report of a Commission convened by the Bishop of Exeter* (The Right Rev Robert Mortimer) (SPCK, London, 1972).
9. J. Richards, *But Deliver Us from Evil. An Introduction to the Demonic Dimension in Pastoral Care* (Darton, Longman and Todd, London, 1974).
10. ——, *Exorcism, Deliverance and Healing: Some Pastoral Guidelines* (Grove Books, Bramcote, Notts., 1976).
11. J. S. Stewart, 'On a neglected emphasis in New Testament Theology', *Scottish Journal of Theology*, vol. 4, pp. 292-301 (September 1951).
12. M. F. Unger, *Biblical Demonology* (Scripture Press, Wheaton, Illinois, 1952).
13. ——, *Demons in the World Today* (Tyndale House, Wheaton, Illinois, 1971).

The books by Richards (9) and Unger (12) contain useful bibliographies.

V. HEALING IN THE EPISTLES

1. F. W. Puller, *The Anointing of the Sick in Scripture and Tradition* (SPCK, London, 1904).
2. J. A. T. Robinson, *The Body. A Study in Pauline Theology*, Studies in Biblical Theology No. 5 (SCM Press, London, 1957).
3. W. D. Stacey, *The Pauline View of Man* (Macmillan, London, 1956).
4. E. White, *Saint Paul: The Man and His Mind. A Psychological Assessment* (Marshall, Morgan and Scott, London, 1958).

VI. THE THEOLOGY OF HEALING

1. D. M. Baillie, *Faith in God and its Christian Consummation* (T. & T. Clark, Edinburgh, 1927). See especially chapter 8, 'Faith and the Gospel of Jesus'.
2. J. P. Baker, *Salvation and Wholeness. The Biblical Perspectives of Healing* (Fountain Trust, London, 1973).
3. K. Barth, *Church Dogmatics* (T. & T. Clark, Edinburgh, 1961), vol. 3 'The Doctrine of Creation', part 4, pp. 356-374 (ET).
4. D. Hoch, *Healing and Salvation* (SCM Press, London, 1958).
5. R. A. Lambourne, *Community, Church and Healing. A study of some of the corporate aspects of the Church's Ministry to the sick* (Darton, Longman and Todd, London, 1963).
6. M. H. Scharlemann, *Healing and Redemption. Toward a Theology of Human Wholeness for Doctors, Nurses, Missionaries and Pastors* (Concordia Publishing House, London, 1965).
7. P. Tillich, *Systematic Theology* (Nisbet, London, 1968), vol. 3, pp. 293-300.

INDEX OF SUBJECTS

Stigmata, 116, 126
Stimulus carnis, 122
Strength, 7, 137, 140
Synagogue, 70, 76, 150

Talmud, 172
Telepathy, 58
Temptation, 122
Textual criticism, 41
Textus Receptus, 91, 122
Theriac, 171
Timothy, 95, 97, 107
Timothy, sickness of, 108, 110, 178
Tongue-tie, 56
Touch, healing by, 49-54, 98
Trachoma, 131
Trinity, 54
Trophimus, 110-111
Trüdel, D., 169, 173
Tuberculosis of the spine, 73-74
Tübingen consultation, 170, 175

Unclean spirit, 76-77
Uncleanness, ritual, 41, 51, 53

Vaseline, 178
Vatican, Second Council, 153
Vespasian, 57
Vulgate, 10, 61, 72, 122, 144

Weakness, 7, 28, 71, 78, 125, 148
Welfare State, 173, 176
We-sections of the Acts, 89, 99-100
Wesley, J., 169
Western text in the Acts, 90, 95, 97, 100
Westminster Confession, 13
Wholeness, 4-5
Wine, 110, 178
World Council of Churches, 170
World Health Organisation, vii, 5

Yahweh-shalōm, 5

Zeller, S., 169

INDEX OF AUTHORS

INDEX OF WORDS

Only those words on which a significant comment is made in the text
are included in this index.

INDEX OF MAIN NEW TESTAMENT REFERENCES

I. REFERENCES TO VERSES

II. REFERENCES TO MIRACLES OF HEALING